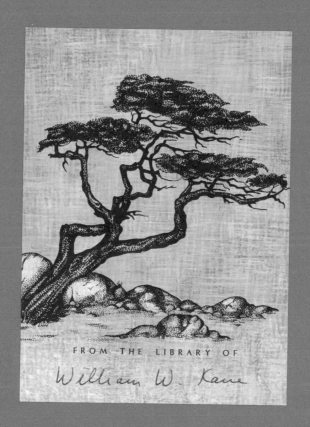

LAUGHTER

is a Wonderful Thing

Joe E. Brown is the author of

YOUR KIDS AND MINE

Other Books by Ralph Hancock

THE FOREST LAWN STORY

BAJA CALIFORNIA

DOUGLAS FAIRBANKS: *The Fourth Musketeer*

CARIBBEAN CORRESPONDENT

FABULOUS BOULEVARD

THE MAGIC LAND: *Mexico*

THE RAINBOW REPUBLICS: *Central America*

OPPORTUNITIES IN LATIN AMERICA

OUR AMERICAN NEIGHBORS

LET'S LOOK AT LATIN AMERICA

MEXICO AND CENTRAL AMERICA

LATIN AMERICA

OUR SOUTHERN NEIGHBORS

LAUGHTER

is a Wonderful Thing

BY JOE E. BROWN

AS TOLD TO RALPH HANCOCK

A. S. Barnes and Company   New York

For

Don and David

Contents

One of the First Families

The Republican National Convention, meeting in Minneapolis in June that year, renominated Benjamin Harrison for President. The Democrats, meeting in Chicago two weeks later, nominated Grover Cleveland for President and a man by the name of Adlai E. Stevenson of Illinois for Vice-President. By the end of July their campaigns were in full swing and the population of Holgate, Ohio (bigger then than it is today), was split down the middle.

The street corner spit-and-argue boys waxed vociferous over their favorites and the major issues, but the bloody strike at Carnegie Steel's Homestead, Pennsylvania, plant also got public attention. The latter was blamed on Russian agitators.

"Them Pinkerton detectives oughta shoot every Roosian in sight." But even this could be twisted into a political argument: "If Ben gets back in office he'll handle 'em." And "Put Cleveland back in office and *he'll* handle 'em."

The back-fence gossip and the small talk in Gillett's Grocery and around the sawdust box in Wildung's General Mdse. Store was mainly local. Mr. P. S. Fitch had invested in a

1

sprinkler wagon and he was going around asking business-men to support him and prevent excessive dust from getting on their merchandise. Kids in the habit of bathing in School Creek south of town had been ordered to "cease or Marshall Knapp will get after them."

Dr. J. D. ("Doc John") Archer, stopping in at Fred Voight's drug store for a cigar and a refill for his black bag, reported an addition to the population. "Another boy for Mat Brown," said the doctor. "Mother fine."

"She was an Evans, wasn't she?" asked Fred, holding out a box of "Cuban Rose" cigars. The cigars were made locally by N. Ritz & Sons, and Doc John always liked to patronize local industry. He was a local product himself, born on a farm near North Baltimore, Ohio.

"She's the daughter of Old Dad Evans, down at the water tank."

Mat Brown's new baby was getting one other mention that day. E. L. Hartman, proprietor (publisher, editor, re-porter, printer's devil), of *The Holgate Times* was writing it down as an item for the column headed BRIEFS: "An-other boy was born to Mat and Anna Brown . . ."

Thus the birth of the town's most famous citizen got only a bare mention in the *Times* (which later became the *Henry County Review*, "Independent in all things—Neutral in nothing."), and he rated that only because Dr. Archer was the town's leading M.D. Any back-fence gossip that covered the event was never recorded, although an old-timer once told me what my father said.

Mathias Brown never found fault with anything. He ac-cepted life's handouts and kicks with equal grace, so his remark on this occasion was not a complaint: "Nice boy, Anna, but don't you think the next one ought to be a girl?" And to show how co-operative Anna was, the next one was a girl.

Eventually there were seven assorted children in the Brown

2

family, though I was not the lucky seventh, as some press agent once said. There were John, born in 1886, and Mike, born in 1889. They were big kids, bossy older brothers, when I came along on July 28, 1892. The girl that followed me fourteen months later was Cornelia. Charles, who came in 1898, was named for my uncle Charlie Evans, mother's brother. Uncle Charlie's proud boast in later years was that he owned a Ford touring car for sixteen years and never had the lights on once. Night driving, he said, was dangerous and hard on a car. Louella, born in 1901, and Paul, in 1904, completed the family.

Today, of the children of Mathias and Anna Brown, only Louella, Charles, and I remain. Mother, at this writing, is eighty-nine and surprisingly active. Charles, in his youth, was the opposite of his namesake, but he settled down in middle age and became a respected citizen of his community. Louella, mother of a big, happy family, is our pride because of the wonderful home she made for her children.

So, looking back on my sixty-four years, I think I can call them full. They each have had their share of joy and sorrow, comedy and tragedy, but if you must have one to appreciate the other, then I'm content.

I knew hunger and cold and hard work before I was ten, but I accepted those things at the time. I never thought of them then as hardships, and I certainly do not think of them now as tragedies. It seldom occurred to me to rebel, or to imagine my fate was different from that of other boys.

It was not from my family that I knew unkindness or cruelty. On the contrary, for the short time I was under parental influence I knew the warm devotion with which large families envelop their clan, even in the face of direct poverty. I came from a line of hard-working Welsh and German folk, and poverty affected neither our family relationships nor our family pride.

Before I was very old, my family had moved several times,

first from Holgate to North Baltimore, Ohio, and then to Toledo, which I remember as the town of my early childhood. But in spite of my father's yen for moving, I do not recall that any of it greatly benefitted our finances. Dad's income seemed to remain about $1.50 a day.

My father never smoked a pipe, as I remember, but he did smoke three-for-a-nickel cigars when he could afford them. When he couldn't, he'd get a week's use out of one by just holding it in one corner of his mouth. We could always tell what our financial situation was by noticing whether or not Dad's cigar was lit.

Dad was a painter, and, in his way, an artist. He painted houses, barns, outhouses, but he took such pride in his work that his honesty was a kind of artistry. He had a talent for giving a full day's work, full value for whatever he was paid. We were on our way to the local ball park one Sunday morning when we passed a house he had painted a month before.

"Now, look at that!" he exclaimed, stopping suddenly to stare at the house. "How could I have overlooked that?"

I tugged at his coattail, impatient to get on to the park.

"Wait, son," he said. "There's a spot on Mrs. Forker's porch I didn't get. I must go back to the house and bring some paint."

"But Dad," I cried, "we'll miss the ball game!"

"The game can wait, son," he said. "Mrs. Forker paid me for painting her house."

That was all he said, or would say on the matter. I was a grown man before I realized examples such as this were the foundation for my own desire to give my best in every job.

My earliest recollections of my father are of his activities at North Baltimore, where we moved when I was four or five. At that time he was clearing land on contract. It was

4

hard work, for some of the Ohio land in those days still bore thick stands of timber and thicker underbrush.

Times were tough—tougher than usual, that is—for Mathias Brown and his big family in those days. There were five children by then, and I was in the middle. I remember especially how, one winter, we depended on Dad coming home every night with a rabbit. It was about the only meat we had that whole winter. I don't remember that I knew the taste of butter except only occasionally in some more prosperous neighbor's home, or when we visited a relative. We used lard, spread on bread and sprinkled with a little salt, or, on rare treats, sprinkled with a little brown sugar.

But people in small towns in those days were like one big family. I remember one evening when all our neighbors came in and helped us put up a barrel of sauerkraut; and other evenings when all the Browns went to some other neighbor's house and helped make pickles. Around ten or eleven o'clock, when such jobs were finished (and most of us kids were sound asleep), they would sit around a big table and have coffee and a snack. One could always count on plenty of helping hands on any big job in the neighborhood.

I guess that's how we got to know one another so well. They knew what we had in our house and we knew what they had in theirs. We knew who had horsehair sofas and parlor lamps and who didn't have parlors. There were no secrets. It was an easy waltz-time rhythm of living. We never thought of ourselves as being poor nor did we think of our lives as hard. I, knowing no better, looked upon it all as normal living. I thought then, as I think today, that it's great to be alive.

My maternal grandfather's name was Evan Evans, and that is where mother got my middle name, and Evan she has always called me. My boyhood buddies never called me anything else.

5

Grandfather Evans died when I was still quite young, but my memory of him remains vivid because he was my first hero. He looked a lot like Lincoln and I think his character must have been very much like Lincoln's too. He ran away from home to join the Army during the Civil War and became a drummer boy. He was in the thick of several battles, but he would never talk much about the war. The horrors of it remained fresh in his mind and he was much too kind ever to put any of it into words. "War's a terrible thing, son," he'd say, and I grew up believing him.

We all admired Grandfather Evans because he was the only one in the family who held two jobs, and held them steadily. He worked for two railroads, The Nickel Plate (our section of it at that time was called the Clover Leaf) and the Baltimore & Ohio. He was a car inspector for the B. & O. and in charge of the water tank at Holgate for the other. Standing with him in the shade of the big black tank while the "Express" high-balled through town and shook the earth beneath us, was a thrill I'll never forget.

The Clover Leaf Express came through Holgate at 6:00 P.M., and we kids would start putting our ears on the track at 5:55 to hear it coming. Moments later we'd see the strong electric headlight—always turned on day or night, for at that time it was the only one on the line—and then would come the "Too-hoo, too-hoo" on the whistle. A minute later it would be roaring through town, shaking the earth under our feet and sending shivers up and down our backs. We'd catch a glimpse of five or six passenger cars all lit up and a white-coated waiter serving food in a dining car. Maybe we'd see a few passengers nonchalantly enjoying a card game. "Gee!" someone among us would say, "They'll be in Toledo tonight!" Toledo was forty-five miles away.

My paternal grandfather lived on a farm about twelve miles from Holgate, at a place called The Ridge, near New Bavaria. All my father's people lived up around there and all were farmers. They were probably of Bavarian extraction, for my most vivid recollections of Grandfather Brown are his long-stemmed pipe and his gaudy vests. My father inherited this taste for colorful vests and handed the foible on to me. To this day I still have a wardrobe full of them. And though the style may come and go, I always insist on a vest with every suit I buy.

I remember my rare visits to the country as orgies of eating. Food was more plentiful on the farm, and we always returned home with the buggy loaded with grandmother's canned fruit and maybe a ham or a side of bacon. In summer there were all the berries and green apples I could eat—and the inevitable bellyache. And, tagging along behind John and Mike, I had my share of thorns, stone bruises, and sore toes.

Toledo in the 90's was "The City," the magnet, the Mecca for places like Holgate and North Baltimore and communities even farther removed. When my father's search for work led us eventually to move to Toledo, we kids looked upon it as a great adventure. Something was always happening to us or our neighbors—a rent eviction, another baby, or something as exciting as our move to Toledo—and these, to us, were the spice of life.

That is why if I began life as an undernourished baby who grew into a gaunt, too-thin little boy, it was a fact that disturbed me not in the slightest. Most of the other kids in my family and neighborhood were equally thin. And if it was a hardship, it was good conditioning for the life I later knew. On those rare occasions when someone did pass around a bag of candy I fought and yelled for my share as loudly as the next. And popped it into my mouth before anyone else could take it away from me.

In Toledo the Browns were one of the first families, that is, one of the first you came to after leaving the railroad tracks. We called the place "Smoky Row," because it was

7

opposite the roundhouse. We moved there in the spring before I was seven, so most of my childhood memories are associated with Toledo.

Living near the railroad had its advantages. I could always find a few pieces of coal along the tracks. One day I discovered a way to increase my "take," and learned for the first time how to use my face to advantage. I made faces at the trainmen and they'd throw coal at me—sometimes enough to feed our stove for days. I did pretty well at it, and sometimes they threw coal when I wasn't making faces. They only thought I was.

We moved to 331 Avondale Avenue about a year later. In those days the neighborhood was known as "The Hill," and it was a little better than Smoky Row. At its center was the Catholic Church and Father Hannen. Our neighbors were the Mullens, Skellys, Scalleys, Dalys, Gilhooleys, Donohers, McGraws, and only two exceptions to these Irish names: Wagner and Jones. Mr. McGraw was our landlord, I remember, and our rent, when we paid it, was twelve dollars a month.

The Hill was a world within itself. Enormous family washes blew in red flannel frankness on the clothes lines. The streets were never still from the shrill voices of too many children in too-crowded spaces. Street corners and vacant lots were our playgrounds.

Against this background, I, at seven, was already beginning to dream of the big things I was going to do. I used to sit on our rickety back stoop, mulling on the activities of my small world and chewing, always chewing. On rare occasions my ruminations might be concentrated on a piece of "Long Tom," a sweet-flavored chewing wax made from paraffin. More frequently it was nothing but a stick. My favorite, when I could get it, was chicory. No one ever thought to question the health-building values or the lack of them in chicory for juvenile "chewins." Families were big and parents

8

much too busy to have time to worry over such trivial matters. We were left alone and let alone. That's one tremendous advantage in being a member of a large, very poor family. One is, in fact, an individualist from the cradle.

As far back as I can remember, I was occupied with two major problems (though I never thought of them as problems). The first was how to get enough to eat; the other was how to get a job to help out at home. Of course, my daydreams on the back stoop were infinitely more grand. If I dreamed of food it was always a whole grocery store all to myself. And dreams of helping out at home were mostly about a fur coat for mother and a big fancy house for the family.

I also had two interests that are a little hard to define. One was a love for shows and any kind of entertainment. The other was more athletic and involved games such as we played at recess, and baseball. Particularly baseball.

Once, with other kids, I climbed a telephone pole and saw the first act of a show through an open window. Though we were chased away, I never forgot it. A few weeks later I got into the balcony from that pole and the window. In the shuffle between acts I worked my way down to the main floor, and when the curtain rose again I thought it was a different show. Strange how a natural view of the stage differs from one almost directly above. Later that year I even got on the stage as a super in *One of the Bravest*, and again in *The Guilty Mother* and *Heart of Chicago*. My pay, and it was generous, was the personal thrill I got.

And athletics and games, well, the more strenuous and the more competitive they were, the better I liked them. I was pretty young to know much about baseball, but I liked to play. Besides, I was one of the proudest kids in town because I had an uncle who was a semi-pro player. Uncle Charlie played on the Holgate Town Team.

When we lived in Holgate, Uncle Charlie would get up

early Sunday morning and put on his uniform. The game wasn't until the afternoon, but Uncle Charlie would wear his uniform all day. The whole team did; it was a sort of advertising for the game. They wore neckties too, and nearly every man on the team sported a huge moustache. My Uncle Charlie's looked like pigeon wings. After we moved to Toledo, I always looked forward to his visits. He was good for a touch—at least a penny or two and sometimes even a nickel—and hours of baseball talk.

I was seven when I finally persuaded Mother I should help support the family. After a daily routine of persistent begging, she finally agreed to finance my first venture into business.

In those days a boy could buy one of the Toledo papers (the *Bee*) for half a cent and sell them for one cent each. I had seen other boys run along the street in the evening yelling the news. It looked like a wonderful opportunity to make money. I could run and I could yell, as fast and as loud as the next. So one eventful afternoon after school, Mother relented and gave me a nickel.

I already knew all the ropes in this business. Five cents bought ten papers which gave me a profit of five cents—if I sold all the papers. I hurried to the alley back of the *Toledo Bee* on St. Clair Street. Already there was a line of about fifteen kids waiting for papers. Seniority or fists (or both) determined a kid's position in that line, so I took my place at the end. I remember some of the kids who outranked me that day. There were Billy and Mickey McGarry, Bill Hirsch (now Sheriff of Lucas County), and Joe Zimmerman. John Gunkle, founder of the Newsboys' Association, had given me a silver badge. It was in the form of a buckeye.

But my first day in business was not successful. For all my yelling and frantic running, I sold only four papers. I was stuck with six, or a net loss of one cent. And the next night it was even worse. I sold only three.

10

The most vivid recollection I have of my mother at this time is how she looked those nights when I came home with a bundle of unsold papers under my arm. I couldn't say anything. Neither could she, but she'd take me on her lap, and there within the circle of her arms a tired little guy would have his cry. The unsold papers would slip one by one to the floor while she rocked and hummed a little tune that had no words but a world of meaning to me. If there were tears in her eyes, she took care that I should see no trace of them.

That first night I stayed out a little later than she wanted me to. Our supper was always around six o'clock, but I wanted to break even, if not make a profit, so I stayed out until nearly eight. I was too tired and disappointed to notice her concern, but as I look back on it, I realize that she must have been worried, for she never scolded me for being late. The others had eaten long since, but she had put aside something for me. There was a big warming oven that hung over the back of our kitchen range, and any member of the family who was unavoidably late for supper could always find something put aside there.

Then came the big day when I sold all my papers. It was the third night, I think, and business was so good I even went back and bought a few more. That night I came home with a profit of eight cents. It was a proud moment when I walked in and handed Mother a nickel and three pennies. "My little businessman," she called me. It was the greatest moment of my life up to that time.

More than Anything Else

One freezing night I ventured into a saloon on Jefferson Street, partly to get out of the wind and partly in the hope of selling a few papers. I had never been in a saloon before and I wasn't sure I wouldn't be thrown out. I timidly offered my papers to the men along the bar. My usually high, shrill voice was hardly more than a squeak. "Get your evening *Bee*," I piped. "One cent."

One of the men at the bar turned, hiccupped, bent over, and put his face almost into mine. "Looka tha funny puss on tha kid!" he said. His laughter caused others to turn and look at me.

It was the first time I realized that my face could be considered funny. The knowledge did not please me. It never has since, though I've grown accustomed to living with it. I even got so I didn't mind the press agents who wrote glowingly about my homeliness, or the make-up artists who made it worse by widening my generous kisser. I even grew to like it, when it was bringing me over $300,000 a year, and the greater reward of millions of laughs.

The biggest week I had in the newspaper business was the

week following President McKinley's assassination. He lived for a week after he was shot at the Exposition in Buffalo and throughout that week interest in the news was at fever pitch. (By this time, I had graduated to selling the *Blade* too, which I bought for one cent and sold for two.)

Though I continued to sell papers after school, I soon ventured into another line. I bought a can of shoe polish and put together a little shoeshine kit which I lugged around on Saturdays. But my first efforts in this endeavor were not successful either. I remember the whole conversation with my first customer.

"Hey, young fellow. You in business?" asked the man.

"You, you mean you want a shoe shine?" I asked, hardly believing he meant me.

"Yep."

"Really?"

"You got yourself a job—go to work."

"Gee! Gee, thanks, mister. Put your foot right up . . . Oh, gosh! I'm sorry," and with that I grabbed my shoeshine box and ran. I can still hear that man yell, "Hey, son, what's the matter?" I was too heartbroken to tell him: his shoes were tan and my only can of polish was black.

However, between the evening papers and my one-color shoe polishing business, I soon had enough saved up to buy a can of tan polish. After that business was a little better. Not so rushing though that there wasn't time to detour past a few favorite street corners.

My route invariably lead me past Burt's Theatre on the corner of Jefferson and Ontario, and I'd spend half an hour looking at the posters and arguing with myself about the relative merits of the featured players. Then, if a softball game was in progress, as it usually was, in the narrow space beside Number 3's engine house on the opposite corner, I'd put a brick on my papers and join in.

My first school chum and my inseparable buddy at this

13

time was Alec Reuben. Allie, as I called him then, now owns the famous Hasty House Farms. And some of his horses have done all right too. (Besides owning one of the most successful stables of thoroughbreds, he has interests in real estate and other activities.) At that time his family ran a saloon in Toledo, but despite the wide difference in the financial status of our families, Allie and I were bosom buddies. We were the same age, we were in the same class at school, and whatever one had he shared with the other.

Though Allie didn't sell papers, he usually walked with me to the paper office and frequently accompanied me on my meandering rounds. That's how we happened to be together the day we saw the man putting up the John Robinson Circus poster.

It was, as I recall, one of those giant 24-sheet things that portrayed every act, every animal, and practically everything connected with the circus, all on one poster. I don't remember having seen one before this time.

We stood transfixed for a long moment, our eyes devouring every detail in the big poster. There was the brave animal trainer, standing with his long whip poised before a semicircle of the most ferocious looking animals I'd ever seen. Tigers and lions and panthers bared their fangs and waved their saber claws as though ready to jump right out of the poster. A parade of elephants all decked out in jewels and colorful blankets filled one side of the poster. On the other side dozens of beautiful horses bore pretty riders in white tights and plumed headdresses. And high above all this swung twenty or thirty acrobats. Some of them were flying through the air, and their graceful movements fascinated me.

"There," said Alec, pointing to the trapeze performers, "that's what I want to be!"

I didn't say anything. In my own imagination I already was one of those acrobats. I could feel myself flying through the air, smiling down on all the other poor mortals bound to earth.

I had had several childish ambitions before. Once, intrigued with the uniform, I wanted to be a policeman. Then, when I saw a big fire, I was sure I wanted to be a fireman. And for a long time I had wanted to be a doctor. Well, maybe not a real doctor, but the kind that sold cure-alls in a medicine show—like "Doctor" Cooper.

Old Doc Cooper made his pitch on a vacant lot on The Hill nearly every year. He always came in a fancy rig drawn by a span of highstepping roans. There was nothing unobtrusive about Doc Cooper. His clothes, his wagon, the brass harness ornaments, and the painted posters proclaimed to the world that here was a man who had gained tremendous success through honest dealings with his fellow man.

On Sunday he drove to church, to several churches in fact. Naturally, a man in his position couldn't afford to favor any single congregation, and besides it was good for business to be seen in as many places as possible. He was very obliging, with a mild condescension, and was never above pulling a tooth, putting a little salve on a sore, prescribing for a sick horse, or kissing a squalling baby. All of it was aimed at only one thing—to draw a crowd to his evening performance on the vacant lot.

And what crowds he'd have! On the back of the lot he'd pitch a tent and here he and his troupe lived during the "engagement." This is where they dressed and also where they mixed the "Sagwa," the world's most remarkable remedy. In front of the tent was the wagon which, lighted by a couple of kerosene torches, served as his stage.

Doc always had high class entertainment. There would be three or four good acts—a blackface (always) who doubled in banjo, sometimes a magician, and maybe a juggler. It was good vaudeville material, and, of course, all the performers helped with the camp chores and in the mixing of the Sagwa.

15

But the entertainment that held the crowd spellbound was the Doc himself. He was suave, glib, and an extraordinary salesman. He was always in complete charge of the situation.

His talk was real entertainment. He'd hold forth for a long while on the history of medicine, with full descriptions of some of the more horrible diseases, and describe in detail (with gestures) the anguish of sufferers. Occasionally he'd drop in an aside, an offhand remark, or even a joke. And from time to time he'd remind his audience that some wonderful acts would follow his talk. This was to keep anyone from walking out on him, but even if he didn't have another act, I never saw anyone walk away. He was good. And toward the finish of his talk he'd come down to the Sagwa, the wonder medicine. His build-up to that was a superb piece of showmanship.

Sagwa was good for anything. If you had a toothache, it would stop it. It got rid of bunions, pain in the back, dandruff, and pimples on the face. It would hasten the healing of a broken arm, settle the liver, stir up the bile, and purify the blood. And the first night he was going to let, *let* them have only twenty bottles.

"Only twenty bottles, ladies and gentlemen. Only twenty bottles." He could have sold a hundred, but making it hard to get was good salesmanship. All these potential customers would be back the next night with dollars in their hands begging for Sagwa.

"But before we distribute these valuable samples," he went on, "is there anyone in the audience who has a bad pain in the shoulder or any other place? If there is, will he kindly, will he please step up on the platform?" He always had a hard time getting the first one up there, but finally some diffident chap would make his way through the crowd to the stage. Perhaps he was only a shill, a stooge, but it

16

didn't matter to Doc. All he needed was one example. The next time it wouldn't be so hard.

"And, kind sir," he'd say. "What seems to be the matter with you?"

"My shoulder, Doc."

"What's the matter with your shoulder?"

"I can't raise my arm, Doc," and the fellow would wince with pain when he tried to raise it. "I haven't raised my arm for two weeks."

"You haven't raised your arm for two weeks?" the Doc would repeat his words in a voice everyone could hear. "Well, we won't worry about that." You could see the confidence with which he was going to take care of it. He reached through the curtain behind him and came out with a huge bottle of Sagwa. "Take off your shirt," he commanded.

"Well," said the victim, starting to unbutton his shirt. "You'll have to help me, Doc."

And the Doc reached over and, as if by accident, tore the man's shirt right off his back. Without a word, but in full view of everyone in the audience, he reached down in his pocket and handed the man a five dollar bill. Then he rubbed a little of the Sagwa on the man's arm and the soreness disappeared, but immediately!

The man raised his arm, smiled sheepishly at the crowd and stepped down off the platform.

The twenty bottles would go like hot cakes then, and when the crowd clamored for more he'd say "I'm sorry, ladies and gentlemen, but Doctor Cooper's word is his bond, as you know, as you must know." And believe it or not, that's all he'd sell—the first night.

So I wanted to be like Doc Cooper. I thought it would be wonderful to sell a medicine that would do all the things he said Sagwa would do. But most of all, I thought how wonderful it would be to be able to hold an audience, make a big crowd do anything you wanted it to do, the way he did. It stuck in my mind a long time, but the day I saw the circus poster I knew at last what I really wanted to be. I wanted to be an acrobat. This more than anything else. Nothing else mattered.

But I didn't see the circus that year. As a matter of record, the first circus I ever saw, I saw from the top of the tent as one of those aerial acrobats!

Cartwheels and Kinkers

The upstairs half of our house on Avondale, on The Hill, was occupied by a widow Jones and her son George.

George Jones was three years older than I and my idol in many ways. He also had an ambition to be an acrobat. He probably also had a real necessity to find work, for sometime during the early fall when I was nine he got a job with an acrobat by the name of William Ashe. That was the first time I realized that one got paid for flying through the air.

"Gee whiz!" exclaimed Alec when I told him. "You mean Mr. Ashe is gonna pay him money?" Our ambition needed no further impetus.

So I remember Alec Reuben and I would come sauntering along the street after school and we'd be trying to turn cartwheels, do handsprings, and walk on our hands.

A small side porch on our house was my own private gymnasium in those days. It was the scene of my first real acrobatic efforts, and hardly a day passed, in rain or shine that autumn and winter, when I wasn't out there practicing or attempting some new stunt.

Next door lived a buxom German lady named Mrs. Wagner. She talked with a thick German accent and I can still hear her mumble as she stood at a little window overlooking our side porch. "That jumping jack iss going again." Other neighbors spoke to my mother. They were worried for fear the frequent falls I took would make me "tetched."

Every new accomplishment that fall added to my confidence, and soon after George started practicing with Ashe I began badgering him to put in a word for me. I wanted to be an acrobat, more than anything else in the world. This, by dint of daily repetition to George, finally made him say he'd talk to Ashe.

Poor George! I must have been an assiduous pest, for every night I would waylay him on the stairs with the same question, "Did you tell him? Did you ask Ashe if he'd take me on?"

This was the stimulus that spurred me on to learn the "back flip-flap."

During the past summer, after we were inspired by the circus poster, Allie and I had got so we could do cartwheels, handsprings, and all the simple tricks the average kids our age could do. By the time school started again in the fall, we were pretty good at it. Actually, we could do more tricks than any of the other kids in school.

Then one afternoon I came home and found Mother doing a thorough cleaning of the house. She had moved a couch out to the side porch. I made a few experimental jumps up and down on the couch and then an idea hit me. I figured how, with the aid of the springy couch, I could do a back somersault. I got up on the headrest of the couch and jumped. The springs gave me enough bounce all right but I didn't know how to handle my body. I landed on my head. I tried it again and the same thing happened. I climbed up once more, my determination only slightly shaken. But the results were the same.

Housecleaning in Mother's day was not the simple gadget-

20

assisted snap it is today. At least with my Mother it was a major offensive that lasted for days. That is why the couch was still on the porch the next day. And after a few more tries, I succeeded in doing a back somersault and, more important, I landed on my feet.

When I had finally accomplished this trick, I could hardly wait to show the kids at school. I chose recess the next morning to show off.

There was a small running track of cinders on the playground of the Illinois Street School in those days and here I took my stand and made my first pitch.

"Hey, kids!" I yelled. "Gather round, everybody. I'm going to show you something."

Almost every place I looked I seemed to see myself taking bows and a large crowd applauding. It was several minutes though before I could gather a circle of pupils around me that eventful morning in the spring of 1902. And when they did join the group the noise they made was not applause.

"Hey, fellas, watch Evan break his neck," and similar derogatory yells only added more heat to the steam that swelled inside me.

I recall seeing my teacher, Miss Fabian, a worried look on her face, watching me from a window in our second floor classroom.

"Here I go!" I shouted. "One, two, three!" and I jumped.

I came down head first and there was a sickening squash as my face plowed into the cinders. The jeering stopped for a moment and someone gasped "Gee, Evan, you're bleeding!"

I was indeed. It seemed to me blood was pouring from a dozen places in my head. But "Gosh!" I said, "I can do it, I know I can."

They all laughed. They thought it was very funny. I had enough presence of mind the second time to move off the cinders onto a corner where there was a little grass.

21

Again I counted and jumped and once more I didn't do it. I wasn't getting sufficient spring into my jump, and I realized the advantage I had had with the couch. Still, I knew I could do the trick. So I tried it again and once more I didn't do it. But, by gosh, I finally did it, after I'd missed three times. It was a back hand spring, a little wobbly, but what the acrobats would call a back flip-flap. This was certainly not something any average kid my age could do, not even Alec, but I did it. And the cheers and applause of that little crowd of school kids was the sweetest music I ever heard, before or since. And when I glanced up, I saw Miss Fabian smiling proudly in the classroom window.

The next day, when George Jones came home, he said Ashe wanted to see me.

"You, you mean me?" I asked, hardly believing my ears. "Mr. Ashe wants to see me?"

"Yeah, he said he needed another kid, and if you want I think he'll take you on."

Well, I could hardly believe it. I was up and down stairs yelling and screaming and my parents thought I'd gone crazy. I'd never told my Mother and Father about my ambition, but it surely was no secret. Anyone who saw me practice day after day could not have doubted that I was aiming at something. But they had the usual objections.

"Why, you're only a little feller," said my Father. "You're not even ten yet."

I begged and cried and altogether made such a fuss that they finally relented, at least to the extent of letting me go talk to Ashe.

"All right," said my father. "You can go down and talk to Mr. Ashe and see what he has to say, but, mind you, this mustn't interfere with school."

I promised it wouldn't. I liked school, but this desire to be an acrobat was greater than I or school. So I met George the next afternoon and went with him to see Mr. Ashe. That was a conversation I'll never forget.

"So, you want to be an acrobat, do you?"

"Gosh, Mr. Ashe, I want to be an acrobat more than anything in the world."

"Well, I told George to bring you in because I think you have possibilities. I saw you do that trick in the school yard."

"Gee, you did? You want me to do it for you?"

"No, no thanks, son, it's all I can do to look at you now. No, it's not your trick I'm interested in. You've already learned the acrobat's hardest lesson. That's to get up and try again whenever you fail. You don't quit until you've done it. You've got the guts to be a kinker."

"Yes. Yessir!"

"Good. Come around for practice with George on Monday after school."

The first thing I asked George after we left Ashe was "Hey, what's a kinker?"

George's answer was no help. "I dunno," he said.

It was six weeks before I found out that a "kinker" was an acrobat.

Winters Ashe devoted to practice and the perfection of new acrobatic tricks, and in lining up summer bookings. This latter task, as I recall, involved considerable correspondence. I still have one of the letterheads he used to advertise his troupe and secure bookings. It shows a troupe of acrobats in action, doing tricks Ashe himself never could have done. Across this is a banner in boldfaced type: THE MARVEL-OUS ASHTONS.

It advertised that the Ashtons could do "single and double backward somersaults, full pirouettes, shoot out forward, and, the most difficult trick in a casting act, double forward cut away." In addition, Ashe wrote that every member of the troupe could do leaps and tumbles.

One day after I first saw this letterhead, I asked George "Do you leap and tumble?"

"I dunno," he answered.

Ashe, the manager, guardian, and professional "father" of the troupe, was an amazing character and this letterhead-circular was typical of him. Athletic and wiry in build, with a complexion a little on the sallow side, he wore his hair in a high pompadour on one side to give him added height. He was rather a beau with the ladies, or at least he so considered himself.

However, in his treatment of the truth, Billy was always a little careless. He frequently bypassed the truth when the plain fact would have served his purposes better. He was a natural born quibbler and though he never prevaricated through viciousness, he misrepresented everything simply as a matter of habit. He'd forge one story and then another one to cover up the first and so on until he himself never knew whether he was shuffling the truth or merely exaggerating. He wrote to all the circuses and described the Marvelous Ashtons in glowing terms, while half the tricks he said his troupe could do they had not yet learned.

When I started practicing with them, the troupe com-

26

prised besides Ashe and myself, my pal George "I dunno" Jones, Grover McCabe, a cross-eyed youth my age, and Otto Lowery (still living, in New York, I hear), who was about Ashe's size and build. When we all stood together to have our pictures made in tights, we ranged in height like steps from Ashe down to me. I weighed then about 64 pounds. Ashe always stood on a block to give him added height when such pictures were made.

I practiced with Ashe for several weeks (always without pay of course) before he was satisfied that I would do. Our act was a "casting act." Billy and Otto would hang by their knees from a stationary bar, with their toes under another bar, and swing George and Grover or me, then throw us from one to the other. Before we left Toledo we were doing single and double somersaults and I was even practicing to do a triple, all over a net. The bars were twenty feet high and the net sixteen feet below. Billy threw us in the most difficult tricks and Otto caught us.

For a few days, I was taught the rudiments—how to swing, how to hold my feet, my hands, my body; how to fall in the net without injury, how to throw my head back for a back somersault and to put my chin on my chest for a cutaway or front somersault. All this without Billy or Otto letting go of my hands or feet—just swinging and dropping in the net.

Each day after school I would walk and run the mile and a half to the Valentine Athletic Club, hoping each day I'd start to "turn over." I practiced a whole week before that great event occurred. That afternoon after school, I hurried along the street repeating over and over to myself "A somerset today, a somerset today. I just know it." And though it was about ten above zero, I was hot and ready to go when I arrived at the gym. Quickly I slipped out of my school clothes and into a pair of bathing trunks and a pair of canvas pumps. And that was the day—January 12, 1903—I did my first "somerset" from Billy to Otto. I did it fifteen times and only fell five times. Once I fell on the back of my neck with my feet over my head and my neck felt as though it was broken. But though my neck and head hurt, we tried it again, and it was successful.

Walking home that night with George, I knew I had taken my first full step toward being an acrobat.

Furthermore, by this time I also knew that Ashe wanted me in his troupe pretty badly, so badly that he was willing to pay me $1.50 a week.

But I am probably the only performer in the history of the business who didn't run away from home to join the circus. When Ashe had decided I would qualify as a Marvelous Ashton (and doubtless after he had a definite booking lined up), he came out to the house to talk to Dad and Mother. I remember us all sitting around the dining room table, Dad and Mother talking back and forth with Mr. Ashe about how much I was worth and how he would take care of me, and what guarantee he'd give that I'd be fed and clothed, and so on. I sat between them, and as they talked my head went back and forth like a spectator's at a tennis match.

Finally, paper and pen and a bottle of ink were brought from the sideboard, and they drew up a formal contract. It specified that Mr. Ashe was to clothe and feed me and pay me the princely sum of $1.50 a week. I remember Dad and Mr. Ashe signed and then Dad got out a bottle of apple cider (or something) and they had a drink all around to seal the bargain.

A few days later, I learned that the troupe was signed to open with the Sells & Downs Circus, and several weeks before the end of the school term, The Five Marvelous Ashtons left Toledo. The great adventure for Joe Evan Brown had begun.

I was ten years old.

28

He's No Larry

Our opening with Sells & Downs Circus did not take place where we expected it to. According to Billy we were supposed to open on Monday in Topeka, Kansas. He saw no reason why we should arrive a day or two early, since that would have meant a hotel bill, and this was something he always avoided if he could. But when we arrived in Topeka on Monday we found that the circus had opened there the Saturday before and had gone on to Chanute over the week end.

We took the next train out to Chanute, and it was there that we finally caught up with it, but not in time to get in any practice before the show went on. There was no time for a green kid to familiarize himself with the confusion of the circus or to fit what he had learned into this strange new pattern. Actually, the afternoon show was already in progress when the equestrian director (stage manager of the circus) signaled for us to go on.

Our rigging was up and, being the smallest, I led our entry into the Big Top. I could hear Ashe behind me whispering "Don't be nervous, kid, don't be nervous."

I was much too entranced to be nervous. I was fascinated by the gaudy colors everywhere. The sound of the band and the noise of the happy, laughing crowd was the most beautiful music I'd ever heard. The mingling odors of popcorn, sawdust, and animal disinfectant were exotic perfumes. The exhilaration of these and my climb to the top of the big tent didn't leave much room for nervousness.

When I got up there, I was forty feet above the ground instead of the twenty feet we had practiced. And the net looked so small down there I couldn't tell whether it was under us or not. But it didn't matter to me. "Hey, Billy," I yelled. "Look at those clowns down there." I was more interested in them than in our act. It was the first time in my life I had been inside a circus tent.

In the evening performance we were supposed to do an entrance trick called "the leaps" that none of us had ever practiced. Ashe had told Sells & Downs that "Every member of this act leaps and tumbles," but neither George, Grover, nor I had ever seen what we were supposed to do. And there was no time to rehearse it even if we had. They excused us from participating in the leaps in the afternoon show and Ashe thought we would have a chance to get acquainted with the routine well enough after the matinee to at least take part at the night performance, but it didn't work out that way.

The strangeness of the Big Top and the unusual height from which we were doing our casting act had caused us to miss a few tricks. We had to spend the interval between the afternoon and evening shows smoothing the kinks out of our own act, so there was no opportunity to practice anything new. The leaps act was only described to us. And then only a moment before we went on. We were to take it from there.

On our entrance, they said, we were to run down a narrow ramp, hit a springboard, and make a big jump over the backs of several elephants. This was the big entrance for all the acrobats and included other acts besides the Ashtons. But there was no opportunity for me to watch how the others did it. As usual, since I was the youngest and the smallest, I had to go first.

Ashe cautioned me to hit the springboard with one foot. If I hit it with both feet, he said, it would throw me into a somersault and probably bounce me clear out of the tent. I was told that there was a big mattress on the other side of the elephants, so all I had to do was run down the ramp, hit the springboard, go into my jump, and land on my feet.

It sounded easy and I wasn't nervous, but I guess I wasn't paying much attention. I hit the springboard with both feet and went flying head over heels through the air.

I realized immediately what I had done wrong, and the thing that flashed through my mind then was that I was going to land on my head and break my neck. I had a fleeting vision of the whole audience crowding around in sympathy and admiration.

But instead of landing on the ground or even the mattress, I found myself being caught like a ball, spanked lightly, and set on my feet. And instead of a crowd, there stood a big acrobat whose job, obviously, was to watch out for fools like me. I was disappointed and humiliated.

But I learned fast, and circus life was fascinating. And at the end of the week Ashe paid me one dollar and fifty cents. Or, rather, he bought a money order for that amount, made out to my parents. I put it in an envelope with a brief note and addressed it to Mother. It was the proudest moment I ever experienced.

I wasn't homesick, much. There were too many interesting things to see and do for that. But thoughts of home did enter my mind frequently, like, for instance, earlier in the week when we were waiting at the station in Topeka for the train to take us to Chanute. There were four railroad tracks there, and they reminded me of home and the days when we lived on Smoky Row. Over on the fourth track lay a huge lump of coal, and I remember saying aloud "Gee, I wish I could take that home." But I was nearly a thousand miles from home.

The shortcomings and the hardships of circus life made little impression on me at first. It was a big, noisy, thrilling world to a ten-year-old, so what if there were a few discomforts and even a little pain? I was an acrobat, an aerialist, and aerialists in the circus rated second only to the equestrians. The circus traditionally favored the horsemen over all performers, since circuses originally were mainly displays of horsemanship. That is why to this day the circus stage director is called equestrian director.

Circus acrobatics, too, I learned, was an old and honorable profession. It began among the wandering minstrels and court jesters of the Middle Ages. Originally they did little more than cartwheels, handsprings, and simple somersaults. Later acrobats developed the backward somersault (the flip-flap); and, after a few pioneers had broken their necks, the more difficult feats that the public takes for granted today.

With the invention of the springboard and the trampoline, additional leaps, twists, and somersaults were added. And of all the acts one sees in a circus today, the aerialists, the high trapeze artists, the death-defying casting acts, always were and still remain the most sensational.

In the casting or flying act, two men hanging heads down from a stationary rigging or even a swinging trapeze "cast" a third, called a flyer, back and forth between them across a space of several feet. In flight, the flyer may execute somersaults and body twists, depending on his ability. We were one of the first troupes to do the passing somersault. In this trick, two flyers are cast simultaneously and pass each other

32

in mid-air. I, being the lightest, did the high one, passing over George or Grover.

Naturally, the smaller the flyer the easier he is to cast, and since I weighed less than seventy pounds at this time, I was the daring young man who flew through the air with the greatest of ease. This was the act that became so popular (the act, not the Ashtons) in circuses during the next decade that it inspired the song *The Daring Young Man on the Flying Trapeze* (only it wasn't the trapeze that flew, it was the daring young man).

Flyers, usually, are not caught by the hands. Catcher and flyer interlock their hands on each other's wrists. But I was too small and my hands too short to do this. I was taught to clench my fists and the catcher grabbed my wrists. That's why the skin on my forearms was always raw and bleeding. My ankles suffered the same way when I was caught by my feet.

Billy Ashe did not consider himself, nor was he considered by his charges, a particularly mean man. In those days, the creed of sparing the rod and spoiling the child was not only believed but practiced by even indulgent parents, and Ashe, of course, was the parent.

He regarded all us younger members of his troupe as his sons. There was a considerable turnover among his heirs, I was to learn later, but his illusions of parenthood never wavered. The billboards said the Ashtons were one family, and that settled it.

I learned about this point of view during our first week with Sells & Downs. The circus postman came through our tent one morning and asked was there a Mr. Brown there. I spoke up in my small piping voice, "Yes, yessir. I'm Mr. Brown." Ashe gave me the back of his hand and knocked me over a trunk.

I had an awful feeling that I was going to cry. The violent

33

blow had hurt and the fall had knocked the wind out of me. But more than all else my pride was hurt. I wanted to cry out, but I just couldn't with all those performers looking at me. Then I remembered *I* was a performer in a fine circus act, and I was making a dollar and a half a week. I was in the most exciting business in the world and I wanted to stay in it. I choked the tears and humiliation back inside me where it really had no room along with the bursting pride I felt in my work.

Ashe had told me in the beginning that one of the first things an acrobat must learn is how to fall. I thought that would be easy. It was one of the most difficult things to learn. Not only must the acrobat avoid injury but he must try to fall gracefully so that it appears to be part of the act. I soon found that even with a net or other safety device under me, considerable skill was needed to fall without injury. Even a "good" fall was sometimes painful because of the hard knots in the rope of the net.

One day, a week or so after our opening with Sells & Downs, Otto missed the catch, and I fell forty feet into the net. I fell awkwardly, and my knee and jaw collided with a crack like a pistol shot. I felt a terrific pain in my head, but a sort of reflex action made me go on with the act. I climbed back up the rope ladder and finished the trick.

Later Ashe took me to the circus doctor who examined my jaw. "Son," he said, "you've got a broken jaw bone."

The bone-setter bandaged it up and advised me to lay off for a week or two.

Ashe devised a special cap for me with straps attached. It fastened under my chin and hid the bandages while the fracture mended. He advised me to forget it.

Lying in my bunk that night, I had a long argument with myself. One part of me wanted to cry out with pain and say to heck with the circus and Billy Ashe. I wanted to write my mother and tell her I was coming home, and why.

34

The other half of me reacted the way it had the day Billy smacked me. This side of me remembered the thrill that came with applause for a trick well done. It remembered the colors, the sounds, and the odors, and some of the swell people I'd met. And hadn't Ashe said "It takes guts to be a kinker?"

I lived on soup and milk for three weeks, but I never missed a performance. Not until years later did my family hear of the accident. And I wore the cap Billy made for me long after my jaw had healed. I didn't want to give it up. It had become a badge of honor among the circus folk.

"He's no larry, that punk," they frequently said, and I learned to translate the circus lingo: "He's O.K., that kid," they said.

Three Sheeting

Ashe was a strict father and ambitious for his children. He punished us and required hours of extra practice for anything less than perfection in our work. It was his theory of education. He felt that a mistake took root unless instantly blotted out by correction. He instructed me over the head and admonished me frequently across the buttocks. He laid it on heavily because of his fixed belief that I didn't appreciate ordinary pain.

Only once was pain too much for me. That was the time both my ankles were sprained in a fall. When I tried to walk, my suffering was unendurable.

"I'll fix you up," said Ashe. He soaked my ankles in liniment and bandaged them tightly. "You'll soon hardly notice those sprains," he said. He was right. The liniment burns made the sprained ankles a comparative pleasure.

There were no secrets to this profession. Co-ordination, timing, and practice, practice, practice were the basic requisites—plus the guts to stand pain. If on occasion I forgot to keep my ankles exactly in the proper position, or one foot was out of line when he reached out to catch me in mid-air, Ashe had a habit of clashing them together as if they were cymbals the moment after catching me or before throwing me to another member of the troupe. The veteran did everything with clockwork precision, and slamming the ankles together helped his timing like the beat of a metronome; and, of course it was educational for me.

At the end of my first week with Ashe, my ankles were swollen double. In a gym suit today, I look like a gamecock. Spurs of bone stick out from my ankles where they were clapped together thousands of times to punctuate Billy's rhythmic catechism.

If I was often lonely and afraid and hungry when the lights went out in the cheap little hotel rooms or the circus bunk I shared with Billy, I never let my family know it. If there were pain and hunger and fear, they were secrets I nursed to myself. The letters I wrote home were almost as glowing and happy in tone as those Ashe from time to time wrote to our parents. Far greater than my fear of Ashe was my dread that my family might learn that my life was not the bed of roses I painted it and order me home.

As a matter of fact, I was very happy every moment I spent actually under the Big Top. All the grown-ups liked the kid who was game for anything even if he did get swollen ankles as a result. And the little guy liked everybody in return.

Billy Ashe always wanted to appear to be a big man, and throughout the years I was with him, I was under the impression that he was big, physically and mentally. I feared him because he smacked me around and I admired him because he really was a great showman. If anyone had asked me his weight I would have said about 190 or so. Then I met him after I'd been away from him for three or four years and after I'd grown a little myself. I looked at him in amazement. He was no taller than I and he weighed about 135 or

37

145 pounds. He was nothing like I had imagined him. So much for perspective.

We lasted five weeks with Sells & Downs and then we were fired. Ashe said he quit because he refused to let us ride in the races.

The customary finale at every performance was a race in which nearly everyone connected with the circus took part. There were horse races, camel races, pony races, chariot races, and a clown take-off on the races. It was a noisy, colorful, high-pitched climax to the show. I always enjoyed it.

"That's what they want us to do," said Ashe, pointing in disgust as the chariots swung into the arena.

"They do, huh?" That's swell, I thought.

"And no more money!" said Ashe, and added "They're not going to get my kids to do such risky work."

He said it was asking too much of an acrobat. But the plain facts were something else. We were fired when it was discovered that Billy had been a little extravagant in his description of our talents.

In addition, Grover McCabe, the cross-eyed boy in our troupe, gave the superstitious circus people the jitters. Living a life of many risks, circus folk come by their superstitions the hard way. Their belief about cross-eyed people probably stems from the feeling that everyone needs all his faculties in good working order to stay healthy around a circus. Poor Grover was blamed for anything and everything that went wrong, from a lost wagon wheel to an elephant on a rampage.

But Grover was a happy-go-lucky kid. And he never changed when he grew up. I was attending a World Series game in 1931 and enjoying myself immensely, until I heard a particularly annoying voice right back of me.

"You need glasses or something?" he was yelling at the umpire. "Get a tin cup and a handful of pencils!"

38

I looked around. It was Grover.

So we were left adrift in the middle of Kansas. But if Billy Ashe was worried, he didn't show it. He got us to St. Louis and installed us in a cheap rooming house and made us live on twenty cents a day. We slept till noon so we wouldn't eat any breakfast.

Meanwhile, Ashe had picked up a copy of *Billboard* on the Sells & Downs lot and had set about answering every acts-wanted advertisement in it. He sent telegrams to all the circuses on the gamble that he could land a booking before his money ran out.

It paid off. We finally got a job with the Busby Bros. Circus and finished out the season with them. Busby Bros. was a little one-ring, one-clown, one-elephant show, so the Five Marvelous Ashtons, being the most important frogs in the puddle, got top billing.

I really enjoyed that engagement, and I soon had a lot of friends among the circus folk.

There was genial "Pop" Erwin and his wife and daughter. Pop worked a dog and ponies act, his wife did a swinging ladder trick that was mostly poses, and the daughter did a head balancing trapeze turn. The daughter and I and all the other youngsters with the circus rode the ponies in the street parades. I always enjoyed this, except that my mount, a little beast by the name of Judge, invariably threw me before the parade returned to the lot.

"Give him his head," Betty Erwin, who knew a lot about horses, would yell.

"I haven't got it," I'd yell back. And then the fun would begin. Fortunately, I had been taught how to fall, and do it gracefully, so I was never hurt.

And there was the clown, One-Eye Murphy, who used to sit in front of three mirrors so he could part his hair perfectly crookedly—from front to down the back. I have thought many times in later years that W. C. Fields must surely have taken his great comic character from One-Eye.

One-Eye Murphy was my particular pal. He used to tell me stories while I sat and watched him make up. "Clown Alley," the section of the dressing room where the "Joeys" put on their makeup was an exclusive area, but One-Eye would turn a bucket upside down and motion for me to sit on it. My favorite stories were about a fabulous character named Popcorn George. And every time he told me about Popcorn George, that amazing gentleman had turned into quite another person. One time he would be a squat little man with coal black hair. The next time he might be a daring athlete with red hair and a long red beard that eventually was his undoing when it got caught in the horizontal bar one night while he was doing a "giant swing."

It was One-Eye Murphy who taught me the secret of pantomime.

"Son," he said, "if you want people to believe what you're doing, always believe it yourself."

I learned values from the people of the circus that were to remain with me all my life. I learned that in spite of the acres of sawdust and mud and dust and the close proximity of animals, circus people are the most scrupulously tidy in the world. And in no place in the show world are the conventions more strictly adhered to. The Big Top had two dressing rooms, one for the men and one for the women and only a sheet of canvas separated them. But no one was ever allowed to be completely undressed in either tent and the sheet of canvas might as well have been a wall of stone.

Circus performers in those days were always hungry. Since we had to eat an early dinner, and a light one, before the night show, we were ravenous by midnight. By then the cook tent was on its way to the next town and we too were in transit. The wise ones, and those who could afford it, kept the makings for sandwiches in their bunks. Even to

40

this day I cannot lie in a Pullman berth and listen to the clack-clack of train wheels without pangs of hunger.

Few circus performers bought insurance in those days. Aerial acrobats were uninsurable and all others had seven years added to their age in computing premiums. There were no circus labor unions, guilds or actors' associations. Never having had them or child labor law protection, I, of course, never missed them. I took the risks for granted, if I thought of them at all.

The people of the circus were glamorous and exciting and interesting to me always. To me they were the most daring and courageous figures in the world. I learned what real courage was when something would go wrong with an act. Someone would miss and a figure would go hurtling through the air. Sometimes the accidents would be very bad and the big tent would be in an uproar. But there were times when only the performers knew that one of their number had been injured, and that gallant soul, in deep pain, would get up and again go through the stunt he had just missed "before his nerve left him." That was the code of the circus. Unless you were actually unconscious, you got up and repeated the daring feat before you had time to think about it and lose forever that steel nerve that made the stunts possible.

Though some of the best acrobats used to get pretty fair money, by far the majority of circus people were underpaid. We never did know exactly what Ashe got for our act.

Sometime near the very beginning of my circus experience, Billy showed me how to pick up a little extra money. He helped me get into the ice water business. For fifteen cents a week I supplied the performers in the dressing tent all the ice water they could drink. Each day I'd buy a big block of ice for a dime and make up a bucket full of ice water. With several performers buying the service, I managed to pick up 60 or 70 cents nearly every week. Of course, I had to supply the Ashtons free.

41

In all small circuses actors and performers were expected to do many other things besides act, and do a lot more acts than in a large circus. They helped raise the tent, place the seats, and strike the whole thing at the end. In the Busby Bros. show the boss, one of the Busbys, wanted us to do another act to fill in.

We were doing a Roman ladder act (which was an extra turn for us), where one acrobat stands in the middle about half way up between two ladders. He acts as a sort of bar holding the sides of an H together. The other acrobats drape themselves around and on these. The boss wanted us to do a comedy act, so we just put on clown make-up and did the same stunt. It was my first attempt at "comedy," and it wasn't very funny.

Busby himself was much more interesting and amusing. One day a near riot broke out in the cook tent and Busby was called to account by his disgruntled employees. The performers complained, among other things, that they were fed insufficient breakfasts. (I didn't complain. I was always hungry anyway.)

Busby feigned indignation that such a thing could happen in his circus. He called for the cook.

"Look here!" he roared. "I want my boys and girls to have all the eggs they want!" and he held one finger in the air. "All the eggs they want, do you hear?" and he kept that one finger in the air as a sign to the cook, who knew exactly what he meant.

I don't recall that the food changed in quantity or quality. We had one egg, two strips of bacon, and hominy grits or fried potatoes for breakfast. And anything left over was carried to the next town where it was warmed over and served up again.

We finished the season with Busby Bros. in Greene, Iowa. We were supposed to go home after that. I had to return to school, but Ashe had an idea he could book us at a local fair that was opening in a few days.

He got us on for the duration of the fair all right and in talking to the management discovered they also booked for the county fair that followed this one in Allison, the county seat.

With two bookings in his pocket and a five-day lay-over before the first fair opened, Billy set about finding a cheap place to stay. It was a good opportunity to finagle a special deal with the proprietor of the biggest place in town.

Ashe stepped up to the desk to register, turned and cast a stern look at the four of us tagging along behind him, and wrote "The Five Marvelous Ashtons, Toledo, O." with flourishes.

Usually Ashe would dicker with the proprietor and in a few minutes would have convinced the poor fellow that it was not only an honor but a privilege to give us a reduced rate. On the rare occasion when the hotel would be full or anticipating a rush business, as it was in Greene, Iowa, then the conversation would take a slightly different turn. In Greene it was this:

Hotel Proprietor: "For the five of you? Well, I'll make it six dollars a day, room and board."

Ashe: "For two grown-ups and three kids you want to charge us six dollars a day? But that's a lot of money!"

H. P.: "Well, I figure it this way. My regular rate is $1.25 per each, but because there are two grown-ups and three kids I make it six dollars." He didn't know that either one of us kids could eat more than the two grown-ups together.

Ashe (lowering his voice to a confidential tone): "Now, look, you are going to have a big crowd here this week end for the fair . . ."

H. P. (interrupting him): "Yep, that's right. That's why I've got to get money for what I've got."

Ashe (undaunted): "I was thinking of that. You're going to be crowded, have a lot of people here to eat. You're going to need extra kitchen help . . ."

H. P. (interrupting again): "Got all the help I need."

Ashe (tenaciously): "Yeah, but think of all those dishes. You'll have to have a lot of help to take care of them." The hotel proprietor was beginning to weaken. "Here," pointing to us kids standing behind him, "are three of the best dish washers you ever saw."

Well, at Greene, Iowa, Ashe wound up getting a rate of four dollars a day for the five of us, and we three kids washed all the dishes while we were there. In-between dish washing, we did our act before a large audience at the fair grounds.

Billy was a great guy. One day he asked me if I loved my mother. "Yessir," I said. "In that case, then," he said, "you ought to make a collection of cigar bands for her." (A popular household handicraft hobby of that era was decorating plates and trays and picture frames with cigar bands.) "There could be no sweeter token of affection for a mother," he assured me.

Well, this seemed reasonable, and for days I haunted the streets and sidewalks in search of examples of this art form. Maybe you remember those miniature gold-encrusted portraits of kings, queens, and princes; artists like Van Dyck and Rembrandt; and stars like Patti and Lillian Russell.

A few days later I found Ashe on the porch of the hotel "three sheeting with the yokels" (relaxing royally while he gossiped with the natives) and gesticulating with a long, black Virginia cheroot. The cheroots were three-for-a-nickel, I knew, so I wasn't impressed. Then suddenly I did a double take. I saw that his old Virginia cheroot was circled with my prized Lillian Russell band, the best and most expensive in my collection.

44

While we washed dishes!

From then on I noticed he never smoked a cheroot with less than a fifteen cent cigar band. In the better hotel lobbies he flourished 25 cent and (when he could get them) 35 cent bands. I guess I just didn't appreciate this high-class showmanship.

Billy's cheroots cost two cents apiece or three for five cents, and were not always worth it. He was unable to make one specimen draw at all one day and after using up a dozen matches, he ripped it open and found a human tooth in it.

Otto had confided to us that the cheroots were made from the sweepings of cigar factories. When he saw the tooth he remarked "Guess they don't sift the sweepings the way they used to."

After playing the Greene and Allison fairs, it was a little late when I got back to Toledo and school. But I was glad to be home. And the reception I got was all any boy could have wished. My brothers and sisters were goggle-eyed with amazement at my stories of circus life. My parents listened for hours to my accounts of the places I'd seen and the things I'd done. I told them about every day, from the day I left home, and the only thing I left out was the way Ashe treated me. I never even hinted about that, or any of the accidents I'd had.

The first morning I returned to school I was up and dressed by six-thirty.

"Why, Evan!" mother exclaimed when she saw me ready for school. "I thought you'd like to sleep late this morning. You must be tired from your long trip." I couldn't explain to her why I wanted to get to school early. I couldn't tell her it was another audience, just like the one I had at home, only bigger.

I never had a better one either, or more appreciative, for Miss Fabian declared a half-holiday while I told the class about my adventures. And at recess Alec proudly rounded up the whole school while I showed 'em how a "pro" did a "somerset."

"You oughta charge 'em admission this time, Evan," yelled Allie, remembering the last trick I did on this school yard. And I remember the warm feeling I had when I glanced up and saw Laura Fabian watching from the window.

I did all right in school too. I thought it pretty soft compared to the schooling I'd had all summer. I recovered from my bruises and sprains, but comfortable, well fed, and showered with affection and admiration, I soon found myself missing something. Within two weeks after I got home I discovered what it was. I missed the pains in my ankles, the hunger, the aching muscles, and my general miseries. I missed the smell of sawdust, the noise of the Big Top, the menagerie, and One-Eye Murphy. I was even nostalgic for an occasional beating. So one day I strolled down to the Valentine Athletic Club and said hello to Ashe.

"Hi, Billy," I said.

"Oh, hello Evan," he said. "How's school?"

"O.K.," I said. "Whatcha doin'?"

"Nothing much. Just keeping in shape. Wanta limber up?"

I said I thought that might be a good idea. I slipped out of my clothes and into a pair of shorts.

"You know," mused Billy, "if you could do a full twist while you're doing the somersault it would be a great trick."

"Yeah," I said, "I think I could do it."

"It would take a lot of practice," said Ashe, shaking his head doubtfully.

It did. It took all winter, but by April we had it down pat, together with a few more new and more difficult tricks. And in April we hit the road again.

46

If You Was Me

We were getting up in the world. Billy booked us with the John Robinson Circus ("Ten Big Combined Shows"), a larger show, and it played at bigger towns than we had hit the previous season. We opened at Norwood, Ohio, a prosperous suburb of Cincinnati.

My winter's practice paid off that summer. It got me my first billing, though not entirely my own name. "Master Joe Ashton, The Boy Wonder," they called me. And, more important, Billy raised my salary to $2.50 a week.

This is it, I thought. No man realizing his first million could have been as thrilled as I was. Doing the work I wanted to do, among people I liked, and getting $2.50 a week for it—well, what more could anyone ask?

I met a lot of nice people that summer. I got to know the famous Orton Family. Claude and Gordon Orton were circus headliners for years. They were real troupers and they always had a good word for the little fellow on the high trapeze. Gordon later went into vaudeville with one of the best dog acts ever staged.

Harry La Pearl, one of the funniest clowns in the busi-

47

ness, was with the Robinson show that year. And looking back on these early experiences, it seems I always had a special fondness for clowns. Perhaps it was prophetic.

Jimmy Dutton was a member of another great circus family. There were four Duttons with Robinson that summer. Jimmy had a pretty good philosophy of circus life and he was always encouraging me, saying little things to keep up my spirits, but mostly he did it with example. Once he was badly hurt in a fall, but he was back in the act in no time as if nothing had happened. It was an adult world, and I was trying my best to live up to it.

We were playing St. Louis sometime in May when I received a letter from home announcing the birth of Paul. Now there were four younger than I in the family, so I felt more grown up than ever.

And this was the summer when I knew for the first time what it was to be in love. I developed an infatuation for a bareback rider in the circus. Her name was Josie Demott, and I thought she was the most beautiful, the most graceful creature I had ever seen. I watched her from the entrance while she did her act in the ring, and, though she never knew it, I followed her all over the circus lot like an adoring puppy. It was a pretty hopeless case, though I didn't realize it, for she was 35 and I was twelve.

Thirty years later I was Billy Rose's guest at a performance of *Jumbo* at the old Hippodrome in New York. Jimmy Durante and Paul Whiteman were featured, I remember, and one of the acts was called "The Circus Fifty Years Ago."

I had a nostalgic twinge as Whiteman's orchestra struck up some old familiar circus tunes. I felt real homesick when a beautiful white horse came prancing on stage. Then suddenly I realized there was something mighty familiar about the rider on the horse's back.

Sure enough, it was Josie Demott, the beautiful bareback rider of my first infatuation. She was a little old lady now, but she sat her mount as poised as ever. She got a tremendous hand from the audience and a real ovation from me.

After the show I went backstage to visit "Pops" and Jimmy and other old friends, and she came by. I stopped her and introduced myself.

"Oh, I'd know you, Mr. Brown," she said, and her voice had a musical quality that matched her silver hair. "I've long been an admirer of your pictures."

"And Josie, I want you to know that I've been an admirer of yours for thirty years," I said.

She paused in thought for a moment. "Thirty years ago I was with the Robinson's Circus," she said.

"Yes, I know, and I was one of the Marvelous Ashtons."

"Oh, I remember them," she said, sparkling with the memory. "Which one of them were you?"

I could see she was thinking that I was one of the men. "I was the smallest," I said.

"Oh, no," she said, "you weren't that funny little one?"

"Yes," I admitted. "And just for your information, I was madly in love with you. You were my first love."

"You, you were in love with me?"

"Yes," I said.

She started crying, and the tears rolled down her wrinkled face. She put her arms around me. "May I kiss you?" she asked.

I said, "May I kiss you?"

I made another friend in Robinson's Circus whom I met again after thirty years, with somewhat the same results.

There weren't many kids with the circus that year, at least not many my age, but I don't recall being lonely very many times. In the first place we were too busy practicing or performing to have time to be alone. Those few moments I could call my own I spent in the menagerie tent, and in a short while I became so attached to several of the animals they were like real people in my life. The babies were my special pets. The trainers, sensing my fondness for animals, would let me hold the baby lions and baby bears, and the animal parents never seemed to mind. Then about mid-season a baby elephant was born, and I couldn't have been more excited about it had it been my own brother. I was the only one the mother would permit anywhere near the baby, and we romped together, in and out around her huge legs and trunk like two of the same species.

Thirty years later I was making a picture for Warners called *The Circus Clown*. Some of the location shots were made at the Barnes Brothers' winter quarters. I had a scene where I was to get on an elephant's back. The gag was that I had the biggest job in the world, washing the elephant.

While the director was explaining to the trainer just what he wanted me and the elephant to do, I strolled over to the animal and fed it a handful of peanuts.

In the script, which the director was still explaining to the trainer, the elephant was to hold her knee out for me to step on and then lift me to his back.

"That'll take a little time," said the trainer. "She'll have to be trained to take the cue from you."

But while they were talking I spoke to the elephant. "Up, up!" I said. "Up, old girl!" She put out her leg, I stepped on it and she hoisted me to her back as neatly as if we had been doing it all our lives. The trainer and picture director looked around and they were flabbergasted.

"How did you do that?" asked the trainer. "She never did that for anyone else without training."

"I don't know," I said. "It just seemed the natural thing to do."

The trainer shook his head, and the next day he was still puzzling over the incident. "Mr. Brown," he asked, "weren't you with a circus when you were a kid?" I told him I was. "I was with Sells & Downs and later with Robinson's show," I said.

50

"What year?" he asked.

"About 1904."

"You were with Robinson's in 1904?"

I nodded.

"That elephant was with Robinson's."

"How old is she?" I asked, but then I already knew, for the whole season of 1904 came back to my mind. I told him about the baby elephant that had been my playmate. There was no doubt in my mind that this was the same animal. And she remembered me. If you saw that picture and remember how smooth the elephant sequences were, this was the reason.

Toward the end of July, the circus route turned south to tour the southern states, and Ashe decided to quit.

"Too hot down there," he said, "and besides, they give everybody a salary cut because they don't make as much in the southern states."

That was his excuse, and for all I know he may have been right. But I heard Fred Fisher, equestrian director of the Robinson Circus, say that there was an old saying in the South: "The three biggest events of the year down there are Al G. Fields' Minstrels, Christmas, and Robinson's Circus." The minstrels and Christmas were winter events, so the circus must have had it good.

Anyway, we finished out the season with carnivals and a short engagement with the Floto Circus.

We were playing at a carnival in East Delaware, Ohio, that summer when I met a team of young clowns called Clark & McCullough. I think they were just breaking in, for this was Bobby Clark's home town. It was also the beginning of a long friendship between Bobby and me.

Carnivals in those days can hardly be compared to the innocuous things they call carnivals today. Bunco squads and civic groups have dry cleaned them. You don't see many performers like my hero "Splash" Johnson any more.

51

Splash was a high-diver. He dived 100 feet into three feet of water, or so it was advertised. I hung around the side shows of the circus for two weeks before I found out how he did it.

The barker would get up on a little platform and start the ballyhoo. Pretty soon he'd have a large gawky crowd around him, and then Splash would stroll out dressed in a smart black and white striped bathing suit that looked like winter underwear.

"Are you ready, Mr. Splash?" yelled the barker.

Splash would bow once to the barker and once to the crowd and then put his foot on the first rung of the ladder. At that moment the band would strike up *The Blue Danube Waltz*. Then the spieler would go into a lengthy build-up of the act and about Splash, "The world's greatest, the world's most daring high-diver."

On each up beat of *The Blue Danube*, Splash would take another step. By the time he had gone up only about fifteen feet someone in the audience would gasp, "My gosh! Is he going higher?"

The barker never stopped talking and he never missed this cue from his audience either. "One hundred and twenty feet, ladies and gentlemen, the most sensational, the most extraordinary feat of acrobatic skill you will ever see." Splash continued his measured steps up the ladder, and by now the crowd was counting them in unison.

"Never in the history of the world has any man attempted such a . . ." Hollywood publicity men got their first inspiration from such side show spielers. "He's going to dive from the top of that ladder, one hundred and thirty feet in the air, into this little tank and only three feet of water!" There was a foot square platform at the top of the ladder. "Watch him, ladies and gentlemen!"

They watched him, counting the rounds, and as he went up and up their heads went back and back.

52

Finally, he reached the top. The music stopped and the barker went into his spiel all over again. Then he'd wind it up with "And now, Mr. Splash." He turned and yelled up at Splash standing on the top of the ladder, "Mr. Splash, are you ready?"

Splash would take an old dirty silk handkerchief out of his tights and hold it up to see if there was any wind. Then he'd wet one finger and hold it up, testing the slightest current. Obviously, any movement of air might mean the difference between life and death in such a dive at so small a target. Splash would hesitate for a moment and then appear to yell back, but his voice was lowered so it sounded as though he were a mile up in the air. "Yes," he'd say.

"Are you ready to take your life in your hands?"

Splash would answer with a little "Yes."

"Have you anything to say before you leap?"

Splash would hesitate for a long moment and then he'd yell so everyone on the lot could hear him: "Yes, go to Flannigan and O'Connor's for your shirts, underwear, and sox." He'd put in a big plug for some local store where he got ten dollars worth of merchandise for the week's advertising. Then he would jump off the darned thing and make the biggest splash you ever saw.

Splash was my hero until I found out how he did it.

In the first place, they would dig down into the ground and drop the tank about seven feet below the ground level. With three feet sticking up above the ground and the tank filled with water, he had a good ten feet of depth to dive into. That was the first fake I discovered.

The other was this. The rounds on the ladder at the bottom were about a foot apart, but as they went up they grew closer together until at the top he could hardly get his feet between them. So it wasn't anywhere near the height they advertised.

Splash would stroll out dressed in the bathing suit for this act, but most of the time he was just one of the canvas men. He helped put up and strike the tents. But for this one event he was Splash, the daredevil high-diver. But he never dived, he jumped. He hit the water in a sitting position and the splash was terrific. Then he'd struggle out like a dog.

That was my hero until I saw them digging in the next town. They went to work early, with a canvas rigged around the spot, so no one could see what they were doing. But several truck loads of dirt would be distributed somewhere about the lot.

These performers may have been daredevils all right, but there was nothing skillful in what they did. There was a fellow who did a loop-the-loop trick with Robinson's show. He rode a little auto on a track that made a complete loop. The car had flanged wheels that kept it on the track no matter what position it was in, and the performer was always strapped in.

The fellow got fifteen dollars a week for this trick— and the other jobs he did around the lot, and he spent most of it on hard liquor. The barker always made a big announcement about the act and about the daredevil rider, and he got to believing it. One day he came in drunk and refused to let them strap him in the car. Someone tried to argue with him, but he wasn't listening. Wasn't he the big hero, the great daredevil the man was talking about?

He got in the car and they started it, but this time it got stuck on the up side of the loop and he fell out on his head. He broke his arm.

Our carnival bookings after we left Robinson's, and the short engagement with the Floto Circus, took us into the autumn. When the circus went into winter quarters in Denver, Ashe was in no mood to go back to Toledo "just to get Evan educated," as he said. We teamed up with a troupe of Arab gymnasts and booked the show at a state fair in Pueblo

54

and an airdrome in Denver. The Arabs did all the familiar tricks with a flourish and a little touch of mysticism. One I remember (because I was in it) was the trick of the disappearing boy in a basket. And when they did their pyramid trick, I was the "top mounter," the one who somersaulted up and stood on top.

Ashe, apparently, had no intention of getting me back to school that fall. When we finished our engagements in Colorado, he booked the act on a cheap vaudeville circuit on the Coast. It was a new experience for me.

I had grown used to the conventional life and the high standards of circus people. I was distressed and ill-at-ease performing in the smoke-filled rooms of honky-tonks and beer gardens. I felt shame and embarrassment that our act had to compete with girls in bangly skirts who "worked" the tables on a percentage basis. And the hours in such places were pretty hard. Frequently we'd start our last show around two A. M., and it would be nearly daylight before I fell into bed exhausted.

There were occasional respites from the honky-tonks, however, when we played the legitimate vaudeville houses. Though they were all small and cheap, the managers frequently were warm-hearted and kind to me.

We played Pantages' theatres in Seattle in the days when he had only two small houses. They were right next door to each other. Both of them were stores that had been made over into theatres. They were his first venture into show business, and I think at this time he was still being financed by Klondike Kate.

Although the stages were small, we had revised our act so we could still do the aerial casting act. (Although, at times, on the backward swing I'd go clear off stage and sometimes my backside would bang the outer wall of the theatre.) But doing four shows a day and five on Saturdays and Sundays

Angeles. We covered the honky-tonks in Butte and Spokane and San Francisco. And it was mid-April before we got back to Toledo and I entered school.

Since Ashe had agreed to clothe and feed me, sometime just before we returned home he would always take me to a store and buy me a new suit of clothes. He never spent more than $3.95, but, of course, to me that was a pretty good suit. And it didn't matter that I had looked like a tramp all season. The idea was to return home in style. I guess the impression we created on the home folks was one of fabulous prosperity.

That spring I went to visit my grandparents in Holgate. Next door lived one of those small-town characters who was obviously amazed at my success. I had been places, done things and seen things, and I got paid for it. Of course no one outside the family knew exactly how much, but it all made a big impression on the other boys in my neighborhood at home, the kids at school, and the neighbors of my grandparents in Holgate. I remember old Barney Poulson about as vividly as anyone of that period.

Long before I woke up that first morning in my grandmother's spare bedroom, Barney was puttering around in his back yard waiting for me to put in an appearance. When I finally did come out, he sauntered over.

"Hi, there, Evan," he said. "They tell me you've been doin' big things out there," and he waved a hand to indicate that "out there" was the whole wide world outside Holgate.

"Well, yessir," I said, trying not to boast. He hemmed on one subject awhile and hawed on another and finally got around to this:

"Say, Evan, I was just thinkin', if you was me and I was you, how much money would I be makin'?"

School work that spring included a lot of homework and it was with considerable difficulty that I managed to finish the term with my class. I could never have done it without the help of understanding teachers, God bless them. Surrounded by such understanding, I could not complain even had I felt like it. And I didn't gripe at home either. There was a greater tragedy there than the small problem of my education. Baby Paul, I discovered when I returned home, was blind.

Steaks and Caviar

With all his sternness, Billy Ashe was a great teacher. He taught me two or three tricks that were not duplicated by any other performer of that period. One of these, and the one that brought me most acclaim, was the somersault with a double full twist. Usually I did it with the help of the trampoline. Bouncing high into the air, I'd do a somersault and twist my body around twice, then hit the trampoline, bounce to the stage, and make my bow.

Lacking the trampoline, Ashe would act as the springboard himself. Lying on his back, he would use his feet to catapult me high in the air. I'd do the somersault and double twist and land on my feet.

I think Billy was prouder of this than of any other achievement of his life. He wasn't satisfied with showing the trick to paid spectators either. He kept me beside him all the time so that we could perform this corkscrew trick wherever we went.

Ashe was also a great talker, and he had only one subject: acrobats. He would sulk for awhile when any other topic came up and then suddenly swoop down on the conversation and switch it to acrobats. He had his own formulas for changing the subject from crops, politics, baseball, or horse racing to acrobats in one or two sentences. If Theodore Roosevelt was being discussed, Ashe would cut in with "Teddy certainly turned a double back somersault on the tariff. Now, speaking of double back somersaults . . ." Or, "Did you ever know that Teddy's uncle was an acrobat? He was the first man that ever . . ." Having thus put the subject squarely before the house, he would rapidly develop it to the point where he had removed his shoes, planted himself on his back, and sent me spiralling upward in a double twist. Once he stole a conversation in the lobby of the Sherman Hotel in Chicago and was soon kicking me at the ceiling. Under the pretense of contributing a simile or a metaphor, he would confiscate conversations from strangers in railway stations and send me corkscrewing toward the roof. In the course of my life I have known most of the great conversation snatchers of the entertainment world, but I have never met the equal of Billy Ashe.

Ashe's insistence on constant practice was the secret of any success the troupe had. But there were times when he used practice as a means of punishment. One night in San José I missed a trick in our aerial act, and he came off stage in a bad mood. I was expecting a beating, but he didn't say anything until we got back to the hotel. When we entered our room he jerked the mattress off the bed, spread it on the floor, and said "Now, jump! I want you to do flip-flaps on that until I come back!" He left with the others and went off to eat.

I was getting a little wiser by this time, however, and I decided that doing without my supper was punishment enough. Any practice would be too much. I left the door open so I could hear them returning, and lay down on the mattress to rest.

About an hour later I heard them coming. I splashed some water on my face and back to make it look like perspiration

61

and went into my act. When Ashe came in I was puffing and laboring at it as if I was nearly exhausted.

"O.K.," he said. "Now get to bed. And let that be a lesson to you. Don't let me catch you missing any more tricks." Nothing was said about food.

A famous psychologist doing some research into the thoughts of working children once asked me what I thought about during this period of my life. About all I could remember was my constant obsession with food. And it wasn't quality but quantity I was concerned about.

Back in the Busby Bros. Circus days, when the performers kicked about the food they were served, I'm sure it wasn't good by modern standards, but hungry kids found little fault with it.

Once we were playing at a dumpy little theatre in Vallejo that was in the same building with a Mexican restaurant. Cooking odors from the restaurant drifted across the stage throughout the performance. I drooled all through the act. I simply couldn't get my mind on acrobatics.

The only time I ever satisfied my appetite during this period was at D. J. Grauman's Unique Theatre in San Francisco. Sid Grauman, later of Hollywood fame (Grauman's Chinese and Grauman's Egyptian theatres), was manager of a theatre in San José and his father, Dave, was proprietor of the Unique in San Francisco. We played several engagements at both houses and I remember the elder Grauman with some grateful feelings.

The Unique was an L-shaped theatre (probably that's what made it unique). The early customers sat in the part of the L that faced the stage. The late-comers had to wait in the part of the L that faced a blank wall until they could get seats within sight of the stage. Grauman allowed the show to run its full time if the crowd was only fair. But if his clients came in large numbers, he cut the acts to half or even to a quarter of their length, in order to shorten the show and increase the audience turnover. He couldn't work the hurry-up system if he let the actors go out to eat, so he fed them sandwiches in the wings. Later, taking a lesson from the zoo, he made a special act out of feeding them before the audience. He kept the house happy by his comments on the table manners of the performers.

He had the right idea about people who played in his theatre, though. He wanted them to come in with the right spirit. He always welcomed everyone and never overlooked the kids. He shook hands with them all.

"Velcome, velcome to Grauman's Unique Theatre," he'd say, in a very marked accent. "Ve are alvays happy to have you here." He shook hands with Ashe and then he shook hands with the kids and then he went back and shook hands with Ashe again. "Vot you fellows vant to eat?"

"What do you mean what do we want to eat?" said Ashe, suspiciously.

"Vot do you like to eat? I vant you should be my guests here today."

"Be your guest?" Ashe was an old hand at this.

"Yes, of course, at the Grauman alvays, between the fourth and fifth shows ve alvays feed our people."

"Between the fourth and fifth shows? We do three a day."

"No, no, perhaps today ve don't do five, but between the third and fourth you'll have dinner with me. You'll be my guests."

"Look, our agreement . . ."

"The agreement? Not more than four on veekdays, that's all it says. But you know today's a holiday, Vashington's Birthday."

"What difference does that make?"

"Oh, ve feed you, don't you vorry. Ve don't vant you should have to go out."

Of course he knew we couldn't go out and get back in time for another show, so he had it all planned. And this is the way it went: The curtain came down and Grauman stepped out and addressed the audience.

"Good afternoon everyone. Happy Vashington's Birthday to everybody. Vell, I guess you're satisfied you got a pretty good show here, huh? These people are the best; nothing is any better than these people. And vhy? Vhy of course, they are happy people. They come here and they are treated like ladies and gentlemen and they are alvays vell fed."

Meanwhile the sets were being changed back stage and a huge table, loaded with food, was rolled in. When the curtain went up again all the actors were seated around the table.

"The best of food. Everybody eats nothing but the best at the Unique. These are my guests, these are my people, these are ladies and gentlemen." He waved his hand in a broad gesture.

"You think the food is not good? Look, I vant to show you something. Meats, ve got nothing but the best." He reached over and picked a steak off one of the plates, walked down to the footlights and held it over toward the audience. "Look at that, did you ever see anything better than that?" He put it back on the guy's plate. "And where do ve get such meat? Vhy, right across the street at Samson's Market. The best meats in town."

And then he went on to the vegetables (from Wong Song's Vegetable Market), and the pies and breads (from Schultz's Bakery), while the "guests" devoured it all with gusto, and the audience drooled. Of course, he got it all, including its preparation (Market Street Cafe) for the plugs he gave it. And the actors made a pretty realistic act out of it too.

As far as I was concerned, I didn't mind doing another show. For a meal like that I'd have done half a dozen more.

In April, 1906, the Five Marvelous Ashtons were playing at a honky-tonk called the Haymarket Music Hall on Mason Street in San Francisco. There had been many changes in the five during the years I had been with the troupe, and at this particular time there were, besides Ashe and me, Julie and Philip Barth and a big fellow in Otto's place, named Ernie Close. Julie was the older of the Barth brothers and one of the greatest flip-flap tumblers of all time. He could do more flip-flaps on a handkerchief than most acrobats could do on a whole stage. And somewhere Ashe had acquired a mongrel dog that he called Frisco.

One day he and the older fellows took the dog and went to Oakland. They left Philip and me at the Turklu Apartments, a fifth-rate rooming house on Turk Street where we always stayed when we were in San Francisco. Billy gave each of us a dime for our lunch.

That morning, as usual, we slept till noon so we wouldn't have to eat any breakfast. When we did, we ate at a small cafe around the corner where we ordered curried lamb. We always picked this dish because they served lots of gravy with it and a big stack of bread.

When Ashe and the others returned around 4 o'clock, he remembered that they had forgotten to feed Frisco. He gave me a dime and told me to run down to the delicatessen and get some roast beef for him.

I'll never forget that delicatessen, and the big aproned Dutchman who ran it. I asked him for ten cents worth of roast beef and he began slicing it off. One, two, three, nice big hot slices which he put on a paper on the scales. The odor of pickles and sauerkraut and sausages and hot pastrami and roast beef made such an appetizing aroma I could hardly stand it. He sliced off another piece and put it on the scales, studied the dial a moment while I held my breath, and then added a half slice.

I paid him and left the store, with the warm package under my arm. I hadn't gone very far before the warmth of the package and its delicate aroma tempted me to open it and sample its contents. I thought, "Billy won't miss that half slice. I'll just eat that." I devoured the half slice and I never before or since have tasted such good roast beef. A little farther on I ducked into a dark doorway and opened the package again. I really intended only to smell it, I told myself. But once the package was open, I couldn't resist taking another slice.

After I'd eaten it I remembered Ashe, and for a moment I debated whether or not I should run away. Finally I decided to go in and face the music. Whatever he did to me it was worth it, I reasoned. It was still the best roast beef I ever tasted.

When I walked in, all of the Ashtons were assembled. I handed Billy the package and held my breath. He opened it, looked up at me and said "Gosh, Evan, you got a lot for a dime didn't you?"

At the Turklu, Billy and I shared a double bed in one room and the other three fellows were bunked together in an adjoining room. Both rooms were at the back of the house and looked out on a blank brick wall. After our last performance on the night of April 17, we trudged our weary way up the hill and practically fell into bed. The act went on at one o'clock and it was around three A.M. on the 18th when we got to bed.

Sometime about five on the morning of the 18th, I was awakened by someone shaking me. It was Ashe. I opened one eye enough to see the wall outside our window. It was weaving back and forth, so I knew I needed more sleep. I turned over and immediately dozed off again. Ashe shook me again and yelled "Come on, get up!" Then I realized the other fellows were in the room and everyone was talking at once.

I got up as consciousness dawned on me and I realized that something terrible was happening to the earth. I ran to the window and saw the brick wall opposite moving like a tree in a hurricane.

Billy was already into his clothes and yelling something about the equipment at the theatre. Ernie tried the lights, but they wouldn't go on. Julie was standing at the wash basin with a blank look on his face. He had tried the water and it was off too. By this time I could hear people screaming and yelling in the street and the sound of fire engines going by.

Ashe and the two older fellows left. "I don't know when we'll get back," he said. "Here's a dime apiece for your breakfast." He was worried about the equipment we had left in the theatre.

Philip and I dressed hurriedly and went out and spent our dimes and then sat on the curb and watched the people hurrying by. A big fire broke out in the downtown section and then another one nearby. We watched excitedly as the sun came up through the flames and smoke. It was the greatest spectacle we ever saw and we thought it was put on for our especial benefit.

Pretty soon Billy came back with Ernie and Julie dragging our big wardrobe trunk between them, the fire and smoke seeming to be right at their heels.

"Let's get our things out of the hotel," Ashe said. "We've got to get out of here before we get burned to death."

We hastily threw our few belongings together and started out. The woman who owned the place was weeping and wringing her hands. She said it would all be destroyed and if we wanted anything in the house we should just take it. "Take anything you want," she said. "Take anything you want."

I remember thinking I'd like to have the big grandfather clock in the hall. I even tried lifting it. But I compromised by taking a couple of pillows, which was a pretty good choice as it turned out.

Ashe said we should try to get to the waterfront and get a ferry to Oakland. We had to detour around fires and streets

67

that were choked with the debris of fallen buildings. Explosions were thundering now all over town as dynamiting crews tried to stop the fire. Once we came on a crew that was preparing to blow up a grocery store.

"Help yourselves, boys," they said. "There's still a few things left in it." While they prepared the dynamite we grabbed the first cases we could lay our hands on. When we reached a safe distance we stopped and examined our haul. All we had was caviar, but we had enough of that to feed an army.

"Oh, fish eggs!" I said, when I saw it. I grabbed a big handful and put it all in my mouth—and I could do it too, even at that time.

What with the detours and the heavy trunk, it was midafternoon before we reached the open stretch along the Embarcadero. Meanwhile, the caviar was disappearing—by the handful at every rest stop. To that bunch of hungry kids even caviar tasted like food, though it was the first caviar that any of us ever ate. Unfortunately, it gave us an ungodly thirst and there was no water to drink. Once we found a broken hose that still dripped a little water and that was all we had throughout that day and night. The caviar was also the only food we had, with the exception of the dimes' worth we had purchased earlier in the morning.

We slept in the open that night and the following morning Ashe wangled passage on a tugboat to Oakland. The first night there we slept in a church and the next in a bowling alley. Then Ashe bought some oilcloth and rigged up a tent in a vacant lot, and we stayed there several days before we finally got a train out. The railroads were carrying refugees away from the disaster free of charge, but they were made up of day coaches and so crowded that the passengers took turns standing in the aisles.

But the heart of the nation was torn in sympathy for these

destitute survivors. All along the way the train was met with delegations bringing wagonloads of fresh fruits, vans of hot food, soup, coffee. I, who had seldom before had enough to eat, crammed so much food into my shrunken stomach that I could neither sit nor stand with comfort. It took us seven days to reach Chicago, and I suffered the entire trip with acute indigestion of a very superior variety.

Our families had given us up for lost. The published lists of survivors had never listed our names and they assumed we had perished. Our homecoming, therefore, was doubly exciting, and we had ready audiences for our tales of adventure.

In my excitement I forgot my usual caution and accidentally let slip something about how Ashe had treated us and how he had beat me from time to time. When Mike and John, my older brothers, heard that they were all for going right down and thrashing Billy Ashe on the spot. Mother restrained them, but she never did forgive Ashe, and to the day he died she never spoke to him again.

It ended my association with him, and, for a few weeks, my career as an acrobat.

In the summer of 1952, I was the guest of honor at a Rotary Club luncheon in Toledo when they made me a life member. They gave me a diamond-studded membership button, and, since it happened to be my birthday, they presented me with a huge cake.

In my speech of acceptance I asked them if it would be all right if I didn't cut the cake. I told them I'd like to take it out to my friend Billy Ashe, the man really responsible for my success, since he gave me my first start. He was then in a little nursing home in Toledo and in very poor circumstances.

I loved Billy despite all the things he did to me and I learned a lot from him. He was a foster father to me during

69

my formative years. And if there is a key to my success it is in the lessons he taught me—stubborn persistence in the face of defeat and enjoyment in a job well done.

I'm glad I took the cake out to Billy and had a chance to tell him these things. He died the following April, at the age of 82.

One Third of a Trio

Among the saloons I frequented back in my paper-selling days were two or three that were my favorites. Johnny Needham's, next door to Burt's Theatre, had a high bar that was so wide it extended out over the footrail. I could walk under it, between the footrail and its base, and no bartender could see me. That's how I got many a good feed.

Between acts at Burt's, everyone would rush into the saloon and have a drink. With the crowd at its height I'd spot the location of the bowl of hardboiled eggs, the dish of pickles, and the basket of bread all in one glance as I sneaked in through the swinging doors. I'd edge myself along the bar until I came to the right spot, reach a hand back up over my head, and help myself. It worked fine until one night Johnny got wise and substituted a bowl of boiling water for the eggs.

But Johnny Needham was a happy Irishman who enjoyed his work and had a lot of friends. He was always humming or singing snatches from some Irish song, usually "Ireland must be heaven, for my mother came from there," and in later years he sponsored a baseball team. I managed the

71

team for him one season and he played shortstop right along side me at second. He was much older than most of us but he was a good player. There was only one other player who was older than Johnny and he was my first baseball hero. Billy Smith was an outfielder on the first Toledo team I ever saw in action. He became my hero when he made the greatest catch I ever saw up to that time. (It still is, for that matter, though I saw Willie Mays make the same catch years later.) Billy was still playing baseball and on Needham's All Stars when I became manager of the team some years later. I didn't recognize him at first. For several days I watched him play and never connected him with the Billy Smith of my boyhood hero worship. When it did finally dawn on me that he was the same Billy Smith, I got the shakes. I was so nervous with awe and stage fright I could hardly play.

Once, en route to a game in another town, Johnny and I got to reminiscing about the old days when I was a newsboy and I told him how I used to swipe eggs from his bar. He laughed and laughed as he recalled those days. "You shoulda asked me for 'em kid," he said. "I'd have given you anything you wanted." And he would have, too, for Johnny was like that.

Crowley's saloon, another favorite, was on the corner of Jefferson and Ontario streets, catty-corner across from Burt's Theatre, and Colonel Bolen's Bar was not far away.

Ollie Pecord was the bartender at the latter place and he was always doing something for the kids in the street. He too lived on The Hill. He organized baseball games and taught us how to box and wrestle. He was popular in all local sports and every kid in that part of town idolized him. He was the man who later (1919) refereed the Dempsey-Willard fight in Toledo. The first baseball team I ever played on, the Young Avondales (I was the youngest), was organized by Ollie Pecord. He was one of the first persons I went to see when I returned to Toledo from my last tour with Ashe. If there was a job in Toledo for a grown-up youngster, then Ollie would know about it.

I've known a lot of people who assumed the responsibilities of manhood before they were fifteen. Theatrical history is full of them. I think I became a man the night my parents signed the contract with Ashe. That is why all the sprains and broken bones I got I simply took for granted. I thought all those things were part of the game. I didn't know there was another way to learn the things I wanted to learn. And I think for that matter, neither did Ashe.

I was not yet fourteen at the time of the earthquake and fire in San Francisco, a seasoned trouper at the time I broke with Ashe. And though I felt some gratitude (and always have) for all that Billy taught me, my brothers and my parents thought I should "settle down." But if anything can be said to get into one's blood, then my taste of this thing called show business had gotten into mine. I gave only half an ear to their counsel. But I did confide to Ollie my need to find steady employment.

"I'd like something where I could use my acrobatics," I told him. It was the only skill I had.

"The only thing I can think of is baseball," he said. "I could get you on a team in the Trolley League and you could pick up a few bucks that way."

Ollie never mentioned my size. I was still pretty small in 1906, but I was well ahead of my years and size in experience and athletic ability, and he knew it. I needed the money and I loved baseball, so on weekends I played a little semi-pro in the Trolley League—the places one could reach on the interurban trolley system.

Meanwhile, since Ollie knew a lot of people in professional athletics and in the theatre, he volunteered to write to some of them for me.

One day he got a letter from an acrobat by the name of

Tommy Bell. Bell wrote that he and a partner by the name of Frank Prevost were getting together an acrobatic act and they thought they could use me if I was interested. They offered me $7.50 a week, but nothing was said about railroad fare to New York where I was to join them. They assumed I would pay that if I wanted the job.

I wanted the job all right and I had saved a little money from baseball, but I still needed another game to make enough to get me to New York.

There was an understanding among the players that if it rained and the game was postponed, no one got paid. However, if a player was on the trolley and en route to the game before he received notice of cancellation, he got paid anyway. The weather had been a little unsettled all week and I was sure it was building up for a good rain on Sunday, the day I was to play in Lima. I got up early Sunday morning, and sure enough, it was beginning to rain. But they didn't catch me with any cancellation notice. I was dressed and on the trolley before anyone tried to telephone me.

The following week I was on my way to New York.

I was favorably impressed with Bell's appearance. He was well dressed and he had the manners of an educated gentleman. His partner, Frank Prevost, was a quiet sort of fellow, older and more conservative. Now, I thought, I'm going to be with two swell guys. No more beatings and no more hungry days. And the routines we practiced were designed for vaudeville. They differed in many respects from the Ashton specialties. We perfected an act in which I jumped from a standing position on the shoulders of one acrobat to the trampoline, which bounced me to the shoulders of the other on the opposite side of the trampoline. In both jumps, down and up, I did single and double somersaults with pirouettes or "twisters." Not difficult tricks for me, but they required precision timing and a lot of practice.

In a few weeks we had the act about ready to sell. It was

74

called the Bell-Prevost Trio. I was "Trio." I was still having trouble getting my name in there. First it was the Ashton family and now it was a trio without my name. But I didn't mind. This was work I enjoyed.

We opened at the Henderson Music Hall, Coney Island, on July 23, 1906. It was a good week, and besides it included my birthday. I was fourteen that week, and with a salary of $7.50 jingling in my pocket at the end of it, I thought I was doing pretty well.

On the same bill that week were Victor Moore and Emma Littlefield in a sketch called "Change Your Act." He was the same great comedian then that he was later. Others on that bill were Annabelle Whitford, in "The Gibson Girl," Avery and Hart, O'Brien and Havel in "Tick's and Clicks," and a man named W. C. Fields, as funny then as he ever was. He opened the show.

We laid off a week after that engagement, during which time Prevost and I continued daily practice but Bell joined us only two or three times. He felt he didn't need any more practice, though subsequent events proved otherwise.

We heard that a certain gentleman from South America was in the city booking acts for a three-month tour in his country. It sounded like a golden opportunity. We wangled a place on the Sunday vaudeville bill at the Colonial Theatre in New York. (We replaced an aerial act that couldn't work Sundays because they wore tights. Under existing blue laws Sunday vaudeville had to be called "concerts.") We were informed that the señor would be in the Colonial at that time.

But everything that could go wrong with an act went wrong at that matinee. It was terrible. And Bell blamed it all on me. He came off stage in a blind fury because he thought we had muffed it. Then, in the dressing room, he really smacked me around. I was shocked to find myself back in the old rut again.

75

Presently Prevost, who had gone out front to see if he could straighten it out with the prospect, came back and said that the señor had not been in the audience. He said he was expected for the evening performance.

But our evening performance was no better. If anything, it was worse than the matinee. We missed so many tricks the audience laughed at us. There were so many wrong moves, slips, and falls we must have looked like rank amateurs.

Looking back on it, I'd say it was probably one of the luckiest performances I ever gave. Had our act been good enough that evening to secure the South American booking I might never have come back. Had we gone to South America, Bell might have figured he could do anything he wanted to and get away with it.

It was a terrible shock to discover that Bell was something like Ashe, only more so. Where Billy had punished me for mistakes much as a father might punish his son, Bell would explode in a fit of temper that was vicious and unreasonable.

A few weeks later we were playing a fair in Sedalia, Missouri. Our stage was a platform in front of the grandstand and our dressing room was underneath the platform. Besides an audience in the grandstand, there was a crowd standing around the platform. I don't know what it was that I did wrong but as we came down the steps Bell struck me with the back of his hand.

A big fellow in the audience stepped up and grabbed Bell by the arm and swung him around. "If you strike that kid again, I'll smash your face in," he said, and I'm sure he could have done it.

When we got under the stage Bell was furious. He said "You go out and tell that damned hick to mind his own business." I knew if I didn't he'd beat the devil out of me, so I went out and told him. All my life since I've wished I knew who that fellow was so I could explain.

My concern in later years for lonesome boys in service

and lonely people in hospitals is the outgrowth of boyhood experiences in small-time show business. I remember all too well some of the homesick days of my own youth.

There weren't many, to be sure. I've been depressed and discouraged and wondered once or twice if life was worth the battle, but most of this came later, when I had greater responsibilities. In these early days it was a rare moment when I felt the blues. Hunger and mistreatment seldom caused me much depression. Usually, I took these things for granted. But there was one Christmas Eve, the season I was with Bell and Prevost, that was especially memorable.

I was a scrawny fifteen year old, sitting alone in a dingy hotel lobby in North Adams, Massachusetts. And this evening was notably sad, because the lobby and streets were crowded with gift-laden strangers while I had no one to wish me one little Merry Christmas. As I huddled down in the old leather chair, my hand felt something under me. It was a silver dollar.

"Jimminy!" I thought. "Now I can do my Christmas shopping just like anybody." I dashed out along the town's main street to look at the glowing store windows and ponder what to buy.

I chose a pipe for Bell and a pair of slippers for Prevost.

Back in our hotel room, I arranged the gifts carefully on the men's pillows and throughout our performance that evening I enjoyed a warm glow of secret pleasure.

I was getting into my cot that night when Bell came in with the pipe in his fist.

"Merry Christmas, Tommy!" I chirped.

"Don't gimme no Merry Christmas business," he said as he yanked me onto the floor. "Where did you steal the money from? You could get this whole act in trouble for stealing."

That incident, although similar to others I went through, was the low mark in my boyhood. But it only stiffened my will to climb. That Christmas I told myself, "Never mind, kid. Someday you'll have thousands of friends. You'll buy diamonds for your mother. You'll build a huge house with your own private soda fountain. You'll even get invited to the White House."

In due course I made every detail of this dreamy, childish resolve come true, but that season turned out to be the toughest I ever saw. Bell cuffed me for the slightest mistake. If I let one foot get one inch out of line I got a beating for it. Prevost was a kindly, easygoing fellow and seldom interfered, but occasionally when Bell was a little rougher than usual, he would stick up for me.

"Let the kid alone, Tommy," he'd say. "He's trying."

It got so I never set foot on the stage that cold terror didn't grip my heart. I could never relax. I always knew that if I made the slightest mistake he would pounce on me. In time the strain became so great that nerves and muscles could take no more.

I was getting older and a little more mature physically. I resented his beatings more and more and finally one day, while Prevost was striking the rigging, Bell and I returned to the dressing room. I knew he was going to beat me. When we got to the dressing room, and hardly explaining what I should have done, he started damning me for the mistakes I made. He hit me with the back of his hand so that I fell against the wall and slid down to a sitting position. A little dazed, I struggled to my feet.

"I'm going to . . ." he said, starting toward me.

I backed up against the wall, and for the first time in my life I swore. "You s.o.b.," I said. "If you hit me again I'll kill you." I meant it, and I think Bell knew I meant it. He didn't come any farther and he didn't stop me when I left the dressing room.

I sought out Prevost and told him I was through. When he saw I was in earnest, he asked me to stay on and fill out the two weeks we had booked. It was a miserable, nerve-wrack-

78

ing two weeks, but I stuck it out and at the end I headed for home.

After a few weeks of idleness, during which Bell and Prevost tried out several new kids, Bell wrote me a letter. None of the other kids were any good, he said, and he added a lot of flattery for me. He wound it up with an elaborate apology and promised that "things would be better" if I'd rejoin the troupe. My idleness was bothering me by that time too, so I went back.

Not long after that we were playing a street carnival at Hudson, New York. We were doing our act on a platform in the middle of the street, right in front of our hotel. In one particular trick Bell threw me in a somersault high into the air. I came down, landing in a standing position on his shoulders.

It was a fairly simple trick, but we weren't doing it cleanly. My feet had to land on his shoulders in the perfect position or the trick would appear wobbly, sloppy. As we mounted the steps to the platform, Bell turned to me and said, "See that you do it right this time."

We went into our act, doing several tricks that led up to this one which Bell and I had worked up. They went off smoothly enough and I was not expecting any trouble with the special trick.

Bell threw me into the air and I went into my somersault. Then, without warning, without telling me that I had done anything wrong, and while I was still up in the air, he just walked away. Too late I saw what he was doing and I tried to brace myself, but I hit the hard platform in an awkward position and broke my leg.

Bell strode off the stage, passed through the crowd and entered the hotel without looking back.

Prevost picked me up and carried me into the hotel and then went back and took down the apparatus. It was the last time it was used by the Bell-Prevost Trio.

Ladies and Gentlemen and Acrobats

The public's low opinion of burlesque today has caused more than one prominent star to soft-pedal his (or her) humble beginnings in this field. I am much too grateful for the things I learned in burlesque to belittle its importance in my story. It was a fortunate thing for me that Frank Prevost decided burlesque would be a good place to try my comedy. It was a fortunate thing for me that he recognized comedy talents in me.

There were funnier looking people than I in and out of show business (though I couldn't name one off-hand), but Prevost had a sixth sense about such things backed up by long experience.

If the history of the acrobats of the circus ring and the vaudeville stage were ever written, one of the most prominent names in it would be that of Prevost. For nearly half a century the name of Prevost was known to the patrons of the circus and the vaudeville theatre. Under the names of Rice and Prevost, Prevost Brothers, Prevost & Prevost, and many other combinations, members of the "family" were constantly before the public for more than forty years.

Originally, there were four "brothers." There were Edward, Solomon, and Howard Prevost and Frank Leroy Guise. Frank was a "Prevost" as I had been an "Ashton." They were seen with every circus of importance that ever toured America, from the days of the old one-ringed shows to the modern tented cities of Ringling Brothers and Barnum & Bailey. Edward Prevost was conceded by the other brothers to have been the greatest tumbler of the family, and his brothers claimed he was the greatest acrobat the world ever saw. He was the first man to turn a double back somersault in the air from the ground without the aid of a springboard or any other apparatus. Only in recent years have other acrobats been able to accomplish this feat.

Frank was always the "understander," catching the other brothers after their somersaults in the air, and doing the work from the ground while they worked in the air. He had a background of long experience. He was the man who taught Fred Stone his first somersault and he had a keen sense of showmanship.

Frank Prevost was in his late forties when the Bell-Prevost Trio broke up, so he was old enough to have been my father. And in many ways Frank was like a father to me. He took me to his home in Cedar Manor, which was about a mile and a half from Jamaica, New York, and cared for me while my leg healed.

Mr. and Mrs. Guise, Frank Prevost and his wife Greta (known in show business as Greta Leroy), were a happily married middle-aged couple and they treated me as one of the family. It was six or seven weeks before my leg would permit me to do any acrobatics, but it was a pleasant time for me. This kind of quiet, convivial home life was something I had nearly forgotten. With Frank and Greta encouraging me, I signed up for the night course at the Jamaica High School, and every evening, after my leg healed, I walked the mile and a half there and back. On weekends

I played some baseball with the Jamaica Woodhulls to earn a few bucks. And, gradually, as my leg regained its normal usefulness, Frank and I began to spend long hours practicing and trying out new routines.

And high school that winter was such a special treat, I enjoyed every moment of it. I never missed a night, rain or shine, sleet or snow, and at the end of the semester I received the honor award for my constancy. I have received a few honors awards since then, but none more prized. And it was my first one.

Prevost and I practiced in a little volunteer fire station not far from his home. We got the use of it rent free in exchange for building a fire in the big pot-bellied stove each morning. It was a cold winter and that stove and fire station were greatly appreciated by two very poor acrobats. Pre's funds were low and except for the few dollars I picked up playing ball, I had no money at all. I had been making only $7.50 a week when the Trio broke up, and most of this I was sending home each week.

Among the many friends that Frank and Greta had in Jamaica and Cedar Manor were some that were to have a strange influence on my life. I met the Sloan family, Tod and Cash, the famous jockeys, and Blanche, who amazed audiences all over the country with her feats of daring in a trapeze and flying ring act. (Blanche Sloan and Mrs. Guise lived together after Frank died.)

Tod Sloan, rated one of the greatest jockeys of all time, and certainly the most publicized, started his career in the United States but became even more famous in England. He was in the spotlight throughout his life. Tod Sloan was the jockey who first popularized the short stirrups—because his legs were abnormally short. He always rode crouched low over the neck of his horse, and this became known as the "monkey crouch." It, too, has become an accepted form. Tod was a great judge of horses and he was daring to an extreme.

It was said of him that "He had the greatest pair of hands ever owned by a jockey."

Listening to the Sloans talk horses gave me my first real interest in them. It was an interest that was someday to bear fabulous fruit.

Prevost said walking was good for my legs, so I did a lot of it that winter. Besides my nightly jaunt to high school, I frequently walked over to the Jamaica race track. I never had money to bet on the horses, but through the Sloans' influence, they held a fascination for me and it was an amusement that cost me nothing. The first time I walked over there, I went through the stable gate because it was handiest. The gateman on duty touched his cap and said "Hi, jock." I looked around but I didn't see anyone else so I assumed he meant me. Then I realized he thought I was a jockey. I was about the right size to qualify, weighing at that time around 90 pounds. From then on I went to the races whenever I felt like it.

Throughout that autumn, Pre kept urging me to develop what he called my "natural talent for comedy." He thought we ought to try out a few routines, do it for a few shows anyway, and see if we couldn't combine comedy with our acrobatic turns.

This was in the day, remember, when everyone in vaudeville, from the grand opera specialty down to the barnyard imitators, pretended to look down on acrobats. Nobody ever addressed a group of vaudevillians except by saying "Ladies and gentlemen and acrobats!" And in the three and four-a-day bills where one show followed on the heels of the next, acrobatic acts frequently were used simply to empty the house. This despite the fact that there were some great ones in the business.

I was keenly sensitive to this attitude. I felt it as a personal slight. But I had been in show business long enough to know that you rate with managements only as you rate with the audience. If an acrobatic act was to get top billing, it had to deserve it. Something had to be added to our act besides new acrobatic tricks. Perhaps Prevost was right, I reasoned. Maybe we could combine comedy with our act.

"If you think I'm funny enough to be a comedian," I said, "then I'll give it a try." I put on a red wig, what we used to call a silly kid wig, and clothes that were too big for me but fit well enough for me to do my tricks in. I spent long hours practicing in them to get used to the feel and additional hours before a mirror experimenting with different facial expressions. Wherever I went I was constantly trying out my facial gymnastics. By Christmas Prevost was getting anxious to try out the act.

"It would help if I could try the routines on an audience," I agreed. I too felt the need of audience reaction. The entire act was silent; neither of us said a word. It depended on the laughs we'd get doing our regular acrobatic tricks in comedy makeup. If I could add a facial gymnastic to get a laugh, so much the better. Pre played it straight.

We persuaded Fox's Theatre in Jamaica to give our act a chance to try out at the end of its regular vaudeville program. We pulled out all the stops and gave them everything we had practiced. I tried out all the facial gymnastics I'd learned and added a few more, but nothing happened—no laughs. They applauded the acrobatic tricks, but they didn't laugh at the "funny stuff."

"What a lot of dumb clucks," said Pre, when we came off. "They don't know comedy when they see it."

If the management had not paid us a cent, I still would have felt indebted to them. I was glad they did not ask us to pay for the use of the stage. But Lew Sidney was manager there at that time and generous, big-hearted Lew paid us for three days. His son directed me in *Show Boat* 43 years later.

Pre kept encouraging me. "It's not your fault," he'd say.

"Wait'll we play an audience that knows comedy. You'll pile 'em in the aisles." He would always chuckle at the things I did and really did a job of building me up. Pre himself was about as dry and humorless as they come, but he persisted in his belief that I was a "natural born comedian."

I was depressed and discouraged and the only consolation I felt was that at least my name was not besmirched. The act was called the Prevost Brothers.

I did not know what the word subtle meant in those days, but I did know that what I had to get into comedy was something in the place of silly kid wigs. We dug through Prevost's attic and found some old opera hats and full-dress suits. They gave me an idea.

Prevost was willing to try anything, and soon we were ready to take another shot at it.

Our first engagement was at a German beer garden over in Newark, a place then called Harburger's Hall. It was not a good audience on which to test a new act. They were usually too busy drinking beer and enjoying their own jokes. But our act was silent and to get any of it at all, they had to look at it.

Prevost came out in his full dress and opera hat. There was nothing funny about him. He looked the part of a well-dressed gentleman. I followed him in identical clothes, but on me they hung slightly askew. Prevost took off his collapsible hat, carefully folded it, and tucked it under his arm. I took off my silk hat and crushed it under my arm as though it were a paper bag. Prevost pulled off his gloves, neatly folded them, and put them in his inside breast pocket. I began to take off my gloves and I kept pulling them off for several seconds. Mrs. Guise had sewed several lengths of her stockings to the cuffs. Finally, I got them off, wadded them up, and stuck them inside my coat.

Meanwhile, we went into our acrobatic act, and throughout it, I imitated everything Prevost did with this kind of buffoonery. It sounds silly and inconsequential, but they giggled and they laughed. I glanced around to see if there was anyone else on the stage they could be laughing at.

They laughed. I kept saying that over and over to myself. It was one of the great highlights of my life. To hear people laugh, to think that they were laughing at something I did! Gosh! I thought, maybe I can do other things, things I haven't even rehearsed, things I haven't even thought of.

That night after the act, the manager of the beer garden came back stage to pay us, and Pre asked him what he thought of the act.

"Fine, fine," he said. "I liked it very much."

"Well," asked Pre, "which part did you like most?"

He hemmed and hawed and finally admitted he hadn't seen the act.

"Well," asked Pre, slightly miffed, "how can you say you liked it?"

"Oh, I liked it when they were applauding," he said, "and they applauded a great deal." He added that he also liked it because the act ran twenty minutes instead of the twelve we had told him it would run. He hadn't seen the act at all but he was pleased because it made his customers applaud and because it ran a long time.

A few days after our short engagement at Harburger's Hall, Pre booked the act with a burlesque show. It was called Williams' *Ideals*. We caught it in Minneapolis. The pay, $60 a week for the act.

Minneapolis was a long jump from New York. Prevost was too proud to ask for railroad fare in advance and somehow or other he scraped up the money and we set out— via the day coach all the way.

The only meal we had on that long trip we ate at a dirty little restaurant between trains in Chicago. I remember we had big stacks of wheatcakes, sausage, oatmeal, and coffee, and when we had cleaned the plates Pre asked for another round of the same. I was worried for fear we'd have to wash dishes, or do something equally drastic to pay for it all. But when we had licked the plates clean for the second time the waiter brought the bill. It was thirty-six cents for the two of us. Big-hearted Pre left a four cent tip.

I always stood offstage and watched the other acts when I was not on or not practicing. In the circus, I was especially interested in the clowns. With Ashe in vaudeville, I studied the comedians until I could mimic their every action and gesture. And when we joined burlesque I had a whole show full of comedians to watch. So I liked burlesque. And burlesque liked the Prevost Brothers. Yes, still no Brown in the billing.

We said nothing during our act at this time, and it was not until weeks later that I uttered any sound. I realized one day that one particularly difficult trick was greatly appreciated by the audience, so I practiced doing it with a great show of ease. Bouncing from a bounding mat or trampoline, I would do a double back somersault and body twist and land standing on Prevost's shoulders. I'd grin and look at the audience as though it were as easy as pie. One day, in a high squeaky voice, I said, "Did you see that?"

I realize how ridiculous it sounds now, and on paper, but they laughed. I made it a catch line.

I was continually trying out different comedy effects, constantly striving to learn what it was that made people laugh. And I was getting more and more opportunity to try it entirely on my own.

Prevost was getting along in years for an acrobat and had to take short breathing spells now and then during our act. This circumstance contributed as much as anything to making me a comedian. I had to do something to hold the attention of the audience while Pre rested.

I first developed an expression of super-idiocy that fascinated our audiences, at least momentarily. Next I invented

87

a comedy head cold. I would make six or seven unsuccessful attempts to sneeze, then sneeze six or seven times, and end up with a smile of unearthly bliss.

Reviews were heady reading for me in those days, but most of all they showed whether or not I was on the right track.

Sime (by-line for Sime Silverman, founder-editor-publisher of *Variety*), wrote: "Looks like real comedy acrobatic turn that needs but little to make the big time. Two men, dressed in ordinary daytime suits, one, the little comedian, going in for a boob effect that he nicely attains. He has a sneeze and laugh, both funny as worked by him, and several other mannerisms good for comedy purposes."

It was the first time anyone had told me I needed little "to make the big time." Sime's tag "and several other mannerisms" kept ringing in my mind for weeks. On the surface it wouldn't appear to be much of a pat on the back, but to me it was a boot in the right direction. It was reviews like this that kept me in show business, though there was a second love competing for my attention.

My love for baseball has been mentioned before. I'm not sure when it began. It predates my first days at school, of that I'm sure, so it probably began when I learned to walk. I was playing semi-pro baseball by the time I was fifteen, in the summers between shows, and I began haunting the knotholes around big league ball parks when I wasn't on stage or practicing. And in the spring, after a season of sore ankles, skinned wrists, and broken legs, baseball as a career held more than casual interest for me.

So that spring of 1908, when Sim Williams' *Ideals* was beginning to fold for the season, I turned to baseball for summer employment. I got acquainted with Tim Flood as he and the St. Paul team were stopping at the same hotel, the Liberty, where the burlesque troupe stayed, and he invited me to work out with the club. The show closed and I stayed

88

This is the earliest photograph in existence of Evan Brown. My father, Mathias, had taken me on a hunting trip when I was four-years-old, and he seemed to have bagged a healthy quota.

The Five Marvelous Ashtons. Those were precious days, in 1906, and I felt like a batboy who's asked to pinch-hit for the star. Billy Ashe, Ernie Close and Phil Barthare are on my left. Julie Barth relaxes on the floor.

This is how San Francisco looked to me (above) after the earthquake and fire of 1906 chased The Five Marvelous Ashtons from this unfortunate city. Fortunately I survived it and the following spring celebrated by wearing my first pair of long pants.

I glide through the air—but not with the greatest of ease. 'Pre' was the pitcher and Tom Bell the catcher when I was the floating part of the Bell-Prevost Trio on the trampoline.

The Busby Bros. big top was my meat in 1902, and if you look close enough you can spot me in the center foreground, holding the head of my pony over my left shoulder.

Otto Lowery and Billy Ashe flank me in my circus days. Now I was an old hand on the trampoline. *(Culver Service)*

It wasn't too many years after I played the human projectile that I moved into burlesque. This serious-minded fellow of 19 is now all dressed up and thinking of new worlds to conquer.

Frank Prevost of the Prevost Brothers comedy-act, was at the height of his career in 1914. I was doing nicely, too, even if the collar seems a bit too dude-ish.

The pupil and the teacher exchange greetings in 1920. My first mentor, Billy Ashe, hadn't changed much over the years, but I had.

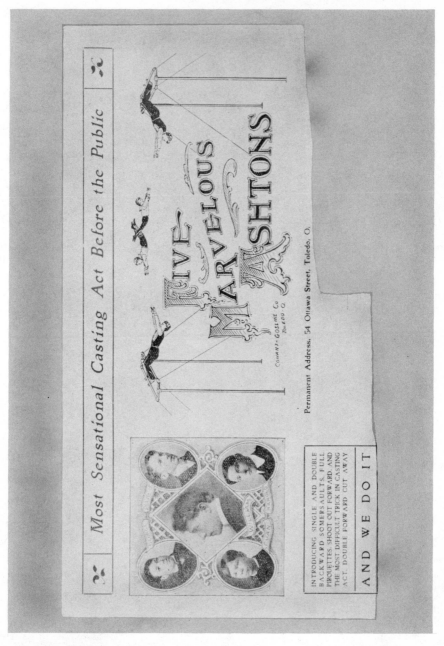

Advertising by letterhead was the thing to do in the early days of the century. The Five Marvelous Ashtons were assigned to a left hand panel, and I was the fellow in the left hand corner. Naturally we didn't fly so smoothly but the general idea is present. *(Culver Service)*

In 1911 (above) I was an anxious passenger with Glenn Martin in his Martin-Curtiss airplane which was launched from a Beatrice (Neb.) cornfield. Thirty years later (below), Glenn and I posed in a more modern Martin design at the Martin factory outside of Baltimore.

My flair for comedy was rather crude in 1908 when I went into this routine with Frank Prevost.

Seventeen years later I was more certain of myself. The stage show *Captain Jinx* afforded me the perfect vehicle for comedy repertoire. *(Culver Service)*

Rhea Cauble, who appeared with me on a General Electric TV show just last year, showed me this old relic—the picture, I mean. Rhea also had a feature role in *Jim Jam Jems,* back in 1920-21.

These are my closest possessions, all of them. The clan all gathered (above) in 1935 while I had a few days between scenes. Joe L. and Mary Elizabeth make a handsome tableau. Don is in style with his white linen suit and Kathryn had just finished bouncing Kathryn Frances on her knee. Mother (below) never looked better when she visited me in 1947 while I was in *Harvey*. (*Culver Service*)

The personal appearance circuit is always easier to take with your family near you. Kathryn and the boys joined me in Atlantic City for this tour in 1931. Joe L. and Don were students at Hollywood's Urban Military Academy.

Kathryn and I celebrate the completion of 16-year-old Joe L.'s first semester as a student at Mercersburg (Pa.) Academy.

We were all so young and dashing then and family portraits were the rage in 1926. Joe L. and Don were growing into fine young men and Kathryn enjoyed her role as a wonderful wife and mother.

Our two darling daughters just after adoption. Mary Elizabeth (above) seemed a bit uncertain about posing with me but Kathryn Frances (r.) is right at home with her new mother.

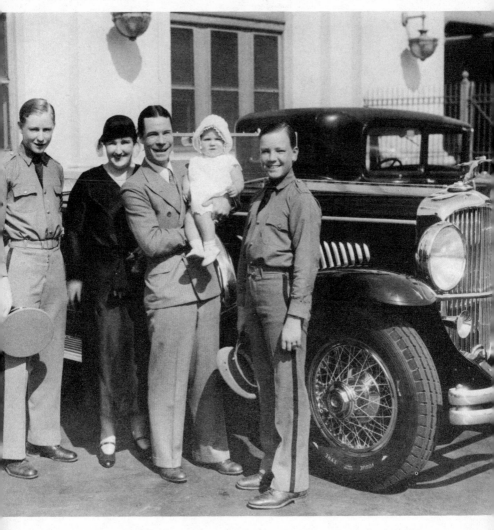

I was living—and riding—high, wide and handsome right after Kathryn and the kids gave me a gift of this snappy Duesenberg in 1931. Price...? $16,500 —and a buck—and a car—had more stretch to a dollar and a mile in those days.

Time takes care of all of us and kids grow up too soon. By 1951 Joe L. had married the pretty girl standing behind him and they had been blessed with a daughter, held by their grandmother. Kathryn Frances and Mary Elizabeth, each to be mothers of two children, already were blossoming into eligible young women.

My son, Joe L., who made the big leagues as general manager of the Pittsburgh Pirates, takes pride in his wonderful family, son Don, wife Virginia, and daughter Cynthia.

on. A few days later Tim came into my room and said "You know, you're kinda dumb."

I asked him why.

"What position do you play?" he asked.

"Second base," I answered. I was pretty good at nearly any position except pitching, but this was my favorite spot and I saw no reason why I shouldn't hold out for it since they were just getting organized.

"Could you possibly play short or third?" Tim asked.

"Not possibly," I replied.

"That's why you're a dope," he said, "because I play second base myself, and I'm the manager, remember?"

Chief Meyers was on the team that year and so was Benny Meyers. Benny, later known as Fog Horn Benny when he was coach with the Phillies, shared his room with me for awhile.

Eventually, Tim gave in and it looked for a time as though I would work in as the regular second baseman of the "Saints." Then in a game a few weeks later I was about to hurl myself into a feet-first slide for third base when the coach at third gave me the "don't slide" signal. Trained through years of acrobatics to exact obedience to signals, I tried to hold up my slide, but it was too late. I hit the ground awkwardly and broke a leg again.

I got paid for a few odd games that summer around Toledo, after my leg healed, and for years I eked out my summers with an occasional game, but I never hesitated when I was faced with a choice between baseball and show business. I was playing with a Toledo team, Needham's All-Stars, at Weston, Ohio, July 3, 1910, when I got one more broken leg. I remember the date because the next day was the day of the Heavyweight Championship fight between Jack Johnson and Jim Jeffries in Reno. I recall lying on a couch with a splint on my leg, reading all about Johnson's k.o. in the evening papers. I remember wondering if Jeffries

89

felt as bad as I did. I decided to stay in show business—at least if I got hurt I was better paid. This is the way my ambition to be a professional baseball player gradually petered out.

However, one player gave me credit for making him a big league ball player, though I'm not sure I should take any bows.

Pie Traynor was going to Summerville (Mass.) High School, back in 1920, and I was working out occasionally with the Boston Red Sox. Ed Barrow, who later became manager of the Yankees, was manager of the Sox at that time, and Jimmy Burke was the coach. Jim saw the kid and liked him and told Barrow about him and they made arrangements for the youngster to get in some hitting practice after school.

So the first afternoon Pie rushed over from school, but the only one to greet him was the club house boy, the flunky who took care of the uniforms, the laundry, and such. While the boy laid out his uniform Pie nervously undressed, and then when he put the uniform on he got it on backwards. Finally, he got it on straight and stepped out on the field. From here on let Pie tell it, as I heard him tell it once in his own words:

"I finally got into my clothes right and went through the dugout to the Red Sox bench. No one said 'hello' to me, or paid any attention to me. I was so scared I was ready to turn around and forget all about baseball. Then I saw a 'pep' game going on near the bench. I was particularly attracted to the game because there were some fellows I recognized from pictures I'd seen of them. There was pitcher Waite Hoyt, catcher Wally Schang, and Mike McNally. There was also a fourth man, a little fellow whom I didn't recognize.

"I stood there watching them for a moment, kinda fascinated, especially with the little fellow. Finally, after a few minutes, I said to myself, 'Well, dammit, Pie, if that

90

fellow is a big leaguer, so are you!' So I went on out and played with them and became a big-league baseball player. They even put my name in the Hall of Fame. And the little fellow? I learned later his name was Joe E. Brown."

I got linked with another one because we looked alike. Thurman Tucker, White Sox outfielder, looked so much like me that my old friend Taylor Spink of the St. Louis *Sporting News* insisted on us having our picture taken together. This was while I was touring in *Harvey*. We were a lot alike, even wore the same kind of glasses, and you had to look at the picture twice to tell which was which. Tucker was a little younger.

A few days after the picture taking event, I dropped by the clubhouse after a game. Tucker had been up nine times with only one hit. He was sitting on a bench looking a little gloomy and I said "Look, you little jerk. If you are going to look like me, hit like me."

He looked up. "I'm afraid that's just what I've been doing," he said.

Always on the Level

Frank Murphy and Jack E. Magee were the star comedians of Williams' *Ideals*. Murphy wrote most of the show, directed it, and he and Magee had several numbers in it. Typical burlesque, it had little pattern except one comedy situation after another. The comedy was low, the gags all off-color, and the situations aimed at a burlesque audience. There were plenty of pretty girls, mostly undressed, who did the usual suggestive dances. When it opened again in the fall, Pre and I rejoined, again as the Prevost Brothers. In October we were in Wheeling, West Virginia.

I never did know exactly what happened in Wheeling, except that the great David Belasco was supposed to have opened a production there and cancelled at the last moment. Left with a cancellation, the management scouted the vicinity for a replacement. Williams' *Ideals* was called in to fill the bill. We were not originally scheduled to show there, but the local management stupidly figured it could hold a sold-out house by ringing the curtain up on anything that was handy.

The Belasco production was advertised all over town,

We were having this discussion one morning while Pre was shaving.

"O.K.," he said. "If you won't change your name, I'll change mine. I don't care." He paused in thought for a moment and his eyes came to rest on a bottle of Rochelle Salt on the dressing table. "That's it!" he exclaimed, and for one whole season we were known as Brown & Rochelle.

I won't take credit for originating what we know today as "doubletalk," but I never heard it before I used it. To me, at least, it was an original discovery. And one of my first uses of it got me into one difficulty and out of another.

We were working the Pantages circuit in company, most of the time, with two or three other acts. Though we did not have the same schedule, we did appear on the same bill with these other acts frequently enough to become well acquainted with them. One of them was a comedy school act in which Jules Held was the teacher with the German accent and Ray and Frank Purcella and Danny Collins were the mischievous pupil comedians. These three fellows were youngsters about my own age and we palled around together a great deal. I think it was in this group that doubletalk was born.

I had tried doubletalk in restaurants a few times, to the great amusement of my friends, and had acquired some facility with the "language." We were returning to our rooms after dinner one evening when we met a waiter in the hall.

"Hey, waiter," I said. "Can you get three orders of vants crass au cral sonomy with a bit of dinton sauce? Of course val scap if you have to cravnetz the havic."

"I beg your pardon, sir?" the waiter answered blankly.

"That's perfectly all right," I replied. "And you might get a do faddis and a couple pam fracks and make sure the comas is snal frack the coddle dit. And bring it right up to room more frenty skevin."

The waiter looked as if he thought he was losing his hearing. Taking a deep breath he said "Well, I . . ."

I interrupted with "If you wilderspack the rannistaff briddle and spractal you'll truffin tab and just bring the troff and forbaz the whole thing."

"Yes, yessir," he said.

"Fine," I said and we went on down the hall barely able to control our laughter.

We were settled down to an after-dinner card game about 45 minutes later when there came a knock on the door. Danny opened it and there stood the waiter with a huge tray.

"Boss," he said, "I had a hard time gettin' the dentin sauce. Don't know whether that's what you want, but I hope the other things are right," and he wheeled the heavily laden tray into the room. "My hearin's been botherin' me lately," he added, apologetically. Then he handed me the check.

It was for $4.25. I was hooked for it, so I paid, but it took almost every cent I had.

Nevertheless, between guffaws at my expense, we ate every scrap on that tray, including the "dentin sauce," and that after a fairly big dinner.

Adventures such as this are sharpened in the memory by other contrasting events that either occurred at the same time or at the same place. This little escapade with double-talk happened at a hotel in Seattle and the piece of good luck that came my way was just the Good Lord's way of balancing the scales—at least, that is the way I always justified my actions in the matter.

We returned to Seattle and this same hotel a few weeks later. Since there were no bellboys (it was that kind of a place!) and we knew where all the rooms were anyway, we were just handed our keys at the desk and left on our own. Mine, I remember, was room 323; that would be third floor (cheapest) back. I entered and started unpacking my suitcase. When I went to hang my other shirt in the closet, I found a brand new tweed suit hanging there. I called the desk clerk and after a little doubletalk mixed in with some words like "suit," "someone," "written back," and "left" I knew that no one had made any inquiry about the suit, and the clerk obviously knew nothing about it. Without enlightening him further, I hung up and tried it on.

It was a perfect fit in every way. Naturally, the sleeves were a little long, but only two or three inches, and the trousers would have to be shortened about six inches, but that was a cinch. In fact, there was enough left over to make a vest. What more could one ask?

But I let the suit hang in the closet the whole week we were there. At the end of the week there were still no inquiries or complaint, and when we left I wore it out, right out of the hotel. It was the first time in my life I had two suits of clothes at the same time.

I always considered that instance one of the strongest examples that religious people could point to, that there is a Providence that looks after us. I needed a suit of clothes and that's the way I was taken care of.

I vividly remember the school act on that bill for another reason. On the same show that year (1913–14) was the great John L. Sullivan, whom I came to know quite well. I knew him well enough, in fact, for me to use the school act as a means to kid him. I always studied all the other acts and spent my spare time mimicking them. I was, in effect, a sort of understudy for everyone on the bill, though I was the only one who knew it. That is how I came to step into the role of the German schoolmaster when Jules Held became sick. I played the part for almost a week.

On March 17th, St. Patrick's Day, we were all in Portland, the school act, John L., Prevost & Brown, and I was still playing the part of the schoolmaster in addition to my own

99

act with Pre. John L. loved all us kids and showed it in a dozen little ways, though he frequently assumed a gruff, fatherly attitude toward us. I was his favorite. He said he was going to make me the champion boxer of the world. But on this particular day, I turned the tables on him. I put on the German makeup . . . wig, costume, and all, except in the place of the flowing black tie I wore a huge green bowtie.

John L. was right in the middle of his famous monologue when out of the corner of his eye he saw me standing in the wings. The combination of shramrock green and German schoolmaster was too much for him. Out of the side of his mouth he roared "Get out of here you s.o.b.!" He didn't think anyone but me could hear him, it was what he would have called his stage whisper, but you could have heard him in the next block. The audience roared. Everyone loved him. And although the books all say John L. had a reputation for swearing, this was the only time I ever heard him do it. He was always careful of his language around us kids.

A lot of books have been written about John L. Sullivan, probably more than about any other fighter, but none succeed in explaining the man's phenomenal popularity.

"Let me shake the hand that shook the hand of John L. Sullivan" was originally a line in a show. Today the name of the show has been forgotten, but the line survives. The season I toured on the Pantages Circuit with John L. was twenty years after he lost the championship to James J. Corbett, and yet his popularity was undimmed. He held the championship for ten years. That is longer than any other American held it before, and he defended it against all challengers. But compared to the large ringside audiences today, very few people ever saw him in action. Yet he was admired by millions. My generation idolized him as much as my father's generation, and yet I was born the year he fought his last great fight. As a matter of fact and record,

100

was spurred on by dreams of various humane projects, but he always felt that he could take everything in his stride, there was no reason to get in a dither about it. He taught me many things that have influenced my own philosophy of living. He would run as hard as he could if he were running a race, but once it was over, win, lose, or draw, he would relax. He said when you need your muscles, use them, but when they are not in use, let them alone.

He continued to write me from time to time long after he had retired to his country place near Boston. In one of the last letters I have from him he said, "Come along, you must come along, and I'll show you how a true Irish gentleman treats his friends. You'll have a grand time, and I will too. You'll have pig's-ass-and-cabbage, that'll be the first dinner you will have with us." I have never heard the expression again, or eaten the dish. But it was like him, as was the famous last line of his monologue, ". . . and so, yours truly, always on the level, John L. Sullivan."

Playing It Big

It has been my great good fortune that wherever I worked I was surrounded by friends. Perhaps it was because I wore a perpetual grin. I had some subconscious feeling that it would cover up and detract from the defects of my features. It won more friends and influenced more people than anything else I ever did. But where women were concerned, I was as backward and self-conscious as could be, though I'd spent half my life in honky-tonks and burlesque shows.

I didn't make enough money for the girls to make a play for me. And I was certainly too self-conscious and unsure of myself ever to force my attentions on them, even if I had had a spare dime to spend on good times or after-theatre parties. Once or twice I had gone through the stages of a childish crush on some lady trapeze artist or circus bareback rider, but I never had the opportunity to meet girls of the home and fireside variety. And I was scared of the other kind; the gilded lilies of the theatre who rated men according to how much they could, or couldn't, spend on them.

It is a strange commentary on the long years I spent in

the theatre, constantly surrounded by women, some of them beautiful, many of them alluring, and all of them sophisticated, that the only serious romance of my life was with a girl who had nothing to do with show business, the girl I eventually married.

I was twenty-one and grown up before I fell in love. Mine had been a man's world, and all the devotion I might have wasted in teen-age love affairs I gave to my mother. I wanted to succeed so that she would be proud of me. I wanted to lavish on her the gifts and affection that boys generally distribute among their girl friends. I was not a "mamma's boy," for she had never coddled me. But she had given me my share of her love and instilled in me the burning desire to succeed, to be somebody.

I wanted to give her a nice home and things back in the days when I was selling newspapers. That desire kept me from throwing money away in later years. Once when we were playing in Buffalo, I bought her a diamond ring. I got it on time, for about $2.50 a week. It was probably the smallest diamond ever cut, but it was the biggest I thought I'd ever own. But she never got the ring. In Philadelphia, a few nights later, I got drawn into a poker game and lost it and all the money I had saved through the entire season. I couldn't have felt worse about it had I actually given her the diamond and then taken it away. That taught me a lesson I never forgot. Though the experience never cured me of gambling, my family never again suffered because of it. (I bought Mother a modest home in Toledo in 1921, soon after I began to hit the big time. Today the house is falling to pieces, but she refuses to move.)

When I read about the difficulties parents today have with their teenagers, I wonder if keeping them busy is not an answer to some of the problems. I don't remember ever having had much spare time on my hands. When we weren't on stage we were practicing, and when we weren't

107

doing either of these we were traveling between shows. To this day I think of travel as a way to relax and rest. It was about the only respite I got from the continual practice, practice, practice. There wasn't much time for girls in my life. I had one date in all these years.

It was the first and only date I had with any girl besides the one who became Mrs. Brown. It was with a young lady in Harrisburg. She saw my show, and when I came out of the stage entrance she was waiting there to tell me she liked the act. She was my first fan. But don't think I told her so! I don't know whether I impressed her with my air of sophistication or not, for air it certainly was. All I remember is that I was impressed with my own importance. She was the nice-looking small-town type. I asked her to dinner and she accepted.

I took her to the fanciest café Harrisburg had (and all the way to the place I kept trying to remember how much cash I had on me).

I think I enjoyed acting the part, and the young lady, apparently, was flattered. Everything went smoothly enough until we came to the end and I paid the check. The waiter, as he had to the other gentlemen in the place, passed me a box of cigars. Others were smoking. I thought it was something I too should do. I took one and lit up. It was my first and my last. I took three puffs and ran. I was too sick and too chagrined to face my young companion again. If she reads this and remembers, I hope she will accept my late apologies.

The Prevost & Brown acrobatic troupe was still getting the last spot on the program when we played the Orpheum Theatre in Duluth, Minnesota, in the autumn of 1914.

Our act was improving. My comedy routines were catching on. Good notices appeared in the press whenever the reviewers sat through the act. But we were still being used to empty the house. There still were people who thought it good manners to get up and leave when the acrobats came on.

I was always keenly sensitive to audience reaction. I thought then and I think today that it is the height of insult, to the actors on stage and the audience who wants to see the show, for anyone to leave or come in while the curtain is up.

I always tried to hide my own annoyance by concentrating on my routine. That's why I usually paid no particular attention to the rude ones who walked out on the act. We had hardly made our entrance that night in Duluth when several people got up and left. Though I didn't know it at the time, one of them was a very superior young lady. (I didn't know until later how Superior she was: she was born there.)

We played in Winnipeg the following week and, though I didn't know it, this same young lady was in the audience. But again showing her disdain for acrobats, she left before the last act.

We were on the Canadian National headed west a few days later when I saw the young lady for the first time. She was in company with her mother, and in the course of the day every male on the train made a point of passing her seat two or three times. She was sitting near other members of our vaudeville troupe and they all flirted with her. Amid such competition, I knew I'd have to use strategy and diplomacy if I hoped to make an impression on her, so I concentrated on her mother.

We got along pretty well. I always had a way with older women. In the course of our conversation I told her we were actors and that we had played Duluth and Winnipeg the previous weeks.

The young lady, I could see, was listening to our conversation with half an ear while she gave her attention to my competitors.

"Oh, we saw that show," she said, breaking into our conversation. "We saw it in both places. But I don't recall seeing you. Were you one of the acrobats?"

Embarrassed, I admitted I was. Then realizing she had walked out on the act, I changed the subject to avoid further embarrassment to either of us.

Day coach passengers in those days brought their meals with them in huge baskets or ate at specified meal stops along the way. The noon stop the next day was at Banff, near the Continental Divide. The ground was covered with snow and the long flight of steps leading up to the station restaurant was ice-coated and slippery. Coming down them after lunch, I suddenly heard a commotion behind me. I looked around, and there sprawled on the steps was the superior young lady.

My heart did a double somersault with a full twist and landed in my throat. But all I could think of as I rushed to help her to her feet was a trite wisecrack. "All the gals fall for me," I said, and immediately I could have cut my tongue out. What I really wanted to say was "Someday you'll be Mrs. Brown," but, fortunately, my smart-aleck remark left me tongue-tied.

Anyway, that's how Kathryn McGraw and Joe E. Brown became acquainted. She and her parents were moving to Oakland, California. I was on the Orpheum circuit, headed for Seattle. But though we were together a lot during the rest of the journey, I wasn't sure I'd made much impression on her. I really concentrated on making a good impression on her mother. I figured that was the best policy at the outset. But on the ferry from Vancouver to Seattle, I did manage to steal a kiss.

I was playing it big between the ferry and the train in Seattle. Though I could ill afford it, I did it up in grand style. I put the young lady and her mother in a taxi, paid the driver handsomely, and sent them on their way.

110

From then on, we kept up a pretty steady correspondence, and when our show arrived in Oakland a few weeks later, we saw a great deal of each other. The courtship continued throughout January and February of 1915, while we played the Bay Area theatres. In March I kissed her goodbye and started east on the last leg of the tour. The last words I said were, "Someday you'll be Mrs. Brown." It was the nearest thing to a proposal I ever made. It was the first time I got up nerve enough to put into words the thought I had had that day in Banff.

I spent that summer playing semi-professional baseball for which I received anywhere from three to 20 dollars a game. I guess at one time or another I must have played on nearly every team in Toledo: the Young Avondales, Needham's All-Stars, the Melvins, the Overlands, Poggemyer's Thads, Crowley's All-Stars, Aiken Dupois' Meccas, Jack Hagerty's Tiffin Club. But this summer should be remembered for something more important to my future.

Larry Gazzola, one of my baseball pals, had a cottage at Toledo Beach on Lake Erie that summer and we spent a lot of time there. One beautiful morning I popped out of bed with the sun and ran down to the water for an early swim. I yelled for Larry to "Come on in, the water's fine!" He didn't hear me. I yelled again, and still there was no answer. I opened my mouth slowly and at the same time began a long, drawn out yell that ended with my mouth wide open. People's heads popped out of tents and cottages for blocks up and down the beach. And that's how the yell that was later "heard round the world" got its start.

I spent a lot of time that summer teaching the neighborhood kids how to dive. We had a diving raft about a half mile out. Having learned the piercing qualities of the yell, I used it thereafter to round up the kids when I was ready to row out to the raft. One yell like that and the kids would come running from all directions. They were the yell's first audience. The first time it was used "commercially" in a show was in *Betty Lee*. Years later it became famous in some of my first motion pictures.

People have said I always repeat my tricks. I do. The fact is they won't let me stop. The yell and the wide mouth always got laughs—and still do. Probably the most amusing (to me) time it was ever used was in the picture *Top Speed*. Audiences had come to expect the yell to pop out somewhere in every picture. (Actually I did it in only seven pictures.) They watched for it, meanwhile building up tension that invariably burst in uproarious laughter when the yell came. But in this picture it didn't come until the very last. The tension audiences built up for that one was worth watching.

Early in September, I returned to New York and teamed up with Prevost again. We had a season booked at all the best vaudeville theatres in the East. Meanwhile, the letters between my beloved and me were becoming warmer, distance, perhaps, having erased many of my faults and defects.

In December, while we were playing at the Hippodrome Theatre in Cleveland, I sat down and wrote a long letter. It was best, I said, to have a thorough understanding. My future did not look very promising, I had no education, could never count on steady work, and when I did work it was frequently dangerous. I had had many accidents. Furthermore, I was as poor as a church mouse. On the credit side I had limitless ambition, and I promised to try my level best to succeed.

If she could accept me on these terms, I said, then I thought we could have a happy life together. My prayer was that she would accept me.

I counted my worldly possessions after I mailed that letter and the inventory wouldn't have used up much paper. Besides my few clothes and theatrical gear, I had exactly $132.00.

112

I told Pre what I had done, but I expressed my doubt that she would accept. Pre smiled. "She'll accept," he said.

Throughout the following week I was torn between my own doubts and Prevost's assurance. I've never been bothered much by fits of depression. I've always had the feeling that come what may I'd accept the terms, grin and bear it. But the long week seemed to me to be a kind of turning point in my life. If Kathryn accepted me, it meant that someone else had faith in my future. If she didn't, then there was some doubt in my own mind that I'd ever be anything but an acrobat.

Then one evening in Baltimore, a few minutes before we were scheduled to go on, I received a telegram. It was from Kathryn. I still have it, so it's easy to copy:

"ACCEPT YOUR TERMS TERRIBLY HAPPY ARRIVING HOBOKEN TEN FORTY AM WEDNESDAY ALL MY LOVE."

Our hotel and the Maryland Theatre where we were playing were both in the same building, I recall, and Pre hadn't come down yet. I let out a yell and literally sailed up four flights of stairs. When I burst in upon Pre I was so excited and out of breath I couldn't talk. I just waved the telegram at him.

"You'll be happy," he said, after he read it. "She's a nice girl." He put his arm around my shoulders and I think he was nearly as pleased at the news as I was.

Never before or since have I given such a performance as I gave that evening. Prevost had tipped off the boys in the orchestra and they played Lohengrin's wedding march just as I poised before the take-off on the trampoline act. I flew into the air higher and my comedy was funnier and, at least it seemed to me, the audience laughed louder and longer than ever before.

I think it was that night, too, that I understood for the first time one of the great axioms of show business. People

113

enjoy watching you do the things you enjoy doing. Enthusiasm is contagious. It was a lesson I was to remember often in the years to come. It was in time to become a fixed part of my personal philosophy.

After the show I wrote to Eddie Darling, circuit manager, and told him I thought we ought to get better billing. We should have a better spot on the bill than opening or closing the show—when the audience was coming in or going out. Furthermore, I said, I thought we should get $50 a week more. (We were getting $175.)

Mr. Darling, apparently, didn't agree with me. Twenty-four hours after I received Kathryn's wire, the Prevost & Brown acrobatic act was out of a job.

But the little pink cloud I was floating around on didn't have much room on it for worry. In any case, I had to be in New York on Wednesday to meet Kathryn, and that was only a few days away.

We returned to New York, and right away we got a booking with the Marcus Loew Circuit. It was a three-a-day with four on Saturday and Sunday (we had been doing only two-a-day), and with my bad ankles I knew I was in for a tough season. But for the next few days, one of which was Christmas, I didn't intend to let anything spoil my happiness.

My New York home at this time was a small apartment on 43rd Street, in the Yandis Court, which I shared with Emmett Callahan. It cost us $18 a month, completely furnished. My most pressing concern was how Kathryn would like it. My excitement had reached an all-time high by Tuesday evening, December 22, so I didn't sleep much that night. I was up at six o'clock the next morning. I bathed and shaved and brushed my hair, shined my shoes, and spent nearly an hour trying to decide which of my two suits to wear.

Though I had plenty of time, I thought the Eighth Avenue trolley would never reach the Hoboken ferry, and once I got on the ferry I wondered if its anchor was dragging. At

114

that I arrived at the railway terminal before nine o'clock.

The morning was sharply cold. The steam and smoke of other trains standing in the station filled the air and nearly obscured the murky sun. I studied and catalogued all the people in the waiting room, read all the magazine covers and newspaper headlines, and listened to the train announcer until I could have done it better than he. And it still lacked a long time till ten. I walked along the platform to one of the huffing engines and stood awhile talking to the engineer. And at long last her train came in.

Few pictures of my Kathryn are clearer in my mind than my first sight of her that morning in Hoboken 40 years ago. If I knew more about women's clothes I could describe her costume better. She was dressed in a brown suit, the skirt coming to just below her shoe tops. The coat was short with a little belt in the back; the sleeves slightly puffed at the shoulders, and the whole topped by a large hat. I guess you'd call it a picture hat. I remember saying to the world as she came tripping down the steps toward me, "Gosh! And tomorrow she'll be Mrs. Brown!"

Neither of us said much as we stood at the rail on the ferry crossing over to New York. I remember thinking, this girl has come all the way across the country just to marry me. How can I justify this? How can I be worthy of her? Of course justify was a pretty big word for me at that time, but that was the essence of my thought. What I would have said, had I put it into words, was that "I have to be right, I have to be good for her."

We took a taxi from the ferry to the apartment on 43rd Street. The fare was 60 cents and I gave the driver a generous fifteen cent tip. This, plus twelve dollars I had spent for a ring the day before, the cost of the license, and a few other expenses, left us less than 100 dollars with which to begin married life.

The first thing that caught Kathryn's attention when I

showed her the little apartment was a towel with the words, "Stolen from Yandis Court" embroidered on it.

"Where is Yandis Court?" she asked, thinking I had stolen the towel.

"You're in it," I said, and showed her that all the linens were marked like that. She blushed.

That night we went to see *Under Fire* at the Hudson. Kathryn remembers that the cast included Frank Craven, Harlan Tucker, E. G. Robinson, Frank Morgan, and Edward Mawson. It was her first Broadway play. But I don't remember much about the play or the players. I was more interested in the drama of my own life.

The following morning we took the subway downtown to City Hall and, with good old Pre and Greta, my closest friends, as witnesses, Alderman Smith performed the ceremony that made Kathryn McGraw Mrs. Joe E. Brown and made me awfully happy.

I knew she wanted a church wedding. With her family background it was almost a necessity. But with less than 100 dollars in my whole world, I couldn't afford to be married on such a grand scale. But on the subway that took us back to Times Square, I put my arms around *my wife* and said, "Kathryn, someday we'll have a real wedding. It'll be in a church, with organ music and flowers and all the rest." She said, simply, "Thank you, Joe."

It was 25 years before I got around to keeping that promise. On the occasion of our silver-wedding anniversary we stood before a minister in St. Thomas Episcopal Church in Hollywood and went through the ceremony again, this time with all the trimmings. Our son, Joe L., was best man; son Don, the eldest, gave the bride away, and our daughters Kathryn Frances and Mary Elizabeth were flower girls.

I have heard that there is no accounting for tastes. Most matrons who have reached their silver-wedding anniversary would be reluctant to face a church ceremonial and in the

116

bridal attire usually donned by young women and girls. The average long-married male would veto the whole idea—church, wedding, bridal party, and all—as dumb foolishness.

The Joe E. Browns, obviously, are different. They may be credited with more than the desire to fulfill their youthful dream of a church wedding with all the trimmings. I think they are, most of all, an old-fashioned pair who believe that a civil marriage is no substitute for one performed in and blessed by the church.

But it didn't end there. A few years later, Mrs. Brown, who was brought up in the Catholic faith, confided to me that she felt she wanted to have her Catholic rights restored, and as the earlier marriage ceremonies were not recognized by her church, this could not be done unless we were married by a Catholic priest.

"If it will make you any happier," I said, "let a rabbi marry us too."

So it is my happy boast that we are the only married couple I know who've been married three times to each other without ever having a divorce.

This Is a New One

The Marcus Loew contract we signed just before Christmas, in 1915, was for $175 a week. Considering the times and the quality of the act, that was probably pretty good wages. Split between Prevost and myself, and deducting our expenses, it left precious little for the days when we wouldn't be working. But if Kathryn felt any anxiety about our future life she gave no hint of it. She continued to bolster my sagging spirits in the face of uncertain prospects.

It didn't matter to me that I seemed to be in a rut professionally. What concerned me most was that I must succeed for Kathryn's sake. I wanted the only girl I had ever loved to have everything in the world to make her happy. And what was I giving her? A ten-cent honeymoon on the subway, to a home consisting of two very small, very shabby rooms, and a future that was apparently leading nowhere. I had been in show business practically all my life but I wasn't much better off this year than I had been the year before. Would I be any better off next year?

It hurt me to see Kathryn scrubbing our cheap little apart-

118

ment, laughing over the insultingly marked linen, going along month after month with no new clothes, and budgeting pennies for our food. For one of the few times in my life, I felt mentally low, heartsick, and discouraged.

My ankles were taking an awful beating from the three-a-day schedule and every night when I came home Kathryn would have a tub of hot water waiting for me. She would fix a warm supper for me and I'd sit eating that while I soaked my ankles. I thought the sore ankles a small price to pay for such devotion.

Then one night I noticed a strange look on her face, and, hesitantly, she said "I went to see a doctor today."

My concern was immediate, but she smiled reassuringly and said "No, I'm not sick."

"What is it then, what's wrong?" I had never been to a doctor when nothing was wrong.

She said "Can't you guess?"

Maybe women are more sophisticated today and maybe they handle such great items of family interest with more nonchalance than my Kathryn did that night. But I doubt if any husband was every more pleased than I was to learn that we were going to have a baby.

"It's gotta be a boy," I said. "It must be a boy."

But my great happiness at the news was almost overshadowed by my worry when I had to leave Kathryn alone. I worried about her health, or for fear she wasn't getting enough sunshine and fresh air, or the right kind of food. She was alone in New York, separated from her family and her friends. When I was out of town on tour I was constantly preoccupied and so beside myself with worry I could hardly concentrate on Pre and the trampoline.

A day before our last engagement that spring I made a big decision. I decided to give up show business. I'd take Kathryn back to Toledo and get a regular job there and have a little home and bring up my family right, like other

119

men. It seemed a shame to walk out on Prevost, good old Pre, the best friend I had in the world. But I had obligations now. I had others to think about besides myself. Pre agreed with me.

I knew Kathryn would object if she thought I was giving up show business because of her and the baby, so I fibbed about my plans. I told her we were just going back to Toledo until after the baby was born. I said I had received a wonderful offer from some old friends, Jack Haggerty and Larry Gazzola in Toledo. They were building a big new billiard and bowling emporium called the Coliseum, and they had offered me a swell position as manager of the place. "Why, in no time at all I'll probably own the darn place. We'll be able to put aside some money and someday, if I feel like it, I'll go back into show business. Might even back my own production."

Part of this was true. Haggerty and Gazzola were old friends and they had offered me a job as manager at $45 a week. I had played baseball with Gazzola and for Haggerty, who owned the Tiffin, Ohio baseball club.

So we went back to Toledo, and my career as a businessman.

It was a happy period. I learned a little about the business and I enjoyed getting acquainted with the customers and building up the popularity of the place. Scott High School was near and that year it had one of its best football teams. (They were national champions that year.) The boys frequented the bowling alley a lot and I taught them some acrobatics. Today a great many of those boys are still close friends.

But most of all I enjoyed the feeling of security, of being at home with Mother and Dad, and knowing that Kathryn was getting the proper care. For exercise, she was in the habit of walking over to the bowling alley every evening

120

about closing time and walking home with me. It was about a mile and a half each way, and with winter and cold weather coming on, it was no little trick for a girl in her condition.

Then the day before Christmas it snowed and the streets became slippery with ice. She wanted to come meet me but I insisted that it was too dangerous. She came anyway and reminded me it was our anniversary. So Christmas Eve we walked home together over the crisp snow.

It was her last long walk for awhile. Before daylight the next morning, she woke up the household. Mother helped her into her clothes and Dad got a taxi. I was much too excited to be helpful in anything.

The taxi driver saw immediately what kind of fare he had and despite my urging him to hurry, he drove slower than a walk. He was afraid to go fast over any bumpy spot for fear the baby would be born in his taxi.

We need not have worried. I waited around the hospital for several hours and still nothing happened. Near ten o'clock I decided I'd better try to open the bowling alley. Since it was Christmas day and a holiday, we were supposed to open at ten instead of twelve, the usual time.

When I got to the alley I found plenty of customers waiting but not a single pin-boy had shown up. We were using Mexican boys at that time and this was one day they always refused to work. But a lot of my high-school friends were there and I told the kids I'd let them roll one game free if they'd set up two games. I got my pin-boys all right, but my mind was across town at the hospital. And everyone in the bowling alley knew what was happening. Around noon a friend, Gary Clash, who had a car, offered to run me over for a quick look-see, and I dashed out.

I got there just as they were taking Kathryn to the delivery room. A nurse threw a white gown over me and I

121

went in with them. I was there for only a moment before I began to get sick. Someone led me out to the hall and I lay down on one of those high narrow carts they move patients around on. I was pretty sick.

Suddenly I heard a loud and lusty squall. Then I heard the nurse say "Doctor, it's a boy." Then I passed out.

When the nurse came out and found me unconscious she was amazed that I hadn't fallen off the cart. I hung around until Kathryn came to and I could tell her the good news myself.

"It's a boy," I said, and my grin was never bigger. "Thanks honey."

I ran out and caught the streetcar back to work. It was a belt line, a long trip back to the Coliseum. But I didn't mind. There were people on it, and I had to tell someone about my good fortune. I told each one, and in considerable detail, about this remarkable child that had just been born to me. I finally worked up to the motorman, and since he was standing at the moment, I took his stool. He had overheard me as I moved along the aisle, talking to each passenger in turn, and he was prepared for me. He stopped the car in the middle of the block.

"Wait a minute," he said. "You think you've got a cute youngster? Take a look at this one," and he pulled a small snapshot out of his wallet. It was a picture of a child about two or three years old.

"Well," I said, "but this one of mine is just a new one. You've never seen one like him. He's the most beautiful child you ever saw," and so on and on, he couldn't stop me.

When I had to transfer to another car, I was tickled because that meant a fresh crop of passengers and a new crew to hear the details of my marvelous son. I didn't mind that people laughed. It was the same kind of laughter I had known in the theatre. The only thing that burned me up was when the conductor of the second car started telling me about his kid too!

Business was great that day. I fairly flew around the place. Gary had taken care of things while I was at the hospital, and during my dinner hour that evening he taxied me over for another quick look.

That was Don, born Christmas Day, 1916, when I was 24 years old.

After the New Year, business at the Coliseum dropped off and my job there began to look uncertain. I couldn't afford to be out of work for a single day, so when Clem Minniger offered me a job at four dollars a day working in the Electric Auto Lite factory as a laborer, I grabbed it. Looking at my son, I knew that any sacrifice I could ever make for my family was a cheap price to pay for the joy they meant to me.

Clem Minniger surely was an understanding friend. When he found I couldn't do the job he had assigned me to, he would move me on to something else. At one time or other during my employment there I must have worked a while in every department in the plant. Clem even tried me out in the offices. But my heart simply wasn't in electric auto lights. The only lights that ever had, or ever would, mean anything to me were footlights, or, impossible dream, my name in big lights over a theatre on Broadway.

One day when Don was about six months old, I received a wire from Prevost. He could get a vaudeville booking for our old act and $150 a week, he said.

Half of that was more than I was getting at Auto Lite, and the prospects for the future were no more uncertain. Besides, it was show business, and, to me, as to Irving Berlin, there had never been any business like show business. I knew that now. I showed the wire to Kathryn.

"I don't think you were cut out to be a businessman," she said.

She has repeated that several times in the years since, not to dissuade me from entering business, for I never tried it again, but to reassure me that she was still at the family helm.

This Is It!

When I look back over my life, I am glad for everything that has ever happened to me. There was a line in Edna Ferber's *So Big* that I shall never forget because it just about sums up my personal philosophy. The line is: "Just remember that everything that happens to you is sheer velvet."

That's a wonderful thought. If you believe that, you can't harbor resentment or hate or malice toward anything or anyone. I have so much to be grateful for that I completely forget the other things in my life. I have found more than my share of happiness in a family, in friends, in work. I have always felt that my work is in the grandest business in the world.

I was always fighting for recognition in my business, but at the same time I knew I'd have to earn it. I was always struggling to perfect my routines, my lines, because I knew you got top billing in this business only if you deserved it. I resented the poor billing we got in the early days, but my resentment never was aimed at managements or the audience. I always knew where the blame lay.

Top spot on any vaudeville program was not the opening

or the end. The importance of a vaudeville act increased from the first place on the program to next to the last. The feature act (headline) was second from the last if it was a full-stage act, and next to closing if it was done in one. (An act "in one" worked in front of the first curtain, back of the asbestos curtain.)

Management's low opinion of acrobatic acts, as I pointed out, is evidenced by the fact that they were invariably placed at the end. Many patrons figured they had seen the show when the acrobats came on (as my Kathryn did, the first time she attended my show), and it was not unusual for us to start our act with half the audience in the aisles on its way out. You had to be better than good to rate any other position, and practically perfect to top the program. And the public itself would tell you and the management whether or not you deserved the position. A good many reviewers had to suggest it before managers scheduled our act to top billing.

In Chicago, Jack Lait wrote "Prevost and Brown came on to the accompaniment of departing footsteps." It was his only mention of our act, inferring we didn't deserve any better. The following year he wrote this:

"The Palace bill has Irene Franklin and Fannie Brice featured and to them, respectively, falls the popular applause, but the bill has a closer—the most unthankful spot such an act can have—a trampoline act that, on its merits, viewing vaudeville as specialties to be judged by their intrinsic excellences, is deserving of the stellar spot on the bill."

Fannie Brice, in a single, twenty-minute skit, did her famous Yiddisher-character singing and comedy act, and inimitable in her line as usual. Irene Franklin did several popular songs, and she was followed by Harry Adler and Anna Arline. Eighth and last on the bill were, as Lait said, Prevost & Brown.

126

As time went on, Prevost needed longer breathing spells, and I had to go in for telling stories. My "Little Mousie" that fell into the barrel of whiskey became a vaudeville favorite. It was the success of my dissipated mouse that gave me my first visions of stardom.

I was also doing more acrobatics on my own. I rigged the trampoline in the orchestra pit, and in the act I backed off the stage, fell into the trampoline, and bounced back on to the stage. I never looked back of me while doing this trick, so if anyone had moved the trampoline I might have broken a leg. I did get a jolt once when some member of the orchestra jostled it out of line a little, and from then on we anchored it down with guy wires. Once a front row customer laid his straw hat on it. My foot went right through the hat and I came up with the brim around my leg. Another time the orchestra leader put his fiddle on it for a moment and I crashed a foot through it. At first I thought I had broken a leg this time for sure. I began to limp, then I discovered pieces of the fiddle clinging to my foot.

Several years later, I used this same trampoline bit as the big finish of an eccentric dance in *Jim Jam Jems* on Broadway. My current idol, Fred Stone, opened that same night in a similar show in which he also used the trampoline in his act. Since the first-string reviewers saw his show first and mine later in the week, they assumed that he originated the trick. When they got around to reviewing my show, they said I stole the trick from him.

As a matter of record, the facts were something else. While I was doing the trampoline bit with burlesque, I met Mr. Stone on the street and he said he had heard that the "tramp" trick was very effective. I was flattered, and I told him then if he could use it he was welcome. He thanked me and said he might sometime. It was several years before he got around to using it, and it was only coincidence that he used it at the same time I introduced it on Broadway.

I called Fred and he, being an honorable man, straightened it out with the press. And thereafter the theatre programs in both houses gave me credit for originating this particular trampoline act.

The season 1917–18 was my last with Pre and my last with vaudeville for several years.

With Pre talking of retirement and vaudeville offering a vague future for a struggling young comedian, I faced the end of the season with more than my usual concern. In addition, Kathryn was pregnant again, and the baby was expected in the autumn (of 1918). I wanted security for my family and I wanted to establish myself as a comedian. I believed that these things went together. I believed that if I could make a name for myself as a comedian there would be a place for me in the legitimate theatre. I had many long talks along this line with Pre, and he encouraged me to go ahead.

"Go back to burlesque," he advised. "You're known there, and it's a good place to start."

Going back to burlesque seemed like a step down, not up. But Kathryn agreed with Pre. "You can do it," she said. "Take whatever they offer you the first year. We'll manage somehow."

"Consider it a step back to step forward," Pre argued.

John Jermon, one of the burlesque producers I interviewed, offered me $75 a week and a spot as second comedian. I accepted with only one reservation. I would not do any off-color stuff.

"O.K.," he said. "If you can get laughs without it, it's O.K. with me." He was dubious.

Rehearsals for *Sporting Widows* began in midsummer and the show opened at the Casino Theatre in Brooklyn late in August. We moved on to Hartford in September and I had to leave Kathryn in New York. It was a difficult time for both of us. She was alone with one baby and expecting another any day. I was trying hard to be a comedian.

The whole cast of that burlesque show was sympathetic, and in our off hours they worked in shifts to keep me occupied. They kept a marathon poker game going between shows until one afternoon in Hartford. I was pretty nervous by then and I was having trouble keeping my mind on the cards when a messenger boy knocked on the door.

"Telegram for Mr. Joe Brown," he said.

It was from Kathryn's doctor and it read:

"BABY BORN THIS MORNING MOTHER DOING FINE."

Everyone in the room had gathered around me and they were all reading the wire over my shoulder. And in one breath we all exclaimed "But what is it? Boy or girl?"

It was several hours before I found out. We named him Joe Leroy, after his Dad and his Dad's old partner, Frank Leroy Guise.

The following week we returned to New York to play the Columbia Theatre at 47th and Seventh Avenue. I made a beeline to the hospital to see the new addition, and all the way over I kept repeating to myself "We now have two fine boys, two fine boys! Gosh! Isn't that wonderful!"

Playing the Columbia, right on Times Square, meant I would be seen by a number of agents and managers and I was anxious to "get at 'em." The laughs had been coming stronger and more often as I became more confident and experienced. The trampoline hidden in the orchestra pit was a surprise hit and it was getting favorable attention. Thus it is not hard to understand why I considered it a matter of life and death when the orchestra at the Columbia wouldn't let me rig the trampoline in the pit. It was a small pit, a narrow space between the front row and the stage.

I said I would not go on if they wouldn't let me put the

trampoline in the pit. I told them it was the most important part of my performance. I didn't want to stay with burlesque all my life, I wanted people to see me at my best, and without the trampoline I simply would not go on. It developed into quite an argument.

Our first show was a 2:30 matinee that day, and the argument began around 11 o'clock when I came in to rehearse and discovered the equipment had not yet been set up. It had to be in place before the audience came in, otherwise the element of surprise was lost.

The argument waxed hotter and curtain time crept closer and little Joey was more determined than ever to hold out for his rights. Finally I walked out and went across the street to a restaurant. The musicians, meanwhile, took their grievance to the management. And the management decided in my favor. (This was before Petrillo, remember.)

"Go ahead," they said, "you can squeeze it in some way," and squeeze it in they did. They put the drummer in one front row seat and his drums in another and split the rest in two sections, one on either side of the trampoline.

The results justified all the difficulty. The stunt was such a hit that afternoon that even the orchestra leader turned enthusiastic.

That victory was more important to me than I realized. Harry Cort, son of the famous producer John Cort, was in the theatre that afternoon and after the performance, he came backstage to see me.

"How would you like to have a part in a new show we are putting together?" he asked. "The title of the piece is *Listen Lester*. I think you'd be good in the title role."

The title didn't mean anything to me. I hadn't read the play and it wasn't even in rehearsal. How was I to know it was destined for one of the most successful runs on Broadway?

130

Anyway, I had a job. I still had to succeed as a comedian in burlesque.

"Thanks," I said. "But I think I'd better stick with burlesque awhile."

Actually, I was doing all right in burlesque, and just before the end of the season I went to John Jermon. My family was growing and I felt I had to have some security for the future beyond the usual one-season contract. On the strength of the good notices I had been getting, I asked him for a long-term contract.

John Jermon was a good showman and a better business-man than most. But he was also one of the fairest I ever knew. He agreed to give me a five-year contract, starting in September at $125 per week on a rising scale that would pay me $250 weekly in the fifth season. Furthermore, to help me over the dull summer months this year he advanced me $300. Now, at last, I had security for the Browns. And, besides, I liked burlesque.

I had virtually forgotten young Cort's offer of a role in *Listen Lester*, although the play by now had all Broadway agog.

I sent Mrs. Brown and the two babies to a farm up in the Catskills, a place run by Suzie Hunt Beers (how well I remember!), and began casting about for something to fill in the summer.

With one of the girls from the *Sporting Widows* show, I teamed up to do a vaudeville act. It was one of those you-say-that-to-me-and-I'll-say-this-to-you sort of things. After a week's rehearsal we booked the act at the U.S. Theatre in Hoboken. We were to get $75 for the act for three days, doing three shows a day.

After our first show the manager sent for me. I went to his office, one of those little cubbyhole places with a small anteroom outside. I sat. Finally, after a long interval, he discovered I was there.

"Oh, Joe," he said. "Come in," and he handed me a big cigar. "Just wanted to tell you that 'Mousie' story of yours is a pip. And you certainly can sing a song. But," and he hesitated for a moment as though this was hard to say, and I thought, here it comes, I'm fired. "But that girl you're working with. Where did you get her? She's certainly no help to you. Don't know how you happened to get mixed up with her. You shouldn't do an act with her, you have too much talent. She's hurting your reputation. If you're smart, you'll call the whole thing off. I'll get another act somewhere, and when you get yourself another girl you get in touch with me."

I was shocked because I didn't have any dough. I was on the point of telling him how much I was counting on this job, but the words just wouldn't come out. With that kind of a brushoff what could I say to the guy? I went and packed my bag.

But as I started to leave the theatre, I thought, what the heck? He engaged us and we played one show, that was worth something. I accosted the stage manager. "Say," I asked, "when an act is let out don't you get paid for the show you've done?"

"Why, I don't know," he said. "That's sort of up to you, I guess."

"Well, I need the money," I said, "and, by gosh, I'm going back to see the manager again." We had done one show, one-ninth of the contract, about eight dollars' worth, and half of that or four dollars was due me.

As I walked into the outer office I heard voices. I sat. The manager was talking.

". . . and you certainly can sing a song. But . . ." and there was a long pause. "But that chap Brown you're working with. Where did you get him? He's certainly no help to you. Don't know how you happened to get mixed up with

132

him. You shouldn't do an act with him, you have too much talent. He's hurting your reputation. If you're smart you'll . . ." I knew the rest of it. I sneaked out of the office and ran. I never saw that theatre again.

Pickings were poor that summer and by the middle of July I was trying to live on five cents a day. Kathryn and the babies were still at the farm, though we were already in arrears there by a week or two. Then I got a call from John Cort, producer of *Listen Lester*.

"You know my current show, *Listen Lester?*" he asked.

"Sure," I said. "Everybody knows about it, Mr. Cort."

"Well, I'm organizing a road company. How'd you like to play Lester in it?"

"Play Lester, me? How would I like to?" I was ready to burst.

"I can offer you a run-of-the-play contract at $150 a week," he said.

This was the role that Hansford Wilson had made famous. Other big names in the cast were Clifton Webb, Ada Mae Weeks, Gertrude Vanderbilt, Fredie Heider, Eddy Garvey, Ada Lewis. A road show of such a big success might be equally popular, the title role my big chance. Then I remembered, and my face fell. "There's only one thing, Mr. Cort. I have a contract, a five-year contract with John Jermon."

"Well, I'm afraid that's your problem, Joe. I'm sorry, but, if you can solve it, come see me."

It was only a little more money than I would be getting in burlesque, and it was less security for the future because no one knew how the play would go on the road. But the important thing to me was the fact that I'd be in a play that was already a proven Broadway success, playing the lead in a comedy role I liked.

One of my greatest dreams was being a comedian in a big

successful show on Broadway. This wasn't it, but it was second best. Except for one hitch.

I went to see Jermon and told him about Cort's offer. "I know we have a five-year contract," I said, and I went on to assure him how much I appreciated all he had done for me. I had been looking forward to a long and happy association with him, I said, but he must know that I also had been looking beyond that to greater things. This offer, coming at this time, was unexpected.

"Well, what do you want me to do?" he asked.

"I want you to release me from that contract."

"Why, Joe," he argued, "I've made great plans for this season. My whole show depends on you."

"But, Mr. Jermon," I pleaded. "All I can do is appeal to your generosity and ask you to tear up our contract. This means more to me than anything in the world. It's my big chance, Mr. Jermon."

"Well, Joe, you've come to me forthrightly. You asked me. You haven't said what you would do if I didn't. So, O.K. But you owe me $300. How about that?"

I said I had no money and I didn't want to go to Cort and borrow from him, at least not until after the show opened, but I promised to pay him back $50 a week every week until it was paid off. He said he didn't want to inconvenience me, he knew I had a family and heavy obligations, so if I would pay him $25 a week it would be all right. I agreed. We shook hands and he tore up the contract. *There was a man.*

I was rooming with Danny Healy at the time and he taught me a little dance that fit nicely into the lines and routines I had in the Lester role. Adding an innovation here and a bit of original business there, I soon had an entirely different interpretation of the role from the one in the Broadway company. I also added the trampoline finish to the dance.

134

In mid-rehearsal one morning I got a call from Mr. Cort. He wanted to see me.

On the way to his office I thought, maybe I'd better stick to my knittin'. He's probably going to bawl me out and tell me to watch Hansford Wilson until I have the role down the way it was written.

"Yessir, Mr. Cort," I said, and the perspiration on my brow was not from running up the steps to his office.

"Well, Joe, how do you feel?"

"Fine, Mr. Cort. You want me to understudy Mr. Wilson? You want me to see how he's playing Lester?"

"No. Hansford won't be playing Lester tonight at the Knickerbocker, Joe. You will."

"Me? With Clifton Webb, Ada Mae Weeks, Gertie Vanderbilt?"

"That's right, Joe. Wilson's leaving the cast."

When I came to, I found myself doing a dance step down Broadway, suddenly conscious that people were staring at me. I ducked into the first doorway and discovered I was in a ham and egg joint. A telephone on the wall near the window caught my attention. Kathryn! I must call Kathryn! It was nearly all a one-way conversation.

"Hello, sweetheart!" I yelled, and she knew immediately something wonderful had happened. "Go out and buy those clothes you've been wanting, get those things for the boys, because we're in, sweetheart, we're in! Tonight I'm playing Lester, on Broadway. Yes, yes, at the Knickerbocker. I made it, like you always said I would. Yes, yes, I can hardly believe it myself. I'll call you right after the show is over. And thanks, thanks honey, for believing in me."

To understand my overwhelming joy at this moment it is necessary to remember the long, hard road I had traveled to this point. I was not a stage-struck amateur getting my break after a season or two of discouragement. From my first appearance before an audience in Chanute, with Billy

135

and the rest of the Ashtons, on through fairs and carnivals, vaudeville, and burlesque, I had loved it. It had been hard work, almost slavery at times, but I never considered it that because I loved the life. *I wanted to be a comedian.* I had suffered from injuries. I had been hungry. I had been beaten and cuffed around. I had been a smalltimer, a nobody for years, an "acrobat." And now out of the clear sky I was chosen for the leading comedy role in an established hit playing *on Broadway!*

Boy! This was it!

It was too much happiness to come all at once, I argued to myself. But I arrived at the theatre at four o'clock in the afternoon to make up for an evening curtain at 8:45. I didn't mind that I was hours early! I wanted to be there on the stage of the "big time." Here were no cheap dressing rooms, lined with torn pictures of girls in tights. I looked out over the dark house, with its luxurious seats, its fine carpets, and beautiful lights, through tears I could not keep back. I wouldn't even leave the theatre to eat dinner. I couldn't have eaten a bite anyway.

I paced up and down in front of the mirror in my dressing room, fussed with my makeup and rehearsed again and again every line I had in the show.

After what seemed years, perhaps it was only hours, I heard the musicians begin their tune up. They played the overture through.

"This is it," I said. "This is the top; this is what I've always wanted." The date was August 7, 1919.

The orchestra began the overture again and played it through.

Someone knocked on my door. I jerked it open. "O.K.," I said. "I'm ready."

It was the stage manager. "No show, tonight, Joe," he said.

"No show?" Disbelief was written all over my pan.

"Yeah," he said. "Equity's called a strike." He went on to the next dressing room.

I sank into the chair before my make-up table. "Equity, Equity?" I said. "What's Equity?" I had never heard of it. I had read something about a strike brewing, but for all I knew Equity could have been a Chinese laundry.

That was the beginning of the great Actors' Equity strike of 1919. It was the end of the world for me. Not only were we in debt to Suzie Hunt Beers and John Jermon; I didn't even have money enough to buy a meal for myself.

John Cort said he intended to keep the show running in spite of the strike. Should I go out with Equity? I wasn't a member. I mixed with the strike crowd and found out what the strike was about. Mainly it was rebellion against long rehearsals without pay (frequently as long as three months), contracts broken at will by the managers, and other complaints of highhandedness on the part of management. The strike also embraced the grievances of chorus girls who used to be required to rehearse for months without pay or guarantee that the show would be a success. This was the time that Marie Dressler earned the everlasting affection of the chorines when she offered her services as president of the Chorus Girls' Union. The girls were getting only eighteen dollars a week, and had to buy their own chorus footgear.

I walked all night, trying to decide whose side I was on.

In the morning I went to Equity headquarters, borrowed five dollars, and handed it back as my dues.

Listen Lester carried on with someone else in the role of Lester.

I sent Kathryn a postcard and told her what I had done. She borrowed money from Mrs. Beers and came storming into town. It was the worst argument we ever had. She was the female of the Browns fighting for her brood. I was trying to hold on to a principle.

137

perate. One gloomy morning Jack said we've got to get some money somewhere if we have to rob a bank. We decided the easiest way would be to get into a card game with some of the wealthier members of the club and cheat. We figured out a way to do it and we won. Our total take between us was only 60 cents, but Healy meanwhile had dug up 30 cents for some odd job, and we feasted.

Another day Jack came in with a big bag of cookies and a can of applesauce. He never did say where he got them and beggars that we were, we never asked any choosey questions. My personal opinion was not that he stole such bulky items but that he found them discarded behind some grocery store.

On September 3, nearly four weeks after the strike began, I came in late after doing a show for returning servicemen on a battleship in the harbor. Kathryn had come to town with the intention of finding some kind of work to help out. She met me at the door and handed me a telegram. It was from Toledo. It informed me that my Dad was dead.

He Should Dance More

I had a chance to catch up on my thinking on that long and sad trip home. It was time, I thought, that I took a good look at my past, present, and where I was going. I was 27 years old. I'd been in show business since I was ten. I had a wife and two children. I was out of work and I owed several hundred dollars. I even had to borrow from Equity again to make this trip. (It was on Kathryn's insistence that I went to Equity and borrowed the money for my trip to Toledo. I didn't think they would do it, certainly it was not customary, and my pride entered into my reluctance to ask them.)

All I had in the way of prospects for the future was ambition, the burning desire to continue in my chosen field. I know nothing else. Now, even that had turned out to be a mistake. It seemed to me I had picked the wrong profession. People didn't want laughs in this world; there was no place for a comedian.

But I didn't really believe that. I couldn't forget how I had studied to perfect my comedy routines and how they had paid off. I remembered how Pre had encouraged me be working again that I must have projected some of my enthusiasm beyond the footlights. And this was the show that taught me how to commercialize on my big mouth.

My part in *Listen Lester* was small and I had only a few lines. And when I say small, I mean it. I had only a few laughs and I wanted them badly. Realizing that a cough or any slight diversion in the audience might lose my line, I hit upon the idea of opening my mouth very wide, waiting for the audience's attention, and then speaking the word in a whisper. From the first time I tried it I always got a laugh.

My notices from the beginning were consistently good. They even praised my dancing. But I was not a dancer. Even in my burlesque days I had confined most of my acting to acrobatics, and it was not until Pre began to drop out of the act that I combined some simple dance routines with the trampoline work. Danny Healy taught me a few dance steps during my first rehearsal of *Lester* and during the strike doldrums I worked with Johnny Boyle, a great dancer and a good teacher. But the credit in those reviews of "Lester" should have gone to Fredie Heider.

I was a little rusty when I joined *Listen Lester* in Washington, so before the show opened in Chicago, our next stop, I had to do some concentrated rehearsing. I was pretty sure the trampoline trick would set me off, but I needed a good dance routine to lead up to it. Fredie Heider taught it to me.

I'll never forget Fredie. He was a comic too and in a way we were competitors—for audience laughs and newspaper reviews. But he reached out and helped me when I really needed it. All day long the day we were to open in Chicago, he stuck with me. When he should have been thinking of himself, getting some rest before his own strenuous performance, he danced and practiced with me right up till curtain time.

144

This number had a spot late in the show, but my number was a show-stopper.

"Joe E. Brown holds the stage alone for ten minutes or more in the last act with a brand of clowning that kept the audience in an uproar," said one review. "Brown can act and dance, and his little spring from the stage to the orchestra and back again in the twinkling of an eye was well received. He should dance more and be given more to do in the first act."

There wasn't more that I could do in the first act, or the other acts either, for that matter, because I was milking every drop from the part. And as for the "eccentric dance" routine they praised so highly—well, they didn't know it, but I was counting one, two, three, four and still practicing just as I had with Fredie. Had they called me back for an encore I'd have had to do the same number over again. But that's what they would have wanted, the same dance and the same trampoline trick. Of course their enthusiasm affected the reviewers, but I learned an important lesson from that act. Even if I had known another dance routine or something different I could have given as an encore, it is best never to give an audience too much.

But there was one thing more the management could do and the more I thought about it the more I built up my confidence to ask for it. I had gone back with the show on my original contract basis or $150 a week, but what with my own day to day expenses, Kathryn's expenses, and the debts we owed Mr. Jermon, Mrs. Beers, and Equity, there wasn't much left out of the week's pay envelope. Finally the good notices and our debts gave me enough confidence to ask for more money. I told John Sheehy, manager of the show, that I had to have a $50 raise. I said I also wanted my name up in lights as a featured player. I wasn't a star yet and I didn't expect any preferential billing, but I had made my part a

145

featured bit and I thought I was entitled to feature billing. "Furthermore," I said, my confidence getting the upper hand above my better judgment, "you can tell Cort if I don't get the raise, I'm giving notice, I'm quitting."

"O.K.," he said, "but I think you're making a mistake."

The following day Sheehy told me Mr. Cort had accepted my notice.

When I told Kathryn what I had done, she said "You go right back and tell Mr. Sheehy you've changed your mind!" I said I couldn't and she gave me the darnedest sales talk I ever heard. The gist of it was that this was my first show, I was just beginning to be known, notices were good, but I hadn't been in long enough to build up a following, and, furthermore, if I left the show others would think I had been fired no matter what I would say.

For a long time, several minutes anyway, I insisted that I couldn't do it. In the end I went to the manager and told him to tell Mr. Cort I'd like to take back the notice, if it was not too late, and that I had made a mistake. "I need the money," I said, "and I would like to have the billing, but if he says no then I'll go along."

It was the biggest and hardest thing I ever did. It is never easy to eat crow. For anyone as cocksure and headstrong as Joe E. Brown was in those days, it was doubly difficult. And, of course, but for Kathryn's insistence, I would never have done it. Mr. Sheehy contacted Mr. Cort and he sent word back that it was all right.

The *Listen Lester* company wound up its successful season in Boston, playing its last two weeks there in May. Sometime during that time Mr. Cort came on from New York and saw the show. Afterwards he sent word he wanted to see me. He offered me a new contract at $200 a week and a featured part in a new show scheduled to open the following autumn in New York. I accepted and borrowed a little advance to help me through the summer.

146

Some people can sing away their blues with songs about clouds that have silver linings. Not me. Whenever I'm faced with a particularly black cloud I can usually blow it away with *Waiting*, or *When the Shadows Fall*, a couple of hit tunes from *Listen Lester*.

Jam on the Bread

The script writer who did Hamlet once expressed some doubt that there was much in a name. Anyone taking a quick flashback at the titles of the Broadway offerings during the season 1920–21 should not believe all they read. It was an indefinite era—half way between the gaslight period and the gasoline age—and the titles of books, plays, and songs reflect it. *Tickle Me, Scrambled Wives, Jim Jam Jems*—there's a triplet of shows that might illustrate what I mean.

I can't speak for the others, but *Jim Jam Jems* made no attempt to be anything but pure entertainment. "Instead of being bored and harrowed by a consistently lowbrow entertainment the audience discovered a corker—a jazzified corker," wrote one reviewer. The piece that opened at the Cort Theatre on October 4, 1920 was just that. Our press agent called it "curried vaudeville," and one reviewer changed the copy to "Lea-and-Perrins-ical stimulus for the jaded appetite." My memory of it was that it was simply a show—and "show" is the word—that had no axes to grind, no rules and regulations to live up to, no great social message to put across, and nothing to do but be jolly. And jolly

I launch my career in the *Hit of The Show*. I also made a hit with Miss Chicago of 1926, Gertrude Olmstead. She's the co-star who accepts my betrothal offer. (*Culver Service*)

The first film I made for Warner Bros. was *Song of The West*, in '29. Peanuts Byron is the girl who appears ill—could be my acting! and John Boles is about to feel that way too.

Sprinter Frank Wykoff held the world 100-yard record in 1930. Didn't mean a thing to me, though. I challenged him in *Local Boy Makes Good.* The glasses?—easier to catch the dust tossed by Frank's feet.

This was not a restrained role. Winnie Lightner pulled the shirt right off my back in *Sit Tight* as we got as enthusiastic as the ring action.

My smile? Slightly restrained, don't you think? This was 'drama in the raw' as the lion paid me a dressing room visit during takes of *The Circus Clown*. I couldn't give with a wide cackle because my furry friend had clawed me earlier.

Who's not an actor? Friends, three Academy Award winners have benefited by my 'tutleage.' In order, Ginger Rogers (*second from right*) in this beach scene with Farina, Preston Foster and Eddie Maxwell in *You Said a Mouthful*....

...then there was Olivia de Havilland, who played her first lead in *Alibi Ike* (1935)...

...and, finally lovely Jane Wyman, peeping behind my finger in *Polo Joe* (1936). Other delicacies with me are Marjorie Weaver (l.) and Carol Mathews (r.)

Just an amateur—my hippo friend. Imagine this fellow trying to match m----s
with me? Harry Hippo was declared the winner, but only after a photo was
taken.

My heart leaped right through my shirt as I expressed my undying devotion for gorgeous Thelma Todd in *Broad Minded*. Poor Thelma later died under sad circumstances. *(Culver Service)*

E-eeemotion, brother, at its best. Joan Bennett is rendered speechless by my performance in *Maybe It's Love* (1930).

That's 327-pound Man Mountain Dean up in the air. I wrestled all day with the Mountain, only to end up in the hospital that night for a double hernia operation.

Flute was my role in *A Midsummer Night's Dream*. Although you can't recognize him (above), that's Jimmy Cagney in his Bottom outfit. What an imposing lineup! I'm in the leadoff spot (below) followed by Cagney, Otis Harlan, Frank McHugh, Dewey Robinson and Arthur Treacher.

Maybe I wasn't Fred Astaire (above), but if the role called for a fancy foot I always managed to lead with the proper pump. I executed—yes?—this simple step in *Bright Lights* with Ann Dvorak. Joan Blondell (below) is the cutie as Lloyd Bacon, director of *Sons O'Guns* tells us how he wants the part played.

Hmmph—a couple of competitors, they think. Ethel Merman (above) makes like you-know-who, but I wasn't even trying. Farina figured to match me with those wide saucers (below), and I felt so sorry for him I kept my big mouth shut for a change.

Three fine looking athletes—eh! Joe L. and Don were on the set of *When's Your Birthday*, in 1936.

The same year I attended a football game with a real athlete—Mike. Since he was 19 Mike has been just like another son. A former UCLA grid star, he's now Columbia Picture chief in England.

After this I gave up golf—after all, what future is there after beating Bobby Jones? Of course, it's only on the screen, though, as the king of the links and I matched pars in *The Putter*. (*Culver Service*)

A really great star of the olden, golden days—Tom Mix. The cowboy hero and his wife (l.) visit Dorothy Burgess and me on the set of *The Circus Clown*.

1932 Olympic Star Ralph Metcalf laughs off my challenge to race my wheel against his legs in *Six Day Bike Rider*.

I slid through a lot of mud (above) under the critical eyes of director Mervyn Le Roy (l.) and umpire Beans Reardon just so I could pop right out of that big New York Radio City Music Hall Screen (below) as *Elmer The Great*, in '33. *(Culver Service)*

all the laughs I had been getting before plus a lot more. And I was doing it without comedy costume or makeup.

That was a great lesson to me and I have profited by it many times since. One must never take away from what he is trying to put over, either by costume or useless gestures. If you are pantomiming with your hands, let the hands do it. If it's an intricate dance step, don't take the audience's eyes off the feet. If it's words that count, make every gesture subservient.

I soon became accustomed to the good suit and found that my dancing was better because they could see my legs in better-fitting pants.

This was the show the reviewers called "a corker" when it opened in New York.

Cort was always worrying about how people would like his show. He used to stand in the men's room between acts and listen to what the customers had to say, and he'd have the colored maid in the ladies' room listen in on what the women said about it. One could always tell how a show was going just by looking at him when he came out of the men's room.

Unfortunately, in the case of *Jim Jam Jems*, it opened the same night that Morris Goetz' *Aphrodite* opened at the Century Theatre, and the latter show, being a well publicized dramatic offering with a famous cast, had received all the prestige advance notice. The first string reviewers didn't get around to our show until Wednesday. Allan Dale, great critic of the New York *American*, came in Wednesday matinee. Cort talked to him during the intermission and then came backstage to see me. "Allan Dale is out there," he said. "He thinks you are pretty good. He wants to know all about you, so I know he's interested, and he can do a lot for you." He was giving me a regular fight talk. But I couldn't do any more than I was doing. (I don't remember having given a single performance, from the "Ashtons" to *Harvey,* when I didn't give all I had in effort. In fact, there were times when I overplayed, became broad or corny, and lost all effectiveness because I tried too hard.)

Nevertheless, I was as anxious to see Dale's review as Cort was, and right after the matinee I rushed out and bought a paper. Of course it wasn't in it. It wasn't even written yet. And it still wasn't in the next edition which came out during the evening performance. After the show that night Danny Healy and I went to a little doughnut place near the theatre and waited for the next edition. As soon as it was dropped to the newsboy on the corner we ran out and bought a copy. Still no mention of *Jim Jam Jems,* though we searched every page. We went back to drinking coffee and eating doughnuts.

They sold about eight different kinds of doughnuts in that place and we sampled two or three of each kind before the last edition was finally delivered about 2 A.M. It contained the review, and it was good. Furthermore, it mentioned me.

That edition of the New York *American* may have been just another newspaper to the rest of the world but I thought it was the greatest newspaper ever published. This is what Allan Dale said:

"I think I should have starred a certain Joe E. Brown, who was a newcomer as far as my ignorant self was concerned. Joe was a scream from start to finish, and with a whole bag of tricks. Joe had a funny face, an amusing diction, and a wonderful activity. He was neither horseplay nor burlesque. The quaint things he did, he did in a legitimate manner, and he won! Also, some wise fore-seer took good care that there wasn't too much of Joe. You clamored for more all the time. That is how a funny man should be staged.

"When Joe stars, I suppose it will be otherwise. Let's hope that Joe won't star. He is too good to star."

154

I'm sure McGregor was pleased with that part about the wise fore-seer. It proved his good judgment.

I couldn't sleep the rest of that night. I hurried home with the paper. We had a small apartment on 101st Street, and Kathryn was waiting up for me with the usual hot foot bath. I was too excited to wait for her to read the review. I read it to her. By then I could have done it without the paper. I was still thinking about it when the boys, early risers as children that age always are, came romping into our room. There was no sleep for Daddy after that, but it was just as well. I had a call a little while later from Cort. He told me to get down to the theatre, he wanted to talk to me.

We sat in the back row of the darkened theatre and he began to talk. He was in a philosophical mood and he dwelt at length on the history and the traditions of show business and the philosophy of the theatre. I don't remember as much of what he said as I do the tone of his voice. I was thinking that there was a two-weeks clause in our contract wherein he could fire me or I could quit, but all I wanted was to stay with the show. It was more money that I had ever gotten before, and no matter what he said I was hoping he'd end the conversation by saying he was pleased with my work and wanted me to continue.

Finally, he said, "By the way, did you see Allan Dale's column? He gave us a nice review." I said, "Oh, he did? Is that so? Allan Dale, huh?" I let on as though I hadn't seen it.

Cort continued talking. He mentioned other actors, what he had done for them, and so on. Then he told me not to worry. "Starting next week," he said, "I am going to pay you $50 more each week. And about that billing, I'm not going to put your name up yet. I'm going to make these reviewers think they forced me to put your name up. They'll like that. Satisfy their ego."

155

Oh, I thought. You're going to satisfy *their* ego.

Three days later Dale was still saying nice things about me.

"There are some singularly amusing people in the show at the Cort—I can't bring myself to give it a name." (Allan Dale was a little highbrow for vaudeville and musicals.) "Mr. Joe E. Brown would make a hit in any community, and yet to me he was new. He had the poise and the makeup of a tremendously popular person." He never knew how hard I studied to achieve that poise and makeup.

And before the week was out this line appeared in another paper:

"Without Brown, *Jim Jam Jems* would be of doubtful entertainment qualities. With him, it is an entertainment that no one who likes musical farces should miss."

And when a nice long review appeared in *Billboard*, Stoddard collected the hats.

John Cort thought the time had come. "But I'm going to wait a couple of days," he said, and then, noticing the look of anticipation on my face, he added, "at least until tomorrow morning."

"When, what time?" I asked.

"Oh, don't worry," he said. "We'll do it tomorrow!"

Gosh! Oh, Gee, Gosh! I thought. Tomorrow I'll be a star. I saw him again that night after the show and asked him again what time they were going to put my name up. He said the painter was to be there at nine o'clock. There was a big marble slab in front of the theatre where the names of the stars were painted in large gold letters, and a space on the marquee for names in electric lights.

I was up bright and early the next morning and waiting in front of the theatre when the sign painter showed up. He had some unexpected help.

He had a can of gold paint and he put it on a step ladder while he wiped off what had been there for ten days. I walked up, picked up the can, and held it while he painted, and saw "Joe E. Brown" form from close range.

When he came to the marquee, I handed him the electric J, O, E and another E. He said, "Huh? Uh, give me the B."

"You forgot the middle E," I said. "Mr. Cort's publicity man insists on the E."

"O.K., mister. Hand it up," he said.

"Yessir, got it?" I handed up the letter.

"Look, bud," he said, pausing to look down at me. "What's in it for you? Ya lookin' for a job or somethin'?"

I chuckled. "Job? Brother, I've got a job! I'm Joe E. Brown!"

"Brown? Never hearda yuh. Gimme that B."

I spent most of the morning walking up and down the street looking at the signs in front of that theatre. I sat on the brownstone steps of a house across the street and watched everyone who passed to see if they noticed the signs. Of course there wasn't one in a hundred who even looked up. The afternoon and evening would be better, I rationalized. People would be thinking more about entertainment then than in the morning. It would be even better when the lights went on. I saw them go on. I hadn't been far away from the neighborhood all day.

Kathryn came down to see the sights and I think it was about as great a thrill for her as it was for me. She stayed backstage until the show was over that night and when we left they were turning all the lights out. She couldn't understand why they would turn off the marquee lights. She thought they should stay on all night. So did I.

Eventually Ada Mae Weeks left and Frank Fay left and someone else replaced Harry Langdon and I was the only name left with the show. In time it became "my" show. *Jim Jam Jems* and Joe E. Brown were almost synonymous terms.

When it had run its season (five months) in New York, Cort sold the show to the Bohemians, Inc. (owned by A. L.

157

Jones and Morris Green). Cort called me in before the deal was closed.

"Joe," he said, "this is your show. I have a chance to sell it to Jones and Green but there's a catch in it. They want you too. I can't sell your contract but I think you ought to go with them. I think it is a great opportunity for you. More than that, I'll tell them you are getting $400 a week and should be given more."

I signed with the new owners and they gave me $500 a week.

Thus, with Cort's help, I got three raises in one show— from $200 to $250 to $400 to $500. It was the best trick I ever did.

The Place to Be Funny

Jones and Green booked *Jim Jam Jems* in some of the best houses in the country, and when it had finally run its course, they offered me a spot in the third edition of the *Greenwich Village Follies* opening in Atlantic City in August, 1921.

They offered me $750 a week, but I felt pretty sure of my worth to them so I asked for $1000. Even my agent tried to talk me into taking their offer. I argued that then they didn't want me. He assured me that they did. "Then they'll pay me $1000," I said.

I thought it would be good diplomacy not to hang around arguing the matter, so I left my address and went home to Toledo where Kathryn and the boys were spending the summer. There, three days later, I got a wire saying they would pay me the $1000. I discovered later that the pressure came from someone else as much as from my "hold out" attitude. The comedian signed for the lead in this show turned up drunk on opening night in New York. The second and third nights he was still loaded and the show was headed for the rocks. I have never wanted to replace anyone in a show, but here was a situation that, obviously, called for emergency action.

Again it was no easy task I faced. The material they gave me was poor and the director, John Murray Anderson, was opposed to having me in the show. He had never seen me work, so he had no basis for judgment, but when I discarded the material they gave me and started to work up my own comedy routines, he began to take notice.

There was an excellent apache dance number in the show and I suggested they let me follow it with a burlesque skit. Jimmy Watts, the English actor, did a very good burlesque of the dying swan ballet and he agreed to play the female role in an Apache dance with me. It turned out to be one of the best numbers in the show. The curtain came down after the original apache dancers had finished their routine and rose immediately as though for an encore. But in the split moment the curtain was down, Watts and I replaced the other act and instead of an encore, we did our burlesque.

Anderson was away from the show for several weeks and when he came back he was surprised at the way business was picking up. He was also surprised that the reviewers were proclaiming me one of the stars of the show. But he saw the show, and later John Murray Anderson and I became very good friends.

This, the third *Greenwich Village Follies*, which opened in New York in the autumn of 1921, was unquestionably the best of the series up to that time. There had been a gradual evolution in the quality of the Follies as originated by The Bohemians, Inc., as evidenced by the "names" they were beginning to get into it. This new production contained Irene Franklin, singing *Broadway Wedding Bells*, Ted Lewis and his band, and the whole of the "revusical comedy" devised and staged by John Murray Anderson. Ted introduced a new song number in this show that was an immediate hit. It was called *Three O'Clock in the Morning*.

The production, however, was cut to the pattern of all such shows: A succession of big scenic costumed song numbers, with dances in many of them, and sketches and comedians following each other so rapidly it was difficult to remember which was what and why. It was taken on the road in January and the Philadelphia *Public Ledger* said "Joe E. Brown carries off most of the honors with his inimitable mouth and his whirlwind buffoonery."

Ted Lewis and his jazz band and Irene Franklin and her red hair were tops too, and the show deserved its success. Ted and I shared dressing rooms throughout the run of that *Follies* (two years) and we shared a lot of interesting experiences. Once, when we were playing Des Moines, the whole company gathered in one little restaurant for a late supper after the evening performance. There was only one waiter in the place, so Ted Lewis and I put on aprons and helped him wait on the trade. It began as a gag, but soon the townspeople passing by saw us clowning through the window. Before we knew it, the room was packed with customers. But Ted and I stayed with it (for two and a half hours) and, for once, really earned our supper.

Word got around town, and the next night the place was jammed. Ted, always a good sport about such things, said "Come on. Let's follow through." And we did. After that, the reputation of the place was made.

The fourth edition of the *Follies*, 1922–23, was pretty much like the one before. I was still pulling my weight—originating most of my own material and sharing star billing with one or two others. It was hard work, especially in the early stages when a lot of rehearsals were necessary.

To an outsider it must have been a fearsome, awe-inspiring thing to watch one whole day in the creation of a musical show. Compared to it, the birth of an automobile is as simple as the evolution of a doughnut.

During rehearsal, labor started at 10:30 in the morning

when the principals reported to work out their special dances, songs, and the proper shading of comedy lines. Work ended for them and the limp girls of the chorus at midnight or one o'clock the following morning, when the assistant stage manager read off the hours at which they must report to the costumers next morning for fittings.

In-between was spread a tangle of dialogue, mass movements for the chorus, endless drills in leg-lifting, steps, changes in head positions, eye-directions, groupings for entrances and exits of the principals, and ten-minute breathing periods while the stage director, the stage manager, the composer, the authors, the musical director, and the chief electrician decided on the next strand to be taken from the script and put into the loom of human beings on the stage.

I was learning more and more about comedy as time passed and my experience increased. I learned that there was even a psychological side to it, and it is important for a comedian to know it. Knowing something of the psychology of laughter will help any comedian to give a better performance because he can get more laughs from the minimum of material.

The entertainment fan would, perhaps, be greatly interested in how comedy stuff is worked up in a revue-type show. It is hardly ever that a comedy hit reaches the public in its original condition. In the *Greenwich Village Follies,* for instance, I was engaged to play the comedy lead, but no one had any idea what I was to do. They left it up to me to dig up my own material or use the other numbers in the show to build my routines. The burlesque of the apache dance was an example. And there was a circus scene, in which a number of girls appeared. I walked into it my first night and gaped around, merely to get the feel of it. The next night I got into an argument with the ticket taker, which made a pretty good laugh. The next night, after the

162

argument, the ticket taker suggested I sell lollypops as a means of getting into the circus. More touches were added to this from time to time and eventually a real comedy episode was developed.

Comedy comes from every source. My skit, *Arrest Me*, which I used later, was adapted from O. Henry's *The Cop and the Anthem*. O. Henry wrote his story to leave a sombre taste, and for all that the skit is a merry one throughout, it too ends on a serious note. But the vaudeville version is even more emphatically ironic than the story, because the contrast is more vivid and sharp.

The plot, if you remember, is typically O. Henry. It is the story of a down-and-out bum who figures the best place for him is in jail. It is cold on the park bench and a news item he happens to read describes the Christmas dinner being prepared for the prisoners. The attempts he makes to get arrested are all good comedy and finally, when he has given up, he suddenly comes into an inheritance. Then, when he doesn't want to be jugged, he is picked up and thrown into jail.

Rehearsals for the fifth annual edition of the *Greenwich Village Follies* got under way in July, 1923. I had scraped the bottom of the barrel for material for the previous two editions, so I anticipated trouble this season. Once I got a look at the script for my routines, I knew what I was up against.

The material they gave me was so poor, out-of-date, warmed-over, and corny there was no way it could be reworked. They thought I'd go out and dig up new material as I had in the previous shows, but I wouldn't do it. It was an expense I felt they should handle. We argued about it, and they finally agreed to buy it if I'd dig it up. I found a couple of skits I thought I could do something with, but they wouldn't buy them. (I tried out one called *The Gob*,

163

a skit by Paul Gerard Smith. The audience screamed, but the producers refused to buy it. In 1931 I made a picture, *Son of a Sailor,* from the same skit. It was a big success.)

It wasn't temperament on my part. I simply felt I had reached a point in my own career where I could afford to turn down poor material. I had already considered parts in plays that were being produced that season. I turned them down because I felt the roles would add no lustre to my name as a comedian. It was a new pinnacle to have reached. It was more confidence in my own ability than I had ever had before.

My argument with the *Follies* management continued right up to opening night. I said I would not go on and they said I couldn't walk out. I wouldn't have to walk out, I said. I could be so sick they'd have to carry me out.

Opening night my first sketch was a scene on a raft. It was a pretty fair piece, so I went on and did it. Returning to my dressing room, I stumbled and fell down a short flight of steps. I yelled and several backstage employees gathered around.

"Think I've sprained both ankles," I said, and they sent for the house doctor. He was probably little more than a common quack. He took one look at my ankles and gasped. He'd never seen such swollen joints in his life. Billy Ashe would have laughed at that.

The doc sent out for bandage rolls and tape and put both ankles in huge casts. Meanwhile they were calling me to go on.

"He's in pretty bad shape," said the doctor, shaking his head. "Better tell 'em he can't go on."

So they cut out all the scenes I was supposed to be in and tried to patch the show together with what was left. And when that doctor got through with me, I found I couldn't walk, but really!

The next night they insisted I go on and do the raft scene.

I sat through it anyway, so I could do that. I did that six-minute skit for three weeks for my $1000 a week. It was the highest per-minute salary I had ever earned.

At the end of three weeks I'd had enough. If I was going to prove anything to myself, now was the time to do it. I resigned from the show and set about immediately organizing my own act based on the *Arrest Me* sketch. I figured I would have no trouble now booking it in vaudeville.

Those were the days when the vaudeville sketch was coming into its own as a reputable form of American drama. There were more comedy sketches than anything else and there was more demand for comedy sketches than any other kind. The vaudeville sketch of those days, comedy or drama, was hurried, jam-packed full of highlights; it carried the idea and got it over with a punch. And all in the space of from fourteen to 30 minutes. Where but in a fast-growing young country could dramatists have been able to do that? It took the American mind, the American psychology, the hurried American type to do it.

I think if we could be said to have a distinctively American type of drama, then it is because it grew up through the vaudeville sketch. The success of *The Show-Off* in New York that same (1923–24) season, was an example. *The Show-Off* was written as a vaudeville sketch and was a success as such for a number of years. Then George Kelly developed and rewrote it without losing any of the original essentials, and made it into a successful three-act play. Critics called it "the great American comedy." (A few years later I was to play in an eventful revival of *The Show-Off*.) Vaudeville was the great training ground for the nation's future dramatic material—for both playwrights and actors.

I got together a full cast for the *Arrest Me* sketch and we played the Orpheum circuit vaudeville houses for the rest of the season.

Toward the end of the season the following spring, we

were touring the Coast. Kathryn was with me on this trip (we had put the boys in school in Philadelphia) and to justify her expenses, I gave her a two-line role in the sketch. It was her first and only stage experience. When we reached Seattle, she decided to go on ahead to visit her folks in Oakland. I said, "What are you going to do, leave us flat?"

For a moment I had her thinking it would really hurt the show. I was reminded of a clown I knew in Robinson's Circus. He complained one day he didn't like something or other that was being done. I asked him what he was going to do about it.

"What am I going to do about it?" he asked. "Why, I'll leave 'em flat, that's what!" As if one clown more or less would have made any difference to Robinson's Circus.

I had managed to combine acrobatics in some form with nearly every routine I had up to this time, and the trampoline was still part of my act. But my back was still giving me trouble (from an injury on the trampoline back in the burlesque days). In the season 1924–25, when I went into *Betty Lee* (adapted from the Rex Beach story *Going Some*), I had such pain after every performance I was sure I'd never make the next one. Finally I went to see a doctor and he said I had lumbago. He put me to bed with a bottle of liniment and I missed my first show in twenty-two years.

The famous tavern owner Billy Lahiff had money in *Betty Lee* and no one was ever more considerate of his employees than he. While I was in bed with my sore back he came in with a quart bottle of Irish Whiskey.

"Here's some good medicine for that back of yours," he said. Then he sat down and started talking about the show and telling me what a fine guy I was and meanwhile poured us each a large glass of whiskey from the bottle. I didn't touch mine, but he never seemed to notice, and in the course of an hour's conversation he finished off the entire bottle.

Finally he stood up, we shook hands, and he said "Well, see you on stage. That medicine'll fix you up."

The old axiom that nothing succeeds like success is nowhere more true than it is in show business. When we arrived back in New York in the summer of 1925, I found an offer waiting for the kind of show I liked and had come to realize was my specialty. *Captain Jinks* was right up my theatre alley. It was the song-and-stocking version of the old Clyde Fitch conceit *Captain Jinks of the Horse Marines.* The original was first staged around the turn of the century and provided Ethel Barrymore with her first important role.

The production, *Captain Jinks*, which dodged a certain kind of criticism by calling itself a "musical pastime" was put on expensively, to say the least. It was one of those productions in which, when nothing else occurs to do, they change the scenery or deck the chorus girls out in brighter colors. They had plenty of scenery and quite a few chorus girls who were pretty enough to justify their elaborate duds.

The plot, which didn't follow too closely the original story, came up for air more frequently than usual, although the poor thing was lost, as usual, in the last scene or two.

The Brooklyn *Eagle* described it this way: "Musically, the production reaches no new level. There are any number of songs and they are well enough sung. However, one can't have everything, and Joe E. Brown's humor is sufficient to make up for more shortcomings than the show has."

I think I can remember the opening nights of every show I've been in. For one reason or another they are always memorable. If for nothing else, I can remember them for their audiences. Opening night audiences are notoriously tough. They are so busy looking at each other and getting others to look at them they offer little response to the action on stage. Their rudeness extends to frequent running up and down aisles, coughing, changing seats, loud whispers, and other things to attract attention to themselves. It is a most disconcerting audience for a comedian.

The opening night of *Captain Jinks* was especially hard for me. In the first scene I drove on stage in an open barouche cab. I stepped down from the high seat and my first words set the pace for the rest of the show.

You may remember the story. I was supposed to be in love with my horse. I loved my horse and wouldn't have anything to do with the girl in the story, although she chased me all through the play. At the finish of the first act I drive off with the girl and her father in my cab and she sings a song something like the echo song from *Rose Marie*. She sings it to her lover, but he doesn't answer. She drops in the seat beside her father and he says "Drive on," and I drive off stage.

We had a five piece band, which they billed as a platoon from the original Marine Band. The band leader was one of those wild baton beaters, and one day in practicing he accidentally hit the horse on the nose with his baton. From then on the horse was frightened of anything that remotely looked like a baton.

Opening night in Philadelphia the lovesick maiden sang to her lover. No answer. She sang again, and again no answer. On cue her father said "Drive on," and as I started the horse she began her *Rose Marie* song again. Just then the band leader waved his baton a little higher than usual and the horse took off. And instead of going off stage he went right off into the orchestra pit. That finished the act. They couldn't even ring the curtain down until we fished the horse out of the orchestra pit.

After the performance, half a dozen people came backstage to tell me how much they enjoyed the show and to say that was the greatest curtain they had ever seen. "But how do you do that without hurting the horse?" they asked.

When we took *Captain Jinks* to the Martin Beck Theatre

in New York a few weeks later, we thought we had all the wrinkles ironed out of it. But opening night, just as I was getting into my first scene, one of the wardrobe women, carrying a big bushel basket of costumes, walked on and right across the stage. Everyone on the stage was dumbfounded, though the audience thought it was part of the act. The stage manager caught the woman when she came off stage and just kept her walking—right out of the theatre.

The Martin Beck Theatre was new then and this was the second show to play there. I knew Martin Beck (president of the Orpheum Circuit) himself, had known him ever since I was a kid doing acrobatics on the Orpheum circuit, and he was always a lovable sort of a guy. But show business was never monkey business with him. We were standing out front one day soon after *Captain Jinks* opened and I made some facetious remark about the show. It was nothing much, just a wisecrack. He didn't laugh. He didn't even smile. He just looked at me a moment.

"Brown," he said, and he had a little accent, "you know my theatre here has a stage. The proscenium arch is 62 feet high. From one side to the odder is 48 feet. From the footlights to the back wall is 60 feet. That's the place for you to be funny."

But it is no wonder I was such a smart alec. Walter Winchell, in *The New York Evening Graphic* for Wednesday, September 9, 1925, said: "Mr. Brown, whom I have enjoyed in other musical comedies, was never better than he was last night, and if space permitted I would like to go on applauding him."

A news item in another section said: "Ethel Barrymore sat in the orchestra of the Martin Beck Theatre last night with her fifteen-year-old son, at the premiere of the musical version of *Captain Jinks,* a comedy in which she captured the hearts of New York theatregoers a generation ago."

Captain Jinks had a long run, was voted the best musical

of the season 1925–26, and gave me all I asked of it. Including the starring role in another show opening the following autumn.

Pre died this year (1926) and I lost the best friend I ever had in show business. When we dissolved our partnership in 1918, and I made my step back (to burlesque) to step forward, he said, "Don't worry about me, Joe. I've got a swell job near home in Jamaica." He didn't want me to feel any obligation to him.

When I learned later that the great Frank Prevost was doing odd carpentry jobs and working at anything he could find to earn a few dollars, I made a spot for him in my *Arrest Me* skit. He was always grateful, though I was the one who was indebted to him.

It was Prevost, incidentally, who was responsible for making me one of the first glider pilots and a pioneer in air travel.

Pre was a natural mechanic who gravitated to any new invention when he heard about it. He built his own home and most of the furniture in it. When we were on the road, he was always improvising little gadgets to improve our rigging. If he found a broken clock in the hotel where we were stopping, he'd spend all his spare time tinkering with it. Sometimes he'd make it worse, but usually he'd have it running before we left.

While the Bell-Prevost Trio was playing Scarborough Park in Toronto early in 1907, Pre was approached by a local inventor who claimed he had made an airplane. Pre was fascinated with planes and pretty soon the inventor was telling him all about it.

"It's not exactly an airyoplane," said the man. "It's more like a kite. But it's large enough to carry a man, a small man who has courage."

Pre said immediately that he had such a man and he nodded toward me. I still weighed under a hundred pounds.

170

Pre explained what an opportunity it was for me and after some hesitation, I agreed to make the attempt. We all went across the road to a vacant field near the Park and I was strapped into a huge box kite, my arms extending out into the "wings," my feet on the ground. Two old nags that couldn't run any faster than I could were hitched to a long rope attached to the kite and whipped into such speed as they possessed.

I ran along after them in the middle of this strange contraption and it eventually left the ground. Complying with shouted instructions from the inventor and Prevost, I then cut the rope. That left me about 30 feet up in the air.

The kite sailed along for about 50 feet and then started down. I maneuvered it as best I could, but in the last ten feet it got out of control and turned over. I landed on my face amid splintered wood and torn cloth. I broke a finger and got a few scratches on my face, but I wasn't hurt otherwise. That made me something of a pioneer in the glider business.

The following year Pre and I were playing a fair in a small town in upstate New York when we met another airplane inventor, a young fellow named Glenn Curtiss. He told me that my acrobatic experience and my size were excellent qualifications for an aviator and he offered to take me for a ride in his "flying machine." I didn't accept his invitation—my kite experience was still fresh in my mind— but I did toy with the idea of becoming a flyer. Who knows what destiny might have been mine had I pursued the idea further? A few weeks later Glenn Curtiss won a trophy for the first public airplane flight of a mile in the United States; and in 1910, he won the New York *World's* $10,000 prize for a flight from Albany to New York. He went on to success and fame as a pioneer in aviation. Perhaps I missed a golden opportunity.

But I was destined still to be a pioneer air traveler. In

1911 we were playing in Beatrice, Nebraska, and in the course of one of my more difficult tricks I overheard one of the spectators say "Gee! What chances that kid takes." I turned to him and grinned, and then, just to show off, I repeated the trick and did it with a great show of ease.

After the performance, the man came back and introduced himself.

"My name's Glenn Martin," he said. "I make airplanes."

He flew them too, I soon learned, but his real interest even then was in perfecting and making better planes and his small factory, one of the first in the country, was already famous. So it was with Glenn Martin, in 1911, that I took my first airplane ride, while a local news photographer recorded the historic (for me) event. It was the beginning of a long friendship. Glenn went on to fame and fortune as a pioneer in aviation. He was working on the basic ideas for his famous Clipper series in the autumn when I opened in my last show on Broadway.

Twinkle Twinkle, with book by Harlan Thompson and music by Harry Archer, authors of such popular works as *Little Jesse James* and *My Girl*, made its bow at the Liberty Theatre in New York, November 16, 1926. Ona Munson, one of the cutest sprites Broadway ever saw, had the feminine lead.

The story was a comedy satire on motion pictures. Alice James (Ona Munson), noted star of the cinema, becomes tired of her surroundings and leaves a trainful of picture people at Pleasantville, Kansas. There she becomes a waitress under an assumed name—just in order to enjoy a complete change in her mode of living. There, also, she finds her true love and, in turn, is found by a correspondence school detective (me). You can imagine the rest with half a guess.

Bide Dudley, writing in *The Evening World*, said: "Miss Munson, while she hasn't voice enough to be put out of

172

modern musical comedy, is petite, pretty, saucy, and dances expertly. She has a fetching little toss of the head that adds to her winsomeness. Joe E. Brown is the most entertaining good-natured gawk I've seen lately. His antics, his dancing, and his spacious mouth make him Exhibit A as a laugh-getter."

Twinkle Twinkle had a long run in New York and then, in the spring of 1927, it was taken on tour. It had its Coast premiere in San Francisco on September 19th that year, and a few weeks later moved to Los Angeles. That was destined to be the best move I ever made.

It's a Great Story

Maybe it is significant that my last stage play before going into the movies was about film folk and my first movie was about stage people. Each gave me a good transitional experience. You might say that the first was an introduction to coming events and the other was a remembrance of things past. But the most interesting story of this period is how my getting into the movies paralleled the *Arrest Me* skit I had played a couple years ago. I had as much trouble getting into the movies as the bum did getting into jail. And, like the bum, when I had finally given up trying, it was thrust upon me.

I'm not sure when the "movie bug" bit me. Seems to me there had always been another goal, another high step, ahead of me no matter what I was doing. I could call it ambition, but in all frankness I must admit that nearly every step was prompted by something much more simple and elementary. For instance, when I was with Ashe and we were playing the circus, my greatest desire was to be someplace where it was dry. Frequently the circus lot would be wet, or our equipment and clothes would be damp from exposure throughout

174

most of the season. My greatest ambition then was to play in theatres and live in hotels—because they were dry.

After three seasons with the circus we switched to vaudeville. I wasn't in vaudeville long before I realized that a lot of people were making a living in show business without working as hard as I did. I remember Julius Tannen, the well-known monologist, was on the same bill with us one season. I watched his act many times and the thing that impressed me most was the fact that he just put on his hat and walked on stage, took it off, and chatted awhile, then put his hat on again and walked off. I wanted to be like him because he didn't risk breaking his leg every time he went on stage and most of all, because he didn't sweat. I thought it would be wonderful if I could do something where I didn't have to sweat.

But I admired Julius Tannen for other things. He was one of the greatest characters in show business. He had been a traveling salesman before he went on the stage, and a lot of his old habits were still in evidence when I knew him. Once, in Harrisburg, he took me to dinner, and on the way back to the theatre we stopped in at a haberdashery. He selected half a dozen shirts, some socks, ties, and underwear and told the clerk to send them over to his hotel. All together it came to quite a large purchase. When we left the store I said "Man! What was that for, how can you afford all that stuff?"

He said, "You've heard my act, haven't you?"

I never missed it, I told him. I'd studied his monologue until I could have given it myself.

"You remember how I always mention the name of some local business firm in my monologue? Well, the first thing I do when I get to a new town, I go around to a store like this one and make a deal with them. I give them advertising by mentioning them in my act and that pays for all this stuff."

175

On the other hand Tannen admired my ability as an acrobat and frequently said he wished he could do some of the tricks that I did. Once he managed to stand on his hands by bracing himself against the wall but he couldn't get down and back on his feet without help. Once I got him to do that trick just before he was scheduled to go on stage. Then I walked away when his call came, and you could have heard him yelling in the next block "Get me down! Get me down!"

When I could walk on stage and get laughs from an audience without comedy costume or makeup I began to think of better ways to use my talents, of bigger audiences and better pay.

The movies seemed to me to offer all these advantages. Several actors with whom I had worked had gone on to Hollywood and fame—Ned Sparks, Harry Langdon, and others.

The ambition to get into motion pictures was prompted and abetted by such examples and by the oft-repeated suggestions of my friends. "Joe, you ought to be in pictures" was a trite phrase to me long before the song with that line. One of the first to make an impression on me was Ed Barrow, manager of the Boston Red Sox. In the summer of 1920 when I played several exhibition games with the Red Sox, Barrow asked me to sign a contract with the team, not because I was a good ball player, I'm sure, but because he thought I was funny and he wanted me along for morale. I didn't care. I never had any illusions about my potentials in the big league and if they wanted a team's jester to influence morale and win games, that was all right with me. Time and again that summer he'd say, "Joe, you're funnier than any of those guys in Hollywood. You ought to be in pictures."

That seemed a little beyond my reach in 1920. I was still trying to pay off the debts I had accumulated during the strike the year before. I was happy if I could make a few bucks that summer playing exhibition baseball, especially when I could wangle a chance to really play.

One of the greatest thrills I ever had was an exhibition game the Red Sox played against Providence that summer. I was sent in to hit for one of the greatest of the game, none other than Harry Hooper himself. I wouldn't mention this except that I got a two-base hit. Joe Connelly, the old Braves' outfielder, gave me that one. In going back for a fly ball I hit into left field, he stumbled and fell. Result, a two-base hit for Joe E. Brown. The fact that I got caught off second on the next pitch has no part in the story.

Barrow's suggestion bore some fruit but it turned out to be indigestible. I took a film test at the old studios over in Fort Lee and the results were terrible. That discouraged me for awhile, but during the season when I was with *Jim Jam Jems* I made several more tests. I made them every time they asked me. I spent several nights at the Famous Players Studios. They experimented with lights, sets, costumes, makeup, but the results were always the same. They would look at the tests and shake their heads. "No," they'd say. "It still looks like Joe E. Brown."

So nothing ever came of any of the dozens of film tests I made from 1920 to 1927. Once, on a tour that brought me out to the Coast, I invested in a whole trunk full of costumes, big shoes and comedy clothes hoping one of the studios would give me a break. No one was interested.

Then, after a nice run in New York, the show *Twinkle Twinkle* was taken on tour. We opened in Los Angeles in October, 1927. By that time, however, I was resigned to my fate. I had decided to quit thinking about pictures and concentrate on a stage career. They weren't going to inveigle me into any more film tests, of that I was certain.

The show had been getting good reviews wherever it appeared. And someone writing for the New York *Sun* even composed a poem about me:

177

A tiptop clown
Is Joe E. Brown;
He has the biggest
Mouth in town;
It reaches clear
From ear to ear,
And makes him quite
A comic peer.

The Los Angeles papers were even more flattering: "There may be funnier things than Brown's burlesque of a picture sheik in a big love scene," said one, "but it's hard to imagine anything more laughable."

During the Los Angeles run, hardly a day passed that someone didn't come back stage and tell me I ought to go into pictures. I thanked them for what they intended as a compliment, and passed it off as such. My concentration on my role in *Twinkle Twinkle* was giving me the satisfaction of a job well done. I couldn't and wouldn't ask for more.

Then one night after the show, a lady came backstage and introduced herself as Jessie Wadsworth. She said she was an agent and she thought I was a "natural" for motion pictures. I told her I wasn't interested, I'd had a lot of screen tests and no one in the business thought they showed promise. She persisted. "Just give me an opportunity," she said, "I'll sell you."

At last I agreed to let her try. I even let Ben Bard, an old friend, make another screen test. He was married to Ruth Roland at the time and he had a lot of motion picture know-how. But this test was just as bad as the others. Then one evening Ralph Ince came in to see the show at the suggestion of Miss Wadsworth. He sent a note backstage asking me to come see him at F.B.O. Studios (now R.K.O.).

I had been through this so many times before that I had

little feeling about it one way or the other. I went to see him with no anticipation that the meeting would result in anything more than I had already had from a dozen other film executives. But Ralph Ince's first words were indicative of the kind of man he was. He told me in some detail about a picture he was planning and then he added, "I want you to play the lead."

"I just want to say one thing, Mr. Ince," I said, "I'm not making any more tests."

"I'm not asking you to make any tests," he said. "I've seen what I want in you. If I don't get it on film, that's my fault."

"I've been turned down before because I have blue eyes," I said, still trying to avoid any further disappointment for both of us.

"That will make no difference," he said. "I'll see that you are photographed right. Now here's a part I want you to read. I think it's a natural for you."

It was a natural, except that it was a completely straight dramatic part and I had never done anything but comedy —and acrobatics. The title of the play was *Hit of the Show* and it was a backstage story.

But I objected again. I said I didn't feel that I should be thrown into such an important part in my first try in pictures. He said O.K., they were shooting another show, a short film, a ten day schedule, and if I wanted to, I could get in that and test my wings.

Those were the days when a rock was a rock, a tree a tree, and most of the outdoor stuff was shot in Griffith Park. When I went to see Bill Le Baron, studio head, he said the title of the picture they were shooting was *Crooks Can't Win*, but that all the parts had been assigned and he didn't see how he could fit me in. I asked him if it was a gangster story and he said it was.

"Have you got a newspaper reporter in it?" I asked.

179

"Why, no, the story doesn't call for one."

"I never saw a gangster picture yet that didn't have a reporter in it somewhere," I said.

"But the story is already written," he argued.

"Couldn't we write the part in as you shoot it?" I suggested.

Finally he agreed to take it up with Ince. Ince said "Sure. It's not a bad idea. Maybe we can get a few laughs out of it. Go ahead."

There was a heavy in the story and the whole picture was built around him. But I had had a lot of experience with small parts. More than once before I had had to build a whole reputation on one line.

The film went to New York for cutting and word came back immediately that they would have to cut the heavy out of the picture to make it a good film. When it was finished, they had cut that character right out of the picture. It made my part more important, in a picture I hadn't even signed to make, in a story that didn't include my role.

Le Baron paid me $500 for my work in *Crooks Can't Win*, and though it was really my first picture, I generally call the next one, *Hit of the Show*, my first, since it was officially the first on contract.

Ralph Ince was a good teacher, an inspired director, a successful producer, and one of the best friends I ever had in Hollywood. He belonged to that old-time school of director-producers who could shoot "off the cuff" with one cameraman, one electrician, and one prop-and-scenery man and turn out better pictures than some of today's directors with their armies of technicians. His scripts generally were only a few pages of notes but he had the story so thoroughly worked out in his mind that he never faltered or paused to think what came next when he was directing.

When he was making a picture he would take up his position just back of the cameraman, or to one side just out of range. On several occasions he became so carried away with the scene he was putting his actors through that his flailing arms knocked the camera over. Of course, this was in the days of the silent picture and all noise, voices, or music off stage were calculated to help the actors through their scenes. He liked to direct love scenes and sequences that exhibited strong human emotions. In a love scene he'd stand behind the camera and yell, "O.K., now, walk towards her. Now take her in your arms. Look at her for a moment as if you'd like to eat her. Ah, you love her, you adore her! Now, kiss her . . . . hold it! O.K., cut!"

The command he had over his actors was nothing short of hypnotic. But he was not above using this power in a practical joke. One day the scene called for the actor to portray a hungry man devouring a huge plate of ham and eggs. He had the food fried in castor oil. The poor victim in this case was Frank Mills. Frank had been a prop man when Ince told him to drop the props one day and take a part in a picture. From then on he was one of the studio's best actors. In this eating scene he came on stage, a restaurant set, threw his hat on the hatrack, and plunked himself down at a table.

"O.K.," yelled Ince. "Waiter, bring the menu. Now take his order. You're a hungry man Frank, you've been out all night, you can hardly wait until the food comes. Now, here it is. Make your first bite a big one." Frank took a big bite and gulped. "Go ahead, you're a hungry man, you're crazy about ham and eggs, eat 'em Frank, eat 'em!" Mills ate every bit, he was that hypnotized by Ralph Ince's voice. "Now, take a piece of bread and dunk up the butter, that's it! That's the stuff, and what a fine meal you've had! Cut!" Poor Frank dashed off stage and heaved for half an hour.

But that wasn't the finish of the joke. When Frank came back on stage Ince said "O.K., everybody. Let's knock off for lunch."

181

Frank said he wasn't hungry, but we finally talked him into it and at the studio lunchroom we all ordered ham and eggs. That night when Frank got home, his wife had dinner waiting for him and she had been tipped off too. Yes, she had cooked ham and eggs.

That's the way they used to carry a joke all day. It was an intimate, big-family sort of a studio and Ince would stop whatever he was doing at any time to explain or answer the simplest question.

But the practical jokes were not always of his making. He suffered from terrific hangovers every time he had too much to drink and his mornings after were something to see. He'd sit a long time with his head in his hands and finally he'd say, "Come on fellows, let's get this thing going, for goodness sake."

Sometimes we'd go through two or three scenes before he could pull himself together enough to look up.

One morning I took all the actors and the cameraman aside and we rehearsed a scene with accompanying dialogue that had nothing to do with the picture we were shooting. I played a king and the leading lady played a chambermaid and the straight man played a comedy lead. We crossed up all our regular roles and broadly hammed the whole act. Ince dragged himself in finally and we could see he had a beaut. "O.K.," he said. "What are we waiting for? Let's get it rolling."

We went into our fake scene and the cameraman started grinding away. Ince let it go on for two or three minutes and then all at once he raised his head and stared. His eyes got big and a wild look came in them. Suddenly he yelled, "Stop it! Stop it! What the hell's going on here? Am I going crazy? What is that? What are you doing?"

We stopped, all deadpan, and I said "Why, are we doing it wrong?"

"No, no, what is that you're doing?" he screamed.

182

"Why, we're doing a picture, you remember, Ralph," I said, with a great show of patience.

"What picture? What picture?" He was fairly beside himself.

"Why, *The King's Night Out*," I said.

"*The King's Night Out!* The hell we are, we're doing *The Hit of the Show!*"

That broke it up and everybody howled. It was half an hour before we could stop laughing enough to get back to work and it was a whole week before Ralph Ince got over the shakes that fright had given him.

The biggest test of my talents and the biggest surprise at the results occurred under Ralph Ince's direction. Not only did he give me my first break in the movies but he saw and brought out of me something I never knew I had.

At some time or other every comedian wants to be a tragedian and every tragedian wants to be a comedian. But comedy had always been my forte, I had never aimed at anything else. And I never suffered from any frustrations on this score. I always considered the physical defects I was born with were tragedy enough. If I could laugh at them and make other people laugh at them, that was enough for me. I never thought I could get a kick out of making people cry.

The difference between tragedy and comedy is often no more than just the turn of a head, the flick of an eye. It is ticklish business for a comedian. If people are used to looking at him and laughing and he is cast in a tragic part and they still laugh that is disastrous. I knew that Joe E. Brown the comedian could not be cast in a heavy part unless they looked at him and believed the part he was playing. Ince was the first who showed me that it could be done. He didn't think the audience would laugh where he didn't want it to laugh.

The first few films I made for him therefore were the biggest test of my talents I had heretofore encountered. And the biggest surprise and one of the greatest kicks I ever got out of pictures was one evening when I stood outside the United Artists Theatre in Los Angeles where *Hit of the Show* was showing. Among the people coming out of the show a number were openly weeping.

I never had the physique nor the natural characteristics of a great tragedian. Any tragedy I played had to be the simple tragedy of the common man, the downtrodden little fellow. It was a character easily identified by 95 per cent of my audience. But this was an audience that needed to laugh too, and so I began to realize that though life included both tears and laughter, I should give my audience more laughter than tears when they paid for entertainment. I began to turn down roles that were strictly dramatic. I felt like a great actor when I could make people cry, but I got an even greater thrill out of making them laugh.

Laughter is a wonderful thing. I don't think I could ever enjoy being in a play that had no laughs in it. Have you ever been backstage in a dramatic show? Notice how quiet and subdued everyone it? It's never like that backstage in a comedy. There is almost as much joviality backstage during most comedy shows as there is out front. Everybody's throwing jokes, pulling gags, doing good-natured tricks. It's a different world. That's my world.

Thus, although the first six pictures I made were highly dramatic stories and I did very little in them that could be called comedy, this is what Ince saw in me, and I found it a welcome challenge to talents I had never tested before. One of them, *Take Me Home*, starring Bebe Daniels, was nominated by Film Mercury Magazine as one of the top ten films of the year (1928), though very little of the credit was mine.

Director Micky Neilan, who was an enthusiastic Joe E. Brown booster, directed this show.

We shot *Take Me Home* during a period when someone

had decided the studio needed a little more efficiency. On one wall of a big studio stage they hung a huge chart listing the pictures being shot, directors, casts, etc., and a shooting schedule. There were also columns marked "Ahead of Schedule" and "Behind Schedule."

We had just gotten started on *Take Me Home* when Bebe Daniels came down with a skin rash or something and couldn't work. We were held up a day or two, but by the third day we were all ready to start shooting. I came in with Neilan and he took one look at the big chart and strode out, saying "I'll see you later." I noticed our picture was listed as five days behind schedule. I thought nothing of it, but like the others went ahead and put on makeup and costume. We sat around for awhile and finally, about 10:30, someone said, "Where in hell is Micky?" I spoke up and told how he had walked off, and the studio executives finally located him at home.

Knowing Micky, I think the wires must have melted while he talked. He could burn 'em up if anyone could. And the gist of it was that he couldn't understand how they could say he was five days behind schedule when he had been working on the picture for only four days. Furthermore, he wanted to know if he was responsible for a girl not being able to work? Etc., etc. He said he wouldn't come back until they took the sign down. The execs said, O.K., they'd take it down right after lunch. Micky said, "Fine, I'll be in tomorrow morning."

Micky was the kind who would sit around and play the piano half the morning getting himself in the mood to work. The technicians would come and say, "All right, Mr. Neilan, it's all ready for you." Still he'd sit and play until he was ready. But he was a good director. His gang was always relaxed.

When the picture *Take Me Home* was finished, he said, "This is your picture, Joe." I said, "What do you mean?" He said, "This is yours. And it's great. If you are not a star after

185

this, you'll never make it." Throughout the production Bebe had been the star, but Neilan had slanted it my way without consciously intending to.

On the strength of that I went off to New York on a vacation. The first day I was back in town I ran into Micky Neilan on Hollywood Boulevard. It was "Hi Micky," "Hi Joe. How's the picture?"

"Picture, Hell! Those s.o.b.s!"

I said, "what happened?"

"What they did to your picture!" He was obviously very angry. "I thought I had something to say about it. They cut you out of the picture, Joe. Bebe Daniels is starred, not you." Of course, she was supposed to be.

The picture was already playing at the Paramount in Los Angeles, so I went to see it. I was shocked. I was hardly in it at all. And I learned what it meant to be cut out of a picture.

John Stahl at the old Tiffany-Stahl Studios was another one who helped me a great deal during my first days in Hollywood. He was another director-producer of the old school, like Ralph Ince, only more so. One of the best pictures I made for him was *Painted Faces*. It was another backstage story. It was in fact a combination of three stories. John Stahl had taken the ideas from three other pictures he had made and written them into one big masterpiece. He was a pretty good man with a pencil.

It was the story of a circus clown, another drama. It turned out to be a good picture, but nothing the actors did was half as dramatic as the private reading Stahl gave me.

I read the story and had pretty well figured out what I could do with my role when Stahl called me to his office. I had no idea what he wanted and I half feared he had changed his mind about casting me.

He greeted me affably and in a full voice asked me to sit down. I realized immediately that he was in a sort of inspirational trance. He was acting a role and giving it all he had.

186

Every movement was highly dramatic, every gesture calculated and exaggerated. He spoke like a Barrymore.

He picked up his phone and spoke to his secretary. "I don't want to be disturbed for the next two hours," he said. Then he locked the door.

"Joe," he said, "I brought you in here because I wanted to talk to you about this story. It's a great story, don't you think?"

I nodded. I didn't dare interrupt his act with the sound of my own voice.

"I saw you in the other backstage story," he said—he was thinking about *Hit of the Show*—"and I think you are the man for this one, though this is a bigger job than you've ever had." So now, I thought, he's going to give me a fight talk. But his next words told me what he was up to.

"I suppose you've set yourself in the part, but I'd like to tell you what I find in this story. I wrote it, you know, from three other plays."

He opened the script lying on his desk and began to read. He started on page one and he read the entire script, acting out every part and describing every scene as he went. Occasionally he'd pause and interject a stage aside like, "Now, don't misunderstand me, Joe. Don't think I don't want you to play Joe E. Brown in this, because I do. But this is what I see in your role," and he'd go through the whole scene detail by detail. Five times during the reading of this story he had to stop and dry his tears. He was crying so he couldn't go on. My insides were hurting from restrained laughter, and when he reached the fade-out we were both as limp as rags, though from different causes.

But John Stahl was a great director and he got great performances out of his actors.

Belle Bennett was another one who was wonderful to me in those precarious early days. While we were filming *Molly and Me* and *My Lady's Past*, she did everything she could to help me. And when she saw the first rushes, she said, "Be sure to put Joe's name up there. He has earned it." Belle is gone now, but the millions who saw her as Stella Dallas (in that great picture) will agree that there was a real trouper.

In the days of the silents, various things were done off stage to help the actors. Besides the voice of the director, there was nearly always a bunch of musicians to help us get in the proper mood. My favorite tune was *The Skater's Waltz* but the song they always played to get me into a serious mood was *Estrellita*. I could nearly always squeeze out a tear or two when they played that one. But on the set of *Painted Faces*, despite John Stahl's good example, it didn't work.

I don't know why I was in such a jovial mood—must have been having a lucky streak at Tijuana—but all morning long I tried to get in the mood to cry and couldn't. They wore out their fiddles playing *Estrellita*, but it didn't work. Finally we knocked off for lunch.

Al Ray, a cousin of Charles Ray, was directing that picture and he was the Job of directors if ever there was one. I never saw a man with so much patience.

After lunch we came back and Al said, "This time, Joe, don't say anything, don't tell me you're ready. Just drop your finger as a signal, get up, and start on. I'll get it."

The music started. I sat down on the set and put my head in my hands and started thinking about all my relatives that had died, all the friends I had lost, all the tragic things I had ever heard about it. It was sacrilegeous thinking, I know, but several dozen studio employees were standing around drawing good pay for doing nothing because I couldn't cry.

Finally I got up and as I did the camera started whirring. I felt perfect for the scene. Just then I looked up, and there on a high catwalk were two electricians. They had made no sound and they didn't even know I could see them from the stage, but they both had huge grins on their kissers. And instead of tears, I burst out laughing. That was the end of the day for the crew and cast of that picture. As a matter of fact we didn't do that scene until weeks later when everything else in the picture was finished. By then I was so dog tired I didn't even need *Estrellita* to get me started, and once started, I couldn't stop.

But underneath all my seeming success in these silent pictures I was beginning to realize that I was selling only half my talents. With a mouth like mine, I could steal any scene by the sheer enormity of it. I opened my mouth and it dominated the picture. But a kisser like mine must be heard as well as seen and I had a hunch that if I could sell sound as well as action I'd have a winning combination.

I did, and back of it lies the story of the luckiest break I ever got.

That's the Way I Was

The invention of sound motion pictures was the most opportune thing that ever happened to me. I might claim I'd spent a lifetime getting ready for the opportunity but if the opportunity had never presented itself, where would I be? No, I consider it pure coincidence, lucky for me, that talking pictures were invented when they were. It was a set-up I might have missed had I been a year earlier or a year later. All the credit should go to Warner Brothers.

It is well known history now that Warner Brothers were facing bankruptcy in 1924–25. Despite its reputation for excellent pictures, their studio was caught in a squeeze play that threatened to put it out of business. Those were the days of cutthroat competition and no matter how good your product was, if you didn't have distribution you didn't have a business. Larger competitors gained control of most of the theatres and Warners' films were left out in the cold. Boxed in with this setup they either had to try something new or quit. With what remained of their capital, they gambled on an entirely new type of screen entertainment.

There had been talk of talking-pictures for years but no

one in the industry wanted to tinker with it. Let well enough alone, they said. Business in the silents was good, so why tamper with a profitable routine?

But the gamble was forced on Warner Brothers, who were desperate for a way out. John Barrymore in *Don Juan* was their first attempt, though only the music was recorded. Then, late in 1926, Warners released *The Jazz Singer*, starring Al Jolson. Compared to today's standards, it wasn't much of a film. Even as a silent it wouldn't have been much. But when the audience heard the voice of Al Jolson as he sang his memorable "Mammy" song, Warners' gamble paid off.

It was 1928 before the executives of the other companies got around to deciding that perhaps they had better investigate sound. Their startling discovery was a shock literally felt round the world. The panic that followed was the worst that ever hit Hollywood. Everyone connected with the business was involved. Stars, directors, writers, producers, distributors, and exhibitors suddenly found themselves fighting for survival. The single test for all was whether or not they could adapt themselves to sound.

This was the maelstrom into which I jumped from the comparative security of an established stage career. Is it any wonder that I considered it at first only a temporary thing? Make a quick buck and get back to the stage before my public forgets me was the thought uppermost in my mind at first. Our boys were still in school in Philadelphia and Kathryn and I rented an apartment in Hollywood on a month to month basis. I had made half a dozen pictures before I began to hope that I had a future in the business.

My original attitude toward Hollywood was not out of character. I never was so sure of anything that I'd count my chickens before they were fully grown. I never knew but what they might turn out to be turkeys. I always worked hard at whatever I attempted, but more than once I'd given all I had and found it wasn't enough.

191

But after I'd made a few pictures, I began to realize some of the potentials in this new field and my hopes began to soar. Now I wanted to succeed in Hollywood and I was willing to take any role they gave me. Anyway, I thought, it was all good practice, it was education in a field I knew little about, and it was a chance to explore my own talents. Once I knew my limitations, I could set some kind of a goal and work toward it.

I certainly couldn't complain about the variety of experience I was getting. The first six pictures I made were dramatic stories and I died in five of them. This was about as different from what I had always done on the stage as night compared to day. But I worked at it just as hard, harder perhaps, as I had with my comedy roles. And, for the first year, at least, I had to be content with less pay.

But this was not a new trick for me either. I had stepped back once before to make a step forward. So I made ten pictures before I was starred. I was co-starred or got feature billing in most of these, of course, but it was not until *Hold Everything* that I actually got star billing.

I had made three pictures for F.B.O., one for Paramount, and three for Tiffany-Stahl before I got a bid from Warner Brothers.

I had an idea I was getting into some pretty big things when the first offer from Warners came and I felt I needed an agent whose business reputation matched the new prospects. Jessie Wadsworth had served me well and our association throughout my early period in pictures was most satisfactory. But when Ivan Kahn came to me with the promise that he could get me a lead in a Warners picture, I felt the time had come to make a change. Just as I had some years before explained a similar situation to John Jermon, I told Jessie of this new opportunity. And like Jermon, she dissolved our agreement with graciousness and good feeling. I have never forgotten either her courtesy in this or her early interest that got me my first break in movies. Not many people in Hollywood would have released a paying "property" with so much grace.

Ivan Kahn was a paragon among agents. Widely traveled, he was a man of varied talents. He had been successful in a number of ventures before he became an agent in Hollywood, but most of all, Ivan was honest. He was completely honest and he always insisted on honesty in those with whom he dealt. Much of my financial success at Warners was due to his shrewd handling.

I did one picture, *On with the Show,* for Warners at a salary of $1000 a week. I knew it was going to be a good picture before it was finished and Ivan thought I should get more for the next one. They wanted me to appear in *Song of the West.*

Our interview with Darryl Zanuck was typical of the finesse with which Ivan could handle a business conference. He said Zanuck had asked to see me.

Zanuck was cordial but cagey. After we had discussed the picture he wanted me to do, we got around to talking about salary. We told him we wanted $2000 a week. Zanuck was on the defensive immediately. "What's the idea," he said, "trying to hold me up?"

I got up and started to walk out of the office. Ivan said "Wait."

I said "No need to wait. I didn't come up here to be insulted. What am I holding him up for? I didn't know I was that important." I talked to Kahn as though Zanuck wasn't in the room. "I can't understand," I said. "I haven't insisted that he has to pay me, I merely said that was my salary."

Zanuck asked me how much they had paid me for my last picture and I told him $1000 a week. "Well, that's your salary, isn't it?"

"No," I said. "I have no fixed salary. I'm allowed to climb. What did you get the first week you worked for Warner

Brothers? Do you still get the same, or has that anything to do with it? I have the same privilege and I'm taking advantage of it. Two thousand dollars is what it's going to be, for you or anyone else. Perhaps the next picture will be $5000." I walked out of the room.

Ivan followed me out to the stairs, trying to get me to go back. I told him if he wanted to talk to Zanuck it was all right with me, but if he talked about anything less than $2000 a week, he wasn't my agent.

Kahn went back and they talked for about fifteen minutes while I hung around at the foot of the stairs. Presently he came out and called down. "Come on up," he said. "He wants to talk to you."

I went back and Darryl apologized, said he was sorry, didn't mean it as an insult, and so on, and he wanted me for the picture. He said he'd pay me $2000 and I signed to do *Song of the West*.

As its name implies, it was an outdoor picture and it was my first on outdoor location. It was filmed near Lone Pine, California, and when it was finished I decided it was about time I made a personal appearance tour in the Middle West and East.

Like the sailor who goes for a boat ride on his shore leave, I never missed an opportunity to see a play. Between personal appearances in Detroit, I saw a played called *Hold Everything*, starring Bert Lahr.

After the first act I went back stage to meet the gang, many of whom I had known for years, and one of them jokingly said "Hey, what's this I hear about you doing a picture of *Hold Everything*?" Of course, he was just ribbing Lahr, because Bert was an easy man to rib.

"What's that?" yelled Lahr, immediately on the defensive.

I fell in with the gag and said "Well, you know, Bert, it's a pretty fair show. I don't know what it would be like in pictures. It's a good stage play and you've been pretty suc-

194

cessful in it. Of course, if I did it for pictures I'd make a lot of changes in it." And I picked out Bert's big laugh scene in the act and said they'd probably cut that out.

Bert went for the gag hook line and reel. I didn't know that he had already been ribbed about it quite a lot. Everyone knew he wanted more than anything to do the picture.

I had been back in Hollywood only a few days when Ivan said Jack Warner wanted to see me. We hot-footed it out to the studio and discovered they wanted me to do *Hold Everything*, at an attractive $15,000 for the picture.

Winnie Lightner was the feminine star, and the picture got excellent notices. Sid Silverman writing in *Variety* made the remark that I was much better in the picture than Bert Lahr had been in the play. And this time it wasn't a rib. Though Bert hadn't seen the picture, he was so mad he wrote an open letter to *Variety* in which he accused me of stealing his character. An article about the "controversy" appeared in the *Saturday Evening Post*, but that was as far as my part of the controversy went. I never answered Bert's letter and I never talked to him about it.

But Sam Sidman, an old-time Dutch comedian, did answer Bert's letter. He gave him hell for claiming anyone could steal what he, Lahr, didn't own. And he went on to say that Lahr had seen him many times and Lahr's makeup and everything he did in the play was taken from Sidman. "And I don't claim any credit for originating the character because I stole it from Sam Bernard," another well-known Dutch comedian of a previous era. "I admit it, why don't you?" he asked.

As a matter of fact, if Bert had taken the trouble to see the picture before he wrote his letter, he would have seen that I was in no way the least bit like the character he portrayed in the stage version of the play. But he would never go to see it.

I have always been sorry for that. Bert Lahr, whom I

consider one of my very best friends, is one of the best comedians this country ever saw. His triumph in *The Wizard of Oz* is the only example I need to offer to prove that.

The picture *Hold Everything* was hardly finished before Warners asked me to sign a term contract for three pictures a year with a starring role in each picture. *Hold Everything* had not been released yet, but I knew it was going to be a good picture, so I asked them to make the star part of the contract retroactive to include that picture. Winnie agreed and so did the studio, but a few days later, huge billboards appeared all over the country announcing the picture. This was the wording: "Winnie Lightner in *Hold Everything*, with Joe E. Brown and . . ." others. I called Ivan and told him to tell Warners the contract was broken.

I heard later that several people responsible for the slip got fired and a general shake-up occurred in the publicity department of the studio. All of the big sheets were recalled and the entire advertising schedule quickly rewritten. My name as co-star appeared as agreed.

That contract with Warner Brothers was probably the most unusual they ever signed. It had more strange clauses in it than a codicil in the will of an eccentric miser. But it wasn't until *Hold Everything* was pronounced a box-office hit that I felt sufficiently secure to sign a full year's lease on a house.

A few months later we brought the boys out and put them in Urban Military School and began shopping for a buy in Beverly Hills. The fact that we could feel sufficiently sure of the future to gamble this much is proof of the confidence I had in myself and in Hollywood, for this, remember, was now in the fall of 1929, when any thought of future security was shaken by the great stock market crash.

Imagine our confidence, then, a year and a half dozen pictures later, when we made two steps we could only dream about before. We bought our first home and we deliberately increased our family.

196

Mike Frankovich was the first addition to our family. He came to live with us in 1930 and though he was never formally adopted, he was soon as much a member of the family as Don or Joe. He was older than they by three or four years, and in no time at all he was their idolized older brother.

Kathryn had always wanted a girl. "Gives a family better balance," she said, though I'd never considered ours unbalanced. With a father named McGraw and a mother named O'Mahoney, she always seemed to hold up her end of any argument. I had had my fondest wish fulfilled and doubled in my two boys. A baby girl, even though adopted, would really fill my cup to overflowing.

But by now everything the Browns did was a news item and we didn't want any publicity on such an intimate family matter. We merely gave out no denials that Kathryn was pregnant, and we never said she was. She disappeared from public social functions for a few months and one of the columnists printed a note that we were expecting. At the end of a respectable period, we went to Chicago.

While I was busy with personal appearances at some of the Loop theatres, she slipped out to Evanston and visited The Cradle. It was not as famous then as it is today and not as large, but Mrs. Walrath had a dozen youngsters for her to choose from.

When she came back that night she said "They've got a dozen of the cutest kids you ever saw out there."

"Shall we take 'em all?" I asked, only half joking.

"You'll want to when you see them," she said, "but I picked out one I think is just what we want." She wouldn't describe the child, she said. She wanted me to look at them first and see which one I would like best. "I'll tell you the one I picked out after you see them."

I went with her the next day and she remained in the waiting room while a nurse escorted me through the nursery.

There were about a dozen babies. One by one the nurse

held them up for my inspection. I looked at six with no more than the average male stranger's interest in youngsters that age. Then the nurse showed me the seventh. It was a little blond four-months-old girl.

"That's the one I want," I exclaimed. "Nothing else will do." I knew it, this was my baby, and I couldn't have felt more sure of it if the child had been my own flesh and blood.

"I'll check," said the nurse. "I'll find out if it is promised. Sometimes one may be promised—just waiting for clearance."

"But that's the one I want," I persisted. "You don't have to look any further for me. That's mine."

"Well, if it's possible," she answered.

Kathryn came in and when she saw which one I'd picked she grinned. I knew then that our hearts were lost to the same little blonde.

We went for a walk while Mrs. Walrath checked her records (she had already checked ours) and we hardly dared to talk about our good luck for fear something might happen to change it.

When we returned, Mrs. Walrath met us at the door with a smile. "She's yours," she said, "if you still want her."

There were some court formalities and papers to sign later, but that was the day, so far as we are concerned, when our Mary Elizabeth Ann was born.

A year and a half later, when we decided to adopt another baby girl (two boys and two girls was the ideal balance, Kathryn insisted), we had need for more secrecy than ever. By then I was a top star at Warners, getting $100,000 a picture, and a reporter or at least a studio publicity agent seemed to be lurking under every seat. I didn't go to Chicago with Mrs. Brown this time. Chicago friends of ours, Pat and Eleanor Barnes, accompanied her and played the role of prospective parents. Pat was one of the first radio announcers in Chicago, a very wonderful guy, and they were a very wonderful couple.

The ruse fooled the press and the first news and pictures ever printed of the babies were those we ourselves released. We named this one Kathryn Frances, for her mother. And this is the first time I have told in print that our two girls were adopted. When they were five or six, we told them, proudly, for it is not every child that is wanted by its parents. Ever since that moment they have felt that they were something really special in our family. We could not love them more were they born to us. The boys, of course, adored and petted them from the very beginning. Both girls are married today with families (two children each) of their own and Grandfather is more popular than ever—as a baby-sitter.

So I got a lot of things I had wanted all my life. It was a full period. If I never got anything else besides those years between 1930 and 1940, I would have had it. There was so much, it made all my living worthwhile in so far as my own personal enjoyment was concerned.

My family was always important in my day to day living and the greatest scene I ever played and the one I always enjoyed most was a private one. It was with my family around the dinner table. (My private variation on Father Peyton's theme "The family that prays together, stays together," is, "The family that eats together enjoys good stomachs.") We enjoyed each other, and it was always a noisy, boisterous hour. It was especially so after Mike joined the family. There were always two or three kids (sometimes half a dozen or more) from the neighborhood who would drop in for dessert. And there were others who seemed to live with us from time to time. I remember Charlie Ewing who lived with us for about a year and Jack Summers who was in the house for a year and a half. Otto Graham, the great football passer, was a member of the household for a short time too. Don met him at a game at Northwestern and said, casually, come out and see us sometime. Otto came out and stayed. And we enjoyed him.

These were the days when Mrs. Brown's standing order for milk was seventeen quarts a day. I liked milk, too, especially in the evening or late at night after long overtime at the studio. But there were so many icebox raiders those days it was hard to keep enough on hand for me to have a glass every night. Finally, in desperation, Kathryn made a big sign POISON DON'T DRINK and stuck it on one bottle.

Three days later the milk was piling up and she asked why I wasn't drinking any. I showed her the sign.

"Oh, that," she said, "I put that on to keep the kids from drinking it all up. I wanted you to have some."

The immediate household was only part of the "family" picture. Obligations one never dreams of increase with every step up in Hollywood. By 1933 I had come to be known as Hollywood's greatest "joiner." I belonged to more clubs than a retired Iowan, appeared at more benefits than the most out-of-work stage luminary who expects to get a job as a result of his religious appearances at such affairs, served as judge of more contests than a tabloid newspaper holds, and appeared at more affairs, social and athletic, than any other Hollywood player.

My numerous memberships, real and honorary, and my constant goings and comings among people made me the screen's unofficial ambassador to the public. While Will Hays was the spokesman of organized Hollywood and Conrad Nagel was the industry's good will builder, I went around joining clubs and opening six-day bike races with the common folk. I was never known to refuse to make a public appearance when it was desired of me and when such an appearance would not conflict with my work in a picture.

And all these activities (not counting fan mail and general publicity which the studio took care of) required con-

200

siderable personal help. I simply couldn't have done half the work or one-tenth the public appearances if I had not had Doug Keaton to organize it all for me. Doug was not an agent, nor even my manager, but a sort of general assistant. I suppose the best title I could give him would be Executive Secretary, though we had the excellent services also of a "Girl Friday," Miss Connie Sherman.

Connie's most vivid recollect of those days is the way her work was interrupted every afternoon by the announcer on the sight-seeing bus yelling ". . . and on your right, ladies and gentlemen, is the home of the famous comedian, Joe E. Brown."

Douglas Keaton was a Pittsburgh boy who came to New York to get into the theatre. I met him soon after he came to New York and liked him. I got him a part in *Twinkle Twinkle* and when I got a foothold in Hollywood, I sent for him. He was with me throughout my Hollywood heyday period.

Doug was a good cook too and he prepared most of my lunches at the studio, after I got big enough to have my own cottage on the lot. Those were memorable meals. Invariably there would be guests for lunch. Pat O'Brien, James Cagney, Frank McHugh, Dick Powell, Eddie Robinson, Arthur Treacher, were among the most frequent.

And in the well-remembered eating scene I did in the stage version of *Elmer the Great* (between pictures in 1931), Doug prepared all the food just off stage. In the course of an hour and a half as Elmer, I consumed a slice of ham, a batch of mashed potatoes, four griddle cakes with syrup, a piece of pie, two cups of coffee, two apples, half a grapefruit, a glass of orange juice, two doughnuts, a slice of toast, and a bit of shad roe.

After a couple of weeks of this, my doctor discovered I was eating too much salt and after analyzing my diet, found that it came from the ham I ate. I hate to think how much ham I consumed at every performance. The appetite of Elmer is so essential to the characterization that I had to stuff. I couldn't cheat on the audience for it always knows if you are only pretending to eat. But the hardest part of the routine was keeping one side of my mouth clear so I could talk and eat at the same time—hard to do even with my mouth.

It was easier in the picture version of *Elmer the Great*, which Warners made the following year. I could fake a lot of the eating sequence in the picture but I still had to talk with a mouth full of food. Besides being one of the most hilarious scenes in the picture, it also "developed" the character of Elmer. It couldn't have been done without sound.

The character of Elmer in *Elmer the Great*, as originally conceived by Ring Lardner, was based on big Ed Walsh of Meriden, Connecticut. Walsh was a member of the old Chicago White Sox when they were called the Hitless Wonders because they dominated the American League for so many years. This was the period when Ring Lardner was known as a good baseball reporter and nothing more. Traveling, dining, and card playing with the noble athletes gave Lardner a great slant on their off-the-diamond characters.

He discovered that even the greatest heroes had their human moments, and he made a special close study of Big Ed Walsh, the greatest hero of them all, and the man Lardner liked the best.

Lardner, of course, made Elmer a composite of several ball players but the foundation on which the literary statue was erected was Big Ed.

Elmer the Great was—well, to put it mildly, he was rather sold on himself. Like Dizzy Dean, he would blandly announce that he'd knock the potatoes out of the other team, and then would make good his bragging by striding out onto the diamond and doing exactly as he had predicted.

It is meaning no disrespect to a grand sports figure to state that Big Ed Walsh was thoroughly convinced of his own abilities. Walsh never suffered from the pangs of an inferiority complex. He knew the power of his mighty right arm and his baseball cap was a lid covering a noodle packed tight with trade secrets about the weaknesses and strong points of enemy batsmen.

A pitcher had to be good in those days, you know, when men like Ty Cobb and Tris Speaker and Nap Lajoie and Sam Crawford were around to make life miserable for the twirlers serving up those hot horse-hides.

Despite the fact that Walsh must have realized that Ring Lardner was using him as Elmer, the two men remained boon friends up to the time of the writer's death in 1933. Walsh never objected to being immortalized in print and on celluloid under another name.

The upstage tendencies of some actors and actresses are the ruin of many good pictures. They have their minds more on how they look to the cameras than on their parts, and the results are contrived and artificial. Winnie Lightner was never like that. For that reason she was wonderful to work with and because of that too, the pictures we made together were good pictures. We never knew where the camera was. Once, for instance, in a scene we were shooting in Busch's Gardens in Pasadena, Winnie and I were doing a love scene on a bench. She was to grab me in a sort of Martha Raye hug and after only slight resistance on my part, we were to go into the clinch. She grabbed all right, but a little too Martha Raye-ish, and we went over backward. The alert cameraman didn't miss a trick. He panned right down on us and we went on with the act, meanwhile crawling out from under the bench. It was one of the most successful bits of comedy in the film. And it was all purely unintentional. It would have been hard to do with a self-conscious, self-centered actress.

It was the unintentional scene, the unplanned shot that frequently made the picture.

Another time, Joan Bennett and I were co-starring in a football picture. In the plot we were to go around to differ-

203

ent colleges and enlist an all-America team. The team we actually cast for the picture were top-notch players and some were All-American. The picture was to open with an introduction of each player, one at a time, each one doing something different. One was to do a drop kick, another to pass, and so on. I'm the eleventh. I'm supposed to catch the ball and streak down the field. I straight arm the first tackle, then bump the next one; shift the ball and straight arm the next, and a huge smile spreads across my kisser. I'm going good when I come to Tim Monahan, former Notre Dame Center.

Monahan is the biggest man on the field. He weighs 240 pounds and it's his job in the plot to stop me. He does and then the whole team piles on top of me, one on top of the other until the last one crawls right up to the top. At that I am to give my famous yell, they all get off, and I get up looking groggy. That was to be my introduction in the picture.

When we were all ready to shoot, the director, Bill Wellman said, "Now, look, Joe. I want you to look groggy, and when you get up, walk toward the camera."

I asked him if he wanted us to rehearse it first and he said no, he didn't think it necessary. Tim came over and suggested we practice the hit once. He hit me and I went down light a light. He said, "That's the way I'll do it, easy like. I didn't hurt you, did I?"

I said no, not at all. I wouldn't admit he nearly killed me. "Well," he said, "I know it'll be a little heavy with all of us piled on you so when you go down I'll make a bridge of my body and hold off some of the weight."

I said, "I'd appreciate anything you can do for me."

So the cameras start grinding and I streak down the field. I straight arm the first, bump the next, twist and shift the ball. Down the field I go with a smile from here to there. Then, Boom! Monahan hit me and I bounced about twenty feet. They piled on and I nearly suffocated under them. I could hardly whisper, let alone yell. (They had to dub that in later.) Finally they all came off and I stood there weaving, trying to find out where the camera was. Then I heard Wellman's voice. "Come on Joe, here, up here. Stagger, now stagger." I staggered right up and fell smack into the camera.

"Great!" yelled Wellman. "That's the way I wanted you to be!"

"That's the way I was," I said.

The risks an actor took in those days made good movies, but they made the movies the most hazardous of occupations.

Once we were on location at Hidden Valley when they wanted to make a lot of stills of me posing with a bear which we later used in several scenes. I posed with the animal, once with a prune in my mouth which the bear took out, and similar nonsense poses. Later, after we had shot several scenes for the picture, I asked the bear's trainer if he ever had any trouble with the animal. He said, "Why, yes, Mr. Brown, we have. As a matter of fact this bear killed a man. He mauled another so bad he never recovered."

I was flabbergasted. "How come," I asked, "you never told me?"

Sheepishly he answered that it might have meant his job.

I was furious. "Yeah!" I said, "and it might have meant my life!" The things they let you do!

In *The Circus Clown* a playful lion clawed my arm in a gentle sort of way, but the doctor had to take six stitches in my hide to sew it up. After that I had to go on with the act and lie on a couch while the lion came up and licked my feet. They put honey on my feet to entice him but there was nothing to discourage him from taking a bigger bite. They employed a double for the long shots, but I had to be the one in the close-ups when the lion was doing his licking act.

That one turned out all right though. When the lion finished licking the honey off my feet, he came over and put his two huge paws on my chest and then put his head down as though he was sorry he hurt me. It was so good, such a "touching" scene, they rewrote the whole sequence to fit it.

It is my opinion that most of the credit for Warners' great success during the 1930s should be given to the fine bunch of directors they employed at that time. They were artists, every one, and though they each had their little idiosyncrasies, they were pardonable faults.

Mervin Le Roy's particular idiosyncrasy was the habit of talking with an accent throughout the making of a picture and using a different accent for each picture. For instance, day after day while on the set he would speak and give directions in a Dutch accent. "Vell, vot's da matter? Come on, come on, let's get dis show rollink!" We'd answer in the same accent.

Perhaps during the shooting of the next picture he would switch to an Irish accent. And the accent was never determined by the subject or any characters in the story. The actors and the technicians all fell in with the gag and any stranger walking on to the set would have thought we were all a bunch of foreigners. Only when the cameras were rolling would the actors speak in their natural voices.

One morning I was half way through a scene before I suddenly realized what the whole crew was laughing at. I was reading my lines in Le Roy's accent.

Every director I ever knew had some little idiosyncrasy that was a sort of trademark. Lloyd Bacon loved to make any picture that had uniforms in it. If the picture he was making didn't have a uniform in it he'd write one in himself. And then throughout the time he was making the picture he'd wear the hat, cap or helmet to match that worn in the picture.

I always thought Lloyd was a frustrated actor. He probably inherited some of it from his famous dad. I remember the lovable Frank Bacon with a great deal of respect. I met him first during the season 1918–19 when his famous *Lightnin'* was having its record run (1291 performances on Broadway alone). It was the play that brought him fame, and competence, and the worship of the multitude. Frank Bacon was co-author of the play, its star, and manager of the show. Still, when the Equity strike occurred, he was one of the first to lead the actors out. His son was much like him, especially in his treatment of the actors and others who worked with him.

Roy del Ruth (who directed *Hold Everything*) was the last person you'd expect to be a practical joker. But once I caught him sitting on the set practicing my signature. And one day he wrote a note to the head prop man whose job it was to build the sets and decorate the stages. The note was signed with Jack Warner's signature. It told the set designer that a certain set he was putting together looked godawful and he wanted him to clear out everything on the stage and replace it with the furniture, files, desks, and equipment from the office of one of the other directors who was away.

The man cleaned out the offices as instructed and left only the absent director's telephones sitting on the floor. When he came back next day and found his office cleaned out he was the most surprised guy you ever saw. Roy del Ruth finally left Warners because, as he said, no one on the lot had a sense of humor.

Ivan called one day and said Warner Brothers wanted me to play the part of Flute in *A Midsummer Night's Dream*, and what did I think about it. I said I didn't know. He said, "Well, you know, Shakespeare might offer a good thing."

"Is he in it?" I asked. The only Shakespeare I knew played for Notre Dame, but I didn't know he could act. Ivan thought that was pretty cute and he told it around the studio, but I was on the level.

Jack Warner gave me a big build-up. "All the principal actors in the studio are going to be in this picture," he said. "Dick Powell, Jean Muir, Olivia de Havilland, James Cagney, Arthur Treacher, Ian Keith, Anita Louise, Victor Jory, Mickey Rooney, they're all going to be in it and we've brought Max Reinhardt over to direct it." Then he talked at length about Reinhardt and about his great success in Germany and what a fine director he was. "It's a wonderful opportunity for you, Joe. Why don't you go talk to Reinhardt?"

So I met the great Reinhardt and I liked him right away. He was an artist, you could sense that immediately. His accent was pretty bad, but I understood him. He said he wanted me to play the part of Flute. I said I didn't know much about Shakespeare. He waved that aside. The first time he saw me, he said, was in the Vendome Restaurant. He had never met me but he recognized me and nodded. "Und den Brown nodded to me und schmiled—und ven he schmiled Brown faded oudt und Flute faded in." That was his way of telling me I was a perfect Flute.

After a half hour of this, I went back to Jack Warner's office. I still was not convinced. And after another half hour with Warner, Ivan, and Hal Wallis all working on me I agreed to think it over. Then Ivan said, "Is this to be one of Joe's regular pictures or is it an extra? And how much will he get?"

Wallis said, well, it was not to be one of my contracted pictures. They weren't thinking in terms of money. Everyone in the studio would be in it, sort of a big family party so to speak. Nice chance for everyone and we thought Joe would want to be in it. He's one of the oldest on the lot in point of service, and so on. Ivan interrupted him. "Hal," he said, "he isn't to get paid?"

208

"Well, no, not exactly."

"You mean he won't get any money?" Ivan was incredulous.

Wallis and Jack Warner acted as if the point were of no consequence. But Ivan was persistent.

"You mean he's to do this whole thing and not get any money? You won't give him anything at all?" Ivan's incredulity was now tinged with scorn.

"Oh," said Jack, "we'll probably give him a present of some kind."

"For instance?" asked Ivan doggedly.

"Well, perhaps a Packard car or a Cadillac or something like that."

Ivan said, "A Packard? A Cadillac?" And Jack, "what would my commission be, a bicycle?"

Eventually, I did play Flute on a contract that gave me afternoons off any day the horses were running at Santa Anita. It was the one and only role I ever signed to play without first understanding the part. Had I known more about Shakespeare I would not have attempted it. If you know your Shakespeare you know the role is that of an addlepated fellow who is forced to play a female role in the amateur show being strenuously put on to celebrate the marriage of the Duke of Athens. One reviewer said, "Joe E. Brown has hair on his legs, muscles in his arms, and a mouth of which the only kind word that can be said is that it's at least masculine." I was outraged, scared, and obviously wrong as a female impersonator. But that's why Reinhardt put me in it. My look of shame and guilt was just what the role required. Reinhardt insisted that I play it straight.

Some of us certainly were hot Shakespearean actors. Besides myself from the circus and burlesque, there were Jimmy Cagney from the chorus and Hugh Herbert from burlesque. At the beginning, we went into a huddle and decided to follow the classic traditions in which Herbert and

209

I were brought up. I really believe Shakespeare would have liked the way we handled his low comedy, and I'm sure the Minsky Brothers did. The Bard's words have been spoken better, but never bigger or louder. It turned out to be one of the most successful things I ever did.

The only fault I ever found with Ivan Kahn was his drinking. It not only got him in trouble, but as my agent it cast some reflection on me. Once he went on a bender at the Roosevelt Hotel and tried to pick a fight with Edward "Mickey" Walker, one-time (1926) Middleweight champion. Ivan had been an amateur boxer himself and he was still in pretty good shape. But Mickey didn't want to get into a fight with him and he ignored Ivan's taunts as long as he could. Finally Mickey knocked him down and they put Ivan to bed.

A short while later, Ivan called for room service and when the waiter came he took his spite out on him and beat him pretty badly. This brought the police in on the fracas and they hauled him off to jail.

Nate Stein, a good friend of Ivan's and a natural fixer for such situations, tried to get Ivan out. The police wouldn't budge. Then Nate decided he'd let him stay in jail and use the instance to teach him a lesson. Ivan was out cold anyway and getting him home would have been a problem. As a matter of fact, he didn't come out of it until about noon the following day.

Meanwhile, with the co-operation of the police officers, Nate rigged a radio set near Ivan's cell but around the corner, out of sight, and connected a mike. When the noon news broadcast began, Nate cut into it with his mike and began to tell about the tragic ending to a party in the Roosevelt Hotel the night before when actors' agent Ivan Kahn in a fistic encounter killed one Joseph Benatti, a hotel waiter. The voice went on to describe how it happened, the bloody details of the fight, and so on.

210

Suddenly Ivan jumped up and screamed, "No, no, I didn't kill him!"

The guard told him to shut up. The radio droned on, giving other gory details. "Oh, oh," cried Ivan, holding his head. "I killed a man, I killed a man."

"Yes, you did," said the guard. "And from what I hear you'll get the chair for it."

At Nate's suggestion, they kept him there for two days and never once let him see a newspaper. He swore if he ever got out of there he'd never touch the stuff again. Finally Nate got him out and told him what a hoax he'd pulled on him and why. Ivan had a good sense of humor and, anyway, he was so relieved to know the truth that he couldn't be mad at anybody. Some people would have gone right back and drowned the whole nightmare in another binge. Ivan didn't. He waited a couple of days.

I believe my final breaking of our contract was the reason for his going on the wagon permanently. He went on a bender right after that and from what I heard it was the bender to top all benders. It was his last. When he sobered up he never touched it again. He wound up as head talent scout at 20th-Century Fox and remained always one of my best friends.

The last picture I made for Warners was *Polo Joe*. One critic said the only false note in it was that I was supposed to be a guy who knew nothing about polo or horses but it was obvious I was an expert horseman. When I made that picture they gave me a mount and told me, "Don't worry, the horse is trained to follow the ball." What they didn't tell me was I had to follow the horse. So that writer never knew what a compliment his criticism was. I never was a horseman, at least in the sense that I rode them. I had hardly been on a horse before that picture was made. The criticism was a compliment to my good physical condition.

I always enjoyed such comments because I at least knew

that nearly everything I did was based on happenings in real life. Situations and characters may have been slightly exaggerated on the screen for comedy effect—you can't condense any period of time or characterization into a 90-minute film without some exaggeration—but in *Elmer the Great,* the Ring Lardner flavor of the character was sympathetically retained in the screen play. *Elmer* is a screwball, more than slightly resembling the great Dizzy Dean. He comes into the big league as a rookie, with enough conceit to outfit a turkey stock company but, like Dizzy, he not only knows he is good, he is good.

When Billy Murray was manager of the Philadelphia Phillies he had on his team a big guy named Harry Frank Coveleskie. Coveleskie came from some mining town in Pennsylvania and he was what you might call unlettered. He was a pretty good pitcher. He had a lunk walk that was funny to watch. I saw Coveleskie play several times and I copied his walk and his mannerisms in *Elmer the Great.*

I also did a very funny gag in the picture that was inspired by Coveleskie. Since a lot of people thought the gag far-fetched, I was relieved when Billy Murray one day, in the presence of mutual friends, confirmed its authenticity.

Coveleskie reported to Murray in 1907 and by 1908 they were calling him the Giant Killer because he beat the Giants three times in the last games of the season. The Giants were in first place but those three loses put them in a tie with the Cubs. When they had to play Chicago over again, they lost. Coveleskie had contributed to their downfall, so he came in for his share of praise.

In his first game with the Phils, Murray handed Coveleskie the ball and said, "It's you today, son."

Coveleskie was so nonchalant it was painful to watch him. He just didn't know any better. He said, "All right. Don't worry about it Bill, I'll take care of it." He had started calling the manager "Bill" the first day in camp.

In the first inning, with a man on first, Coveleskie spit on his hands, fingered the ball, and took a full wind-up. And of course the man on first stole second without a play being made to get him.

When the side was retired and Coveleskie came in to the dugout, Murray was waiting for him.

"What the hell's the big idea?" yelled Murray.

"Huh?" said Coveleskie. "Didn't hear what you said, Bill."

"I said what's the idea of winding up with a man on first?"

"Doin' what?"

"Winding up with a man on first! Why did you do that?"

"Why, Bill, gosh. I never knew he was there."

Murray turned around, called all the players off the bench, called the hitter back and the coaches, and gathered them all around him.

"Listen, you fellows," he said. "I've told you before, with this ball club we play as a team. We don't play as individuals. It's not every man for himself. *I want you to have no secrets in this club, understand? If there's a man on first, I want the pitcher to know about it!*"

Coveleskie stood there with the rest. "That's the stuff, Bill," he said. "Give 'em hell. They deserve it."

We didn't change the dialogue or the action very much when we used the story in *Elmer*.

On his death bed, Billy Murray said, "See that Joe E. Brown gets my National League life pass." It's one of my most treasured trophies.

I have always felt that a tremendous responsibility rests on the shoulders of the man in the public eye. When I found myself in a celebrity's shoes, I remembered the days when I had my idols and the influence they had on me. And if I had not remembered, there were always plenty of things happening to remind me.

When I was a little fellow my two ideals were Ty Cobb,

whom I still consider the greatest baseball player of all time, and "The Great Commoner," William Jennings Bryan. I saw Bryan deliver a speech from the back of a dray once and though I don't remember what he said or what he stood for, the sincerity and zeal of his delivery has been an inspiration to me ever since. No one could revere such idols and be guilty of misconduct without a twinge of conscience.

In the picture *Elmer the Great* I had to drink a cup of coffee. For a gag and to point up Elmer's uncouth ways, I left the spoon in the cup when I drank. Every time I tried to drink the handle of the spoon would come around and hit me in the eye. After five or six tries (I milked the gag as long as I could) I bent the spoon and put it back in the cup, then drank the coffee successfully.

That was the gag, but a few weeks after the picture was released, I received hundreds of letters of complaint from irate parents telling me they didn't have a straight spoon in the house. That made me realize my great responsibility to children, and there never was another similar complaint.

One mother wrote me that she and her young daughter had just seen one of my pictures. As they came out of the theatre after the show, the child—just six—said to her mother "Mommy, when Joe E. Brown dies, will he go to heaven?"

"Why of course darling," replied the mother.

"Golly, Mommy," the child said, "won't God laugh!"

I always counted my wealth by the number of children who thought I was all right. Children seldom do much that you tell them to do, but they will follow an example and do as you do if they think you are worth following. And since adults are only grown-up children, a lot of this theory applies to them too. If children like us they will do what we do, so it is up to us to be what we want them to be. We can be an influence for good or bad.

214

Once, when I was playing in burlesque (*Sporting Widows*) with Harry "Heinie" Cooper, he remarked that I never used "hell" or "damn" before an audience. Heinie was "first comedian" in that show and probably got twice what I was earning. He was a lot like Frank Murphy of Williams' *Ideals*. He thought his success depended on smutty jokes and the dirtier the better. Watching his audience I was convinced (as I was with Murphy) that he could clean up his act and still get the laughs. He had a lot of talent, but he covered it up with some of the oldest jokes and crudest language you ever heard.

I had a song and dance number with one of the girls and a Utica paper had said "Brown's business during 'Oui, Oui, Marie,' brought encore after encore and came mighty near stopping the show." That was typical of the reviews we were getting and Cooper knew there was no off-color stuff in our act. When he remarked about my lack of smut on stage, I asked him why he didn't clean up his scenes, get some new jokes, and cut out the cuss words. He argued, "Well, they still laugh at it don't they?"

Then one day he came off stage yelling "I did it! I did it!"

I said "Did what?"

He was as excited as a kid with a new toy. "I cut out all that dirty stuff, and you know what? They laughed more than ever!"

Years later I appeared in the stage version of *Elmer the Great* in San Francisco, during a respite from pictures, as I mentioned. After I returned to Hollywood, I received a letter from Heinie's mother. She said Heinie had been to see the show five times, but he didn't want me to know because he was blind. I didn't know he was in San Francisco. I didn't know he was blind. It touched me that the great Heinie would do that.

Fan mail is the big barometer of a star's popularity as everyone knows, but few understand what it means to a star.

The upstage actress, the shrinking-violet "I want to be alone" type, the cocky ham, the careless comedian, the serious actor, and the extrovert all feel the same when it comes to fan mail. They may never read it or even answer it, but without it they are dead, a property no one wants, a drug on the studio market.

I read all the fan mail I got my first year in Hollywood. It wasn't a big job. But it began to mushroom after that and by the time I made my first picture for Warners, we had to hire a whole staff to take care of it.

But though I could not attempt to read any great portion of it, I did keep a careful check on the type of letters that were being sent, the complaints and criticisms of my pictures and any good suggestions for improvement that they contained. These were depression years, too, remember, so there were always many requests for money and financial help. The really worthy ones we did try to help, but by far the majority of them had to be ignored. Occasionally my secretary would hand me a letter that was for some reason or other particularly interesting. Here's an example:

Dear Joe Brown:
The other day me and another fellow had an argument. He said Joe Cook was the world's greatest comedian and I said you was. We finally came to blows about who was the greatest comedian and I socked him one and broke his arm. It cost him $12 to get the arm fixed and he's going to make me pay for it. Could you please send me the $12 to pay the expenses on account of I was fighting for you? Whether you send it or not, I still think you're the greatest comedian in the world.

As I said in the beginning, everything in my background had fitted me for talking pictures and the industry's switch over from silent to sound happened at the opportune mo-

216

ment. The timing was right—and so was Warners' contract. At $100,000 a picture and three pictures a year, who could ask for anything more? By the use of all my talents in sound and sight, I had a winning combination that brought me a lot of things I had wanted all my life. So let me repeat, if I never got anything else besides those years between 1930 and 1940, I would have had it. There was so much, it made all my living worthwhile in so far as my own personal enjoyment was concerned.

This Fellow Is a Ball Player

Each spring when I left school to rejoin the circus or to begin
a vaudeville tour, all the kids in school would beg me to
bring them souvenirs. One season I hit on what I thought
was a novel idea. I collected a rock, just any kind of a rock,
from every town we visited. I wrote the name of the town
on the rock and I had visions of lining up all these rocks on
the window sills of our classroom.

In those days all five of the Ashtons dressed in one trunk,
that is, all of our stage clothes and all our street clothes were
kept in one trunk. Ashe began complaining that the trunk
seemed to be getting heavier and heavier and one day near
the end of the tour he went through the trunk and down on
the bottom he found my collection, a whole layer of rocks.

That was the end of my first experience in souvenir collecting, but it was not the end of my desires in that field.

Those who are not too sophisticated for sentiment or too
hardened for hero worship will understand my "Room of
Love." It began when I started collecting sports trophies
25 or 30 years ago. These were not cups and trophies that I
won, nor even asked for, but a variety of keepsakes whose

218

sentimental value to the giver made them doubly cherished by me. When I gave the collection to U.C.L.A. in 1946, it was probably the finest privately-owned sports trophy collection in the world. The collection then included over 200 different items (counting all of more than 200 autographed baseballs as one item).

The collection comes from virtually every sport, and every item has a particular significance in the history of the sport. I started the collection with the autographed baseball used in the 1906 World Series. It bears the signatures of Ed Walsh and Three-Fingered Brown (who real name was Mordecai Peter Centennial Brown), and is so black with age one can barely distinguish the signatures.

The trophy room grew from that until I had to build a special room in our home in Beverly Hills to hold it all. I called it my "Room of Love."

I turned it over to U.C.L.A. because I have always been a big booster of the school and because my boys went there, and because I felt that more people should have the pleasure of viewing it. Youngsters, from nine to 90, are always thrilled and inspired by these reminders of great sports heroes.

What are some of the trophies?

Besides the ancient baseball I mentioned above, there are the shoes that Tris Speaker wore in the 1920 Series, gloves belonging to Herb Pennock, Chief Bender, Mickey Cochrane, and Roger Bresnahan; Paul Waner's bat the year he won the National League bat crown, and Babe Ruth's bat the year he hit 60 homers; and Dizzy Dean's uniform from the 1934 Series (later transferred to the Baseball Hall of Fame).

Then there are the trunks that Jimmy Braddock and Gene Tunney and Jack Dempsey wore when they won the heavyweight title; Primo Carnera's shoes, size 23 (we'd like to have them back now—we'd live in one and rent the other!); the uniform Tommy Harmon wore in his last college game; the uniform Red Grange wore in his last pro game; the driver

Bobby Jones used the year he made the grand slam; tennis rackets belonging to Don Budge and Bill Tilden; the football used in the 1927 Rose Bowl game when Pittsburgh defeated Washington; the shoes that Frank Wyckoff wore when he broke the world's 100-yard sprint record, and, oddest of all, two University of Southern California athletic trophies— of all things in U.C.L.A., because they were given to me first and were among the other trophies I gave to U.C.L.A. Of the latter, one is the basketball U.S.C. used in winning the Pacific Coast basketball championship in 1931.

Anyway, you get the idea. That's only a small part of the list. Of them all, there were a few that I wouldn't part with even for an exhibit at U.C.L.A.

One is Tris Speaker's World Championship medal of 1912 (Boston Red Sox). Tris and his Frances are today two of our best friends. It has been a long and happy acquaintance.

My love for sports is pretty well known. It is deeper than my portrayal of Elmer in the old baseball movie classic, *Elmer the Great*. Actually, I was once offered a contract to play with the New York Yankees. I didn't accept it because it came at a time when I was beginning to get a foothold on Broadway, and weighing together my future in the two careers, I figured my best chance for success would be the stage. Nevertheless, I did don a Yankee uniform and spent several weeks working out with the team. Once Miller Huggins and Jake Ruppert were watching me work out with Hoyt, Jones, Ruth, and some of the pitchers, fielding bunts along the side lines.

"Well," remarked Huggins, "he's not the first comedian I've seen in a Yankee uniform."

"Comedians," said Jake, "yes, we've had our share of them. Only some weren't so funny."

Lou Gehrig, one of the greatest to wear the Yankee emblem, was also a very close friend, so it is fitting that in my

220

years of collecting sports paraphernalia, one object should represent the immortal Iron Man of Baseball.

Lou had been a guest at my home in Beverly Hills, not once but several times. And it was there that he, like many others, first marveled at my trophy collection.

I said I never asked for a gift. There was only one exception. I asked for one from Gehrig. To me he was Mr. Yankee. I felt my trophy room would never be complete without something from him. I had been told that Lou's health was failing. He had long since passed the 2000 consecutive games mark. So I wrote to him, asking if, when he retired, he would give me the first baseman's glove he used all that time. I wanted to include it in my collection.

A week or so later, I received a reply.

Lou wrote that he knew how much the glove would mean to me, but as it meant everything to him, he wished I had asked for anything but the glove. To be sure, it was an ordinary first baseman's glove, he said, but he couldn't part with it. He offered his favorite bat—even his uniform. I wasn't hurt. I understood. But in my embarrassment, I blushed.

Shortly after that, Lou's long string of consecutive games was broken in Detroit. After 2130 games he took himself out of the game because he felt he was hurting the team, his team. He never played again. He was stricken shortly afterward with multiple sclerosis.

That fall I went to New York to see the Yankees play in the World Series. My seat in the stadium was just a couple down from the Yankee dugout. Joe McCarthy, Bill Dickey, Earle Combs, and some of the other players came over and chatted with me. Then, just before game time, the bat-boy came over and told me Gehrig wanted to see me on the Yankee bench. I left my seat and made my way around to the dugout. There, standing at the end of the dugout, was Lou.

By this time he was in very poor health. It was a shock to

221

me to see the once erect, powerful, handsome Lou with his hair now turned prematurely gray, his face wan, and his frame thin.

Looking up from the bench as I walked toward him, he was unmindful of the eyes of the Yankee players watching us.

"Well, pardner," he said. "Here it is," and he held out his glove.

For once this big voluble mouth of mine didn't have a thing to say. I glanced at that line-up of tough, healthy, wonderful ball players and there wasn't a dry eye on the bunch. I took the worn glove, though I too could hardly see it through my tears.

That glove is another trophy among my most cherished.

My "Room of Love." I think the name was appropriate. Every one of the items I received certainly was dear to the person who gave it to me. They really made a sacrifice to give them to me. And the amazing part of it is that all but one of them came to me unsolicited. People found out about my room, and sent me the trophies. And I think that people have to like me a lot to give me keepsakes that they treasured.

Somehow or other I've always managed to combine a little baseball with whatever I was doing. I played in the minors between off-seasons in vaudeville; and during vaudeville seasons, I played on the National Vaudeville Artists team. One season I played on that team it was managed by Joe Schenck. Gus Van caught for that team; Bob Grody was one of the pitchers, and Ernie and Val Stanton were other players.

I think my best motion pictures were baseball stories. But pictures are only fantasies. My real-life interests were stronger than that. I even mixed baseball with business.

My contract with Warner Brothers, as I said before, was probably one of the most unusual ever signed in Hollywood. One of the clauses it contained was one that said Warners must supply me with a baseball team. It was they who first suggested calling it Joe E. Brown's All Stars—probably because they thought it would never amount to much.

Buster Keaton had a team about the same time, and it was comprised of stage hands and extras, legitimate studio employees. Not mine. I went out and hired professional athletes and some of them were experienced ballplayers. I did my own scouting too. That's how I discovered Mike Frankovitch, who later became a member of the Brown family. I found Mike playing baseball at Belmont High School, but he was a big boy and plenty qualified to play on my team. We licked the pants off the other studio teams and most of the others in our circuit.

Unfortunately, the publicity department at Warners kept building up my past as a baseball player until I was one of the all-time greats of baseball. I've been trying to live up to it ever since, although its foundation in fact was no more than an occasional season in the bush leagues and the invitations mentioned above—but never accepted—to join the majors. I have stood alongside some of the greatest ball players in the world and heard them say (about me) "This fellow is a ballplayer." Of course I don't know just how they meant that, what reading they gave it. Maybe they said "This fellow is a ballplayer?"

I have always loved baseball more than any other sport, but I didn't buy into the Kansas City club alone because of my love of the game. It had always been my ambition to own at least a part of a big professional club, but I bought into this club more because of my love for Tris Speaker. I wanted to help him. I admired Tris long before I knew him personally and more after we became friends.

I bought into the Kansas City Blues in 1933 at a time when I was pretty hot publicity-wise. The team had been making such a poor showing they figured some of my popularity might rub off on them if I'd stop off on my way to New York and pose for some pictures in the ballpark. Several news-paper reporters were on hand to interview me, though I tried to evade any predictions on the future of the Blues. They persisted. One chap asked "What do you think the chances are for the Blues this season?"

"I don't know," I said. "That's something you ought to ask these fellows here, they know more about the team than I do." Tris Speaker, who was in the deal with me, was standing there and I pointed to him.

"We already got Tris' opinion," sportswriter Ernie Mehl said. "This is your story, Joe. We want to know what you think."

I kept trying to back out of it. Finally, the president of the club, Lee Keyser, said "Go ahead, Joe. Tell 'em." So I thought, O.K., if they really want my opinion, they'll get it.

"O.K.," I said, "if the ball club we have now is the one that will open the season I don't think we're going to go very far."

At this Lee turned and looked at me in amazement. "What do you mean?" he asked.

The newspapermen were right on the ball.

I said "Well, you insisted. I had to give my opinion and I have to be truthful."

"But why don't you think so," Lee persisted.

I said "O.K., now I'll answer your question. How can you expect more from a ball club that last year finished fifth in the American Association, with only five additions which you brought from your own ball club at Des Moines? Espe-cially, when you remember that the Des Moines club, two classes lower than the Blues, finished in seventh place. Can we expect more from our team now that we have five new players from a team that finished seventh in a lower league?"

That was it. I told the truth, but until he died I don't think Lee ever forgave me.

Honesty may be the best policy, but frankness doesn't

224

always pay off. Frequently, at ball games, the sportscasters would ask me up to the broadcasting booth to do an interview. Often it would turn into a monologue with me doing the whole inning for them. So once in Chicago, when a sportscaster friend of mine, Bob Elson, asked me up to the booth, I thought nothing of it. And when he left the booth and told me to carry on with the inning, I thought nothing of it. "Take care of it for me, will you, Joe?" he said. "I'll be right back."

After the inning, the technician in charge of the mike shoved a piece of paper over to me and motioned for me to continue. I glanced at the paper. It was a commercial for a cigarette. I said no, I'm not doing a commercial too.

"But this is the place for it," he said. "We'll have to do it."

I looked out the window and there was Bob sitting way down front enjoying the ball game. I turned to the mike.

"Look, ladies and gentlemen," I said. "I'm on here for free. I'm not getting paid for this broadcast. But this is the place for the commercial, so here goes, this is reading," and I read the commercial.

"Well," I added, "I suppose these people are honest. But I don't smoke, so what do I know about it? They say their cigarette is full of Latakia. It's full of a lotta something, I don't know what. I only know they are popular."

The radio people didn't care much for the way I handled it, but they couldn't say anything. As it turned out they got a lot of compliments on that broadcast and a few years later, another radio announcer gained stardom and a fortune with similar frank treatment of his commercials.

I always played baseball the same as I do anything else. Just because there are two men out and we are ten runs behind in the ninth doesn't make the game finished. As far as I'm concerned, no game is over until there are three men out in the ninth inning.

225

I remember how John L. Sullivan used to put it in his famous monologue.

"*Now* is the time," he said. "Live hard, leave nothing undone, work for success in a decent way—then you won't be wasting time having regrets for things you left undone."

I expounded this philosophy to a group of boys in their final year at the University of California at Los Angeles— seniors who belonged to the football team—one night when they were chatting informally at my home after dinner.

"Don't go off the field saying 'I wish I'd done so-and-so,'" I said. "Play every game knowing that you'll never play it again—play it to the utmost." The boys took the theory to heart and went off and formed themselves into a group called the "Club of No Regrets."

I went to Pittsburgh in 1933 to attend one of the first dinners held by the Variety Club (another one of my life memberships) and to see the Pittsburgh-Nebraska football game as a guest of my old friend John Bain "Jock" Sutherland. Jock, at that time, was head football coach at Pitt. It was one of his best years at Pitt and they wound up the season playing Southern California in the Rose Bowl. They lost to S.C., but they were practically unbeaten otherwise that season. Their only defeat was in a game with Minnesota when they lost in a 7–3 score.

In the Pitt locker rooms after the Nebraska game, Jock and I were watching the post-game horseplay of the victorious Pitt team when Nebraska's coach, Dana Bible, came in. Dana and Jock and I were friends of long standing, and so I felt torn between the pleasure of one's victory and the pain of the other's loss. We talked awhile and then Dana said, "Joe, would you do me a favor?" I said, of course, anything in the world.

"Well," he said, "my kids think you're a pretty swell guy Joe, and I think they'd listen to anything you had to say. Most of them have dressed and gone but there are a couple

226

over there who just don't want to go home after losing the game. It meant a lot to them. I wish you'd go over there and talk to them. I'd appreciate it." I started out the door and he said "I'll take you over."

"No," I said. "I'll find my way. I'd rather go alone."

I went into the visitors' locker room and there were these two kids still in their uniforms, sitting there crying. One was Bernie Masterson and the other was George Sauer (both were lettermen in 1931, '32, and '33, and Sauer became All-American in 1933). I told them about our little Club of No Regrets at U.C.L.A. and what a fine thing I thought it was to be able to say you'd given your best. And if you felt in your heart that you'd given everything you had, then there wasn't any more you could do.

We kicked it back and forth like that for awhile and joked a little and pretty soon the boys were on their feet. I don't think it was the words so much as the fact that I'd take the trouble to say them. My interest in those kids was worth more than any platitudes I could hand out.

And I got to thinking, after I left the field, what a lot of callous people there are in football stadiums. Somewhere in the stands at every football game there sits at least one Big Noise. He has two dollars bet on the game and he doesn't care how many bones are broken as long as he wins that bet. You can hear him shouting after every play "What a dumb quarterback," he roars. "Why didn't he pass?"

No one answers him, so he thinks everybody agrees with him. "My five year old boy could carry the ball that far," he bellows.

The chances are that he hasn't any five year old boy and that if he has he will be singing a very different tune if his son ever plays football. For the Big Noise isn't necessarily mean, he is just thoughtless—and he doesn't want to lose his two dollars.

And possibly the mother or dad of the boy he so thoughtlessly criticizes is sitting just behind him. We are all good second guessers—and fast-thinking Monday morning quarterbacks.

The boy is doing everything possible to win the game. He would give his right arm at the moment for a victory and that is no figure of speech. On such a day there is nothing in a boy's life so important as that football game.

A football game is something to be seen and forgotten by the spectators. But it is something that will always be remembered by the boy who plays in it, more especially if he happens to have made a mistake. I suppose Roy Riegels will be haunted, unfairly, all his life by the ridicule of the crowd when he made his long run in the wrong direction. The public remembers that mistake, but it forgets that he was hurt just before he made it and that the following year he was the captain of his team and an All-Coast center. The spectator demands only victory and seldom looks behind the scenes.

Looking back upon my long love affair with sports and especially baseball, is one of the happiest things I do. Educators tell us that we remember best those things we like to remember. I guess my reputation as a walking encyclopedia of baseball history is due entirely to my love for it. This knowledge came in handy many times during the late war when I was touring the battlefronts. Whenever I found myself stumped for something to talk about, I just asked some G.I. in the front row where he was from. Generally, I could mention some ballplayer from his home town, or at least from his state, and I'd take it from there. A little kidding and a story or two and we had a program. Some of my recollections went back before these kids were born, but it didn't seem to make much difference. A baseball story is a baseball story whether you know the main characters or not.

Mine Also Ran

I have always had a soft spot in my heart for animals. No stray dog or cat ever got turned away from my door. I think most people in show business are like that. The itinerant life most of us have to live doesn't leave much room for pets of our own. It's a frustration we overcome by kindness to all animals.

My entrance into movies made a big difference in this pattern. In Hollywood I put in a workday like any other businessman, and in the evening I went home to a family and my own fireside. And, of course, with children in the house, we had our quota of pets. But Hollywood provided something else for me besides the settled life of a studio worker. The additional income bought luxuries beyond the dreams of a struggling young comedian.

It was Bing Crosby's race horses that were so slow of foot that they became a national gag, but I raced horses before Bing got the bug. Furthermore, I had a stable of old nags that were by far a worse lot, horse for horse, than the shabbiest Crosby had in his barns. And I never did get the credit that was due me for racing such terrible plugs. Could have been that Bing had a better publicity man than I did. Looking back on the experience, I'm not sure whether I should call the memories fond or poignant. They provided me with two of the greatest thrills of my life. The memories of these two experiences alone is worth the $150,000 and the eight or nine years I spent as the owner of a racing stable.

It all began in a weak moment at Santa Anita. I had followed the ponies for years as a spectator and frequent win-place-and-show contributor. There were no tracks near Los Angeles during my early days out here, but Tijuana (and later Agua Caliente) was just across the border and not far away by car or plane. We were just beginning to enjoy our new bonanza and taste some of the sweets that money can buy, when I discovered this Mexican pleasure resort. Those were the days when the casino and gambling rooms were operating in addition to the track and one could lose more money in more ways than you could imagine. Though gambling never was the cause of hunger in our home, I did play poker and the horses when I could afford it. And for my money, the ponies always had an edge over poker because I knew they couldn't be shuffled as easy as cards.

So the border resorts held more than casual fascination for me. That is, they did until a momentous weekend when I really lost my shirt. Mrs. Brown had refused to watch my foolish spree and had in fact returned to Hollywood after a day of varying luck on her own account. But like any other sucker who has gone in over his head, I swore I could beat the game if I could hold on a little longer. By the end of the next day I was cleaned out. I even had to borrow money to get home on.

I'll always remember coming into the house that night. Kathryn was already in bed and I thought she was asleep. I tiptoed in, feeling like a dog with his tail between his legs.

I crawled into bed and then, out of the darkness, she said "Well?"

230

"I'm ashamed," I said, "terribly ashamed."

"How much did you lose?" she asked.

"More than you should know," I answered.

She was silent a moment and then she said "Well, it's your money. You've worked hard for it and you have the right to lose it. Good night."

That is why when Santa Anita opened in 1935 I was one of its first patrons but I didn't buy any stock in it. I was too smart to get caught in anything like that. I remember when it was being promoted and "Doc" Strub (Dr. Charles Strub) sent out 400 letters to prospective stockholders. I received one of them and tossed it in the wastebasket. I said oh, no, not this time. I'm wise to these schemes. I've always gone in on these things and I've lost a thousand here and a thousand there, but this time, not me. I was too smart for them.

Claiming a horse in a race was a much safer investment, I figured. At least you would have something to show for your money, and if you got a good horse you might even make a little on the deal.

So one historic afternoon at Santa Anita I claimed a horse named Straight Jacket. Mrs. Brown was in the East at the time, and when reporters told her I had become the proud owner of a horse named Straight Jacket her remarks made headlines.

"They ought to put Joe in one," she said.

My experiences with that horse should have discouraged me from going any further into the business. He was not a horse one could learn to love easily, and soon after I got him I shipped him off to Bay Meadows with trainer Frank Farrell. Frank was a nice old chap who had more patience than I and many years of experience as a trainer. He would call me about once a week and say "I'm entering Straight Jacket tomorrow."

At first I would ask him what about it, has the horse got a chance, and he'd say he didn't think so. After we had repeated this conversation four or five times and the horse ran last each time, I said don't call me any more. "I don't want to know anything about the horse. You run him Frank and have fun with him, that's all."

Then one day he won and I didn't have a dime on him. It was a muddy track, one of those days when the "dogs" were up, the guards they set up on the track to keep the horses away from the rail where most of the water lay. It has to be pretty wet when they do that. It was tough going for most horses, but Straight Jacket seemed to enjoy it. Of course he paid a good price but since I didn't have anything on him I don't remember what it was. I wasn't interested. It was the only race he ever won for me, though we kept trying that whole season. And I believe his 1.18–4/5 was the slowest six furlongs ever run to win.

Trainer Farrell had a chance to take some other horses back to New England that summer and asked me if it would be all right to take Straight Jacket along. I said, sure, that was O.K. with me. "Take him farther than that if you want. About a hundred miles out to sea and drop him, if you like."

Mrs. Brown and I went east that summer also, and one evening after the races at Narragansett Park we were dining with my friend Percy M. Pike at the Biltmore in Providence. Pike owned some stock in Santa Anita and he had several horses entered at Narragansett. Two of his horses had won that day, and so we were celebrating, in a mild sort of way, his double victory. Conversation eventually got around to Santa Anita and how it had caught on and how successful it was and what a fool I'd been for not buying some stock when I had the opportunity. Percy said he had three shares. I said "You don't want to sell any of it do you?"

"Any time I can sell anything and make 50 per cent profit I'll sell," he said.

Par at that time was $5000 a share. I was convinced that it

232

would be no risk at $7500. "I'll take it," I said. "All you've got."

Percy said he wanted to keep one for himself and one he had promised to lay away for his grandson, but he said I could have the other one. I said O.K., and we shook on it.

This was in midsummer. It was October before we got home and Percy got home and we got around to collecting our stock. He delivered it all right, and for $7500, even though meanwhile its value had risen to $12,000. I made $4500 on the deal before I spent my money. That is why I say Percy Pike is the best illustration of a gentleman and a sportsman that I could give.

The second horse I acquired by outright purchase. I paid $10,000 for Barnsley, and horsemen in the know advised me it was a good deal. It was just before the $10,000 Breeders' Handicap at Santa Anita in December, 1936. They assured me if I would enter him he would win himself out in that one race. He ran second, but only because of a bad racing break. The jockey pulled him a little too wide coming into the stretch and a horse owned by Alexander Pantages and named A.P., beat him by half a length. There was mud along the rail that day and Barnsley didn't like mud, so the jockey had been instructed to keep him out of it. But swinging into the last turn he had pulled too far to the right and thus lost the race.

Also Barnsley wasn't an easy starter. This was in the days before the starting gates, and no jockey was ever able to get his head facing the right way when the barrier went up. But after many disappointments, Barnsley did win for me one day and gave me one of the two biggest thrills I ever experienced in horse racing.

I was probably the most thrilled fellow in the horse-racing business anyway, so you can imagine how I felt on the rare occasions when my nags won. February 23, 1937, was one of those days. I was sitting in our box at Santa Anita when the horses hit the finish wire in the seventh race. Suddenly it dawned on me that my horse had won.

"He made it!" I yelled, and everyone at Santa Anita must have heard me. At least a thousand did, for that many gathered around my box and cheered like college football fans.

Barnsley, from my own stable, won the race. It was his first win, too, under my colors.

Tom Gwynne, a local sports reporter, covered the story this way:

"Despite the stiff counter-attraction of two disqualifications, Joe E. Brown stole the show yesterday at Santa Anita. His horse, Barnsley, performed an afternoon miracle by actually winning a race. There was a hushed silence as Barnsley galloped home on the chin strap in the seventh. Countless programs were thumbed quickly as No. 3 went up in the lights. Suddenly, the fact of his victory slowly dawned upon the half-dazed customers.

"Then the stand rocked with cheers!

"Joe E. Brown stood up in his box and took a bow. But the cheering mounted in volume. The racegoers were paying tribute to a game guy and they weren't doing it in any half-hearted fashion. In a moment, his box was surrounded by admirers, he wrung more hands and signed more programs than a Democratic Congressman in the deep south. Traffic in the aisle was blocked—the crowd was 200 deep. A dozen guards rushed to the scene to protect the women and children in the crush."

Well, consider the facts leading up to that race:

Here I was, an eager racing enthusiast, and a horse owner for three seasons at Santa Anita. I fed my horses well, gave them tender care and loving attention, but they ran like milk wagon steeds on a sit-down strike. A hard luck stable, they hadn't cracked the ice in three dreary winters.

234

Barnsley, my special pride and joy, drew such glowing tributes from the handicappers as "Might do with zebras." "Lion farm is bidding for him." "Would be 20 to 1 in funeral procession." And so on.

Insults, to be sure. But all that was changed, and the crowd that came to laugh remained to cheer. Barnsley, showing an effort which could only be described by such wild adjectives as stupendous, colossal, epic, gigantic, and terrific, ran a race that touched the heart of humanity and especially me. He paid 53 bucks for a two-buck ticket and I had 30 bucks riding on his nose, 35 to place and 30 to show.

Because the horse was a 25 to 1 shot, few of the fans had tickets on the winner. Nevertheless, they went right on cheering Joe E. Brown and his race horse. It was a remarkable demonstration. I was so tickled I cheered with them. Waving both arms wildly, I stopped long enough to pull a rabbit's foot from my coat pocket.

"That's what did it," I shouted. "I rubbed that on Barnsley's nose this morning. He couldn't miss!"

At a party the night before, I was talking with Tom Bragg, wealthy turf owner, and George Breen, New York businessman.

"By the way, Joe," said Breen. "I understand your Barnsley is running tomorrow. Well, here's a rabbit's foot for good luck. I won on Fairy Hill and Colonel Ed with it today and you can't miss tomorrow." Both horses had been long shots.

Funny thing about this particular race, though. I seldom gave my trainer instructions. I figured he knew more about horses than I did or I wouldn't have had him on the job. Once in awhile, however, I did offer a suggestion. On this particular morning I said, "Why not let the jockey run him hard on the way to the post? Maybe that'll help." My trainer said "O.K."

Well, Jockey Roberts followed instructions and I don't

know whether it really made any difference, but it might have been just what the horse needed because we had never run him hard going to the barrier.

It was only later, after the race, that I realized I had not tipped off anyone at the studio or at home that the horse was going to win. I was worried.

One of the judges presented me with a photo finish picture showing my horse crossing the finish line all alone.

I thanked him, but on second thought I knew when I took that one home and showed it to Mrs. Brown, she'd laugh. There was not another horse in the picture and nobody could tell by the picture whether my Barnsley finished first or last!

It may strain the imagination of the cynical, but I contend that I was in the racing game not for the publicity value, not to make money, but for fun.

Publicity? People who bet my horses didn't go to see me on the screen as a result. Why should they? My horses didn't get into the pictures. And people who went to see my pictures didn't care whether I owned a horse or a duck farm. I'm an actor. I never was a jockey.

And as to financial gain? Huh!

My second acquisition was a horse named Captain Argo. The day he raced at Narragansett, I was invited to be a guest in the judges' stand. I was new at the game, obviously, and the elder judge, Mr. Bryan, took it upon himself to explain the rules for claiming a horse. I kept mum as though I knew nothing. When the feature race came up I asked him which was the favorite. He said, "Why, Captain Argo should win this race but he's not too game." I had heard someone else say that earlier in the day and I asked, "What do you mean, not too game?"

"Well," he said, "when another horse begins to crowd him a little he doesn't put up a battle."

I never did believe horses were like that. I had the feeling at that time that the judge's criticism simply wasn't true. I felt the horse was being maligned. I was so sure of it I had already put in a claim for him and placed a bet on his nose. But I didn't tell the judge this.

The race was run and Captain Argo lost. Judge Bryan took me down to the lower part of the judges' stand to explain the further details about claiming. He was a little flabbergasted when he discovered I had a claim for the horse. I got Captain Argo for $5500, a pretty fair price for a horse in those days.

We took him out to the ranch I had acquired and turned him out to pasture for awhile. He looked like a different horse after two or three weeks of rest and we brought him back. I told the jockey I'd like to win but I didn't want him to beat the horse. He ran all right and the jockey never gave him more than a slight tap coming in to the last stretch. He won easily.

I fell in love with Captain Argo and I think he became fond of me. I spent hours in the stable talking to that horse and he would nudge me and whinny and carry on as though he understood every word.

We shipped him east again to Rhode Island's Narragansett Park. I was tied up on a busy picture schedule at the time and unable to leave the Coast, but on the day Captain Argo was scheduled to run (in the Weybossett Handicap) I got a direct telephone line in to the track and stood by. We had four phones in the house and three servants. I was alone except for the servants that day and I had specifically told them not to bet on my horse. But they all had and though I didn't know it at the time, each of them was on an extension when the race began.

There was a five-minute delay at the gate before the field of six broke from their stalls. F. A. Carreaud's Ajaccio showed on top briefly, then Captain Argo streaked down the track and quickly took the rail position. At the five-furlong pole, Captain Argo was leading, but George D. Widener's Sation, the favorite, was only a head off his keen pace. He was the favorite.

Against this fast footing, Ajaccio shuffled back to third and stayed there. From the half-mile pole home it was clearly a race between Captain Argo and Sation.

At the three-eighths pole, Sation seemed to move ahead by inches. He was just showing on top when they came to the head of the stretch. The voice on the other end of the wire sounded almost as excited as I was.

"Looks like there's only a pencil line between them as they come pounding around the turn," he said. "Now they straighten out and Captain Argo is in the lead, but by nothing more than a nose."

I am holding my breath and the sweat is popping on my forehead. "Here they come," yells the voice in my receiver. "Sation's moving up . . ." and suddenly the telephone connection is broken.

I hear gasps on the extension and I nearly pass out. About a minute and a half later the phone comes to life again and the first thing I hear is that a foul has been claimed. I yell, "By whom?" The track voice answers, "Sation's jockey." So I knew it was Captain Argo and a moment later the voice announced: "Foul disallowed. Winner Captain Argo!"

But Captain Argo also gave me my first bad shock. A few weeks after this fine race, he became sick and died shortly afterwards. I was so saddened by his loss I never left the house for a week.

Then there was the Argentine horse, Cascabelito, I purchased for $17,000. I got him to win the Santa Anita Handicap and I think he had some kind of a chance, but something went wrong with that horse too. He lost the $10,000 handicap, but a week later and against the same field, he won a $2500 race. (Three years later, when I finally got rid of my stable and quit the racing business, he was the last horse to go—for $500!)

238

About that time I got a filly whose sire was the famous Phar Lap of Australia. She caught a cold and never raced.

Later I sent my trainer to Kentucky and bought five youngsters I was sure had the makings of great race horses in them. Four were fillies, so I named them all after Mrs. Brown: Kath, Royal Kate, Kate Em Bee and Battling Kate. I didn't realize at the time what effect all this had on my wife, but years later we were having a little spat one day when she said: "And furthermore, I never did like your idea of naming that horse Battling Kate!"

When I claimed a horse named American Emblem from owner Bert Baroni for $3500, I was elated over the acquisition. The horse was a grandson of Man O'War and a son of American Flag. We entered him in a race or two at Bay Meadows, but he was a tired hoss and I decided to give the old boy a rest. I told my trainer, who then was Jim Headley, to turn him out to grass for a few weeks. And there, during the first week of his vacation, he was kicked in the knee (right forefoot) by a frisky pal of the corral.

Jim called me and told me about the accident and said he believed the horse's leg was broken. He had called in a vet and it was the opinion of both of them that the horse should be destroyed.

The horse was insured for what we had paid for him so I phoned my insurance broker and friend, Lew Rowan, and told him to send me a check because the horse would have to be destroyed.

"Well," he said, "we'll have to send our doctor up there to confirm it." I said, O.K., but do it quickly. I don't want the horse to suffer.

A few days later, Lew called and informed me that he could not pay me for the horse. I said, why, am I not insured? He said yes, but only if the horse can't stand. "This horse can stand."

I asked him who told him that and he said their vet. When

I asked him who the vet was I discovered it was the same doctor who had told Headley to destroy the horse. I was getting madder by the minute. "I'm sorry," he said, "but that's our report and I can't do any more about it."

I slammed the receiver down and sat for a moment stewing in my own anger. Presently I began to reason. If that horse can stand he can walk and if he can walk he can trot and if he can trot he can gallop and if he can gallop he can run. That's the way I figured it. So I called Jim Headley and told him. He said, "Well, I don't know, Mr. Brown, but I'll try it."

Jim got a leather boot and made a cast and put them on the horse and every time the horse wanted to get up he had to have a lot of help.

We kept the cast on him for about four weeks, after which we had the leg X-rayed and noted that it had set fairly well. Jim had an electric current apparatus of some sort which he used in connection with regular applications of liniment. It was slow and tedious work and if there was any improvement in the horse's condition, it was hardly noticeable from day to day. But after a few more weeks the useless leg was sufficiently mended to walk, and American Emblem took a few steps. Still he could put little weight on the foot.

"Just let him take things his own way," I said. "Don't hurry him."

American Emblem was a co-operative horse. I'm sure he understood what we were trying to do for him and he was just as anxious to do his bit as we were. His few steps grew to a daily walk around the corral and though he continued to limp terribly and favor the bad leg, Headley persisted.

A month later the horse was beginning to trot a little and as the weeks slipped by, he gradually increased that to a gallop. Finally one day I asked Headley, "What do you think, will he ever run?"

"Our chances are pretty good," he said. "I think he'll run.

240

He still limps after a work out but I'm going to put a light jockey on him next week and let him breeze through a furlong."

I asked him if the horse seemed to be in any pain and he said he didn't think so. "He eats well," he said, "and that's the first place we'd know if anything were very wrong with him."

Our enthusiasm increased in proportion to the horse's improvement, and I cautioned Headley to keep him under wraps and let no one know what we were doing. I had discussed the case with a few horsemen in the beginning when we began treating him, but they had just scoffed. They told me I was kicking the gong around or simply that I was crazy to think that I could ever race the critter.

But we fooled 'em. American Emblem came back at Santa Anita. On his first reappearance he ran eighth, but only because we had put the wrong jockey on him. Next time he ran second and was claimed by "Doc" O'Connell, much to my chagrin. I had come to care a lot for that horse despite Mrs. Brown's opinion that I was well rid of the animal.

But when Mrs. Brown was looking the other way, I reclaimed American Emblem next time out and after he had won. After that he won three more starts and earned a place in my pasture and my heart for life. American Emblem, son of American Flag, and grandson of Man O'War, proved he had the blood of champions in his veins and gave me my other great thrill in horse racing.

I never regretted the money my racing experience cost me. I never regretted any of the luxuries I had because I enjoyed them as few people could enjoy them. The memory of hard times and the days when I didn't have enough to eat was never very far from my mind. You have to have that contrast for pure enjoyment. Only the hungry man can enjoy a meal, only he who has been ill can fully enjoy good health. Anyone who spends the first 35 years of his life scrabbling for pennies and finds himself suddenly earning $300,000 a year could appreciate the difference.

I did, and I was never able to forget the first half of my life, nor those who helped. People today may question my interest in Pony League Baseball, for 13- and 14-year-olds. (60,000 members, Joe E. Brown, President) or in the many other organizations for boys of which I am a member. The time and effort I put in on these things seem little enough when I remember the gratitude I felt for similar attention when I was a boy. I remember, for instance, a certain overcoat.

John Mockett ran a clothing store in Toledo. Though it wasn't generally known, Mr. Mockett gave away ten or a dozen overcoats every winter to poor kids, mostly newsboys, because those were the ones he saw most. I doubt if John Mockett had what he would have called a philosophy about such things. I have discussed it with his son and his grandson in later years, and I think he just gave the overcoats because he felt like doing it, not after any philosophical musings on the matter. In other words, he had a philosophy all right but he never knew it. But it meant a lot to the boys. I know because one wintry day he called me in off the sidewalk and gave me one.

It was a beautiful little box coat that came half-way to my knees, and I'll never forget the feeling I had of warmth inside and out as I thanked him and strode proudly out of the store. I sold a lot of papers that day because I knew someone cared enough about my small world to give me an overcoat.

Thus the symbol for my salad days in Hollywood had to be the most expensive thing money could buy. For me it was a $16,800 Duesenberg automobile. It was Mrs. Brown's gift to me after a strenuous personal appearance tour and a year of hard work. It and the whole family met me at the station in Los Angeles when I returned from the tour. I never saw such a beautiful car. I was flabbergasted. I didn't know whether to be angry with her for buying it or pleased that she could think so highly (expensively) of me.

Every time I drove that car I thought how many hungry people could eat and for how long on that much money. But I drove it and I got to love it. And I got to be a pretty good speed merchant too. Given the room I could outrun any motorcycle in California and 105 miles an hour was an average speed when I was going farther than the studio.

But it wasn't its speed that got me into the most trouble. The fact that anyone (in 1932) could afford a Duesenberg was enough to start a riot wherever the car appeared. I resented that feeling because I felt I had earned every bolt and nut in the thing.

I was breezing down Highland Avenue early one morning when a big truck ahead of me decided to hog the whole street. No matter which way I dodged he kept me hemmed in. I gave him the horn and got a lot of abusive language in return and, finally, in desperation, I squeezed in between the truck and the curb and we both came to a sudden halt.

I asked him what he had said and he called me a dirty rich s.o.b. who was trying to show off. I invited him to come down out of his cab and repeat it. In a moment we were at it, and a lively brawl ensued. He was considerably bigger, but my lifetime of acrobatics easily compensated for my smallness.

Meanwhile, I was pouring out all the pent-up feeling I had about people who envied me my luxury. I knew more about hard times than anyone, I said. I came up the hardest road any man ever traveled and by golly anything I had now I had earned by blood, sweat, and tears and no truck driver was going to tell me I wasn't entitled to it. I told him that I knew what it was to be hungry and I had worked thirty years to get the money to buy things I had wanted for forty years.

He apologized and we shook hands and went our separate

ways, but in the years since then I have come to realize that you can't change the world by licking its individuals. There are too many of them. And it's too much wear and tear.

Comedy Is Serious Business

In the summer of 1936, when I stepped off the air-conditioned Santa Fe Chief at Chillicothe, Illinois, the nearest stop to Peoria, to face a welcoming committee of Peoria's most prominent citizens, a 40-piece band from Peoria's famed Caterpillar Tractor Company, and a blast of 110 degrees from the baked prairies, I began one of the most extraordinary public appearance tours ever dreamed up by a Hollywood press agent.

And no doubt the hottest. On the triumphal seventeen-mile motor jaunt into Peoria, through highways and small-town streets lined with cheering fans, two of the 50 motorcycle police forming an escort dropped off their bikes from the heat. The guest of honor couldn't get out of it that easy. He sat high on the back of an open car and waved and beamed all the merciless way.

But if you think that was heroism, you should have followed me that afternoon. After a luncheon given at the Père Marquette Hotel by the Great States Theatre chain to the local press and dignitaries and the visiting critics

245

from Chicago, I left the air-conditioned dining room to carry through my afternoon's program to the bitter end.

The Chicago critics, who had intended to carry through with me, abandoned me to my good deeds and remained in the iced restaurant throughout their stay, while I, the intrepid man from Hollywood, visited orphanages, hospitals, and went through the huge Caterpillar Tractor Company, which served as the background for the picture that started all the trouble.

It was the world premiere of *Earthworm Tractors*, made from the currently popular series of magazine stories by William Hazlett Upson, who used to be a Peoria tractor salesman himself, that brought me across the continent to be guest of honor at the Madison Theatre in Peoria, where the picture had its initial showing.

The thriving little city virtually suspended business to celebrate Joe E. Brown Day, and so the least I could do was to return the courtesy by being a guest to be proud of. It was the most strenuous tour I ever made, and it followed on the heels of the most exhausting picture.

I had played in motion pictures with horses, bears, lions and elephants and bicycles but never with anything as tiring to handle as those big tractors. They weren't hard to operate, once I got the hang of it, but no one on the lot ever trusted me with them, least of all Guy Kibbee, who played a lead role in the picture. In a number of scenes he was supposed to ride with me, but when I went a little wild with the tractor and started tearing down buildings and running over automobiles, he hollered for help.

He yelled so loud and swore so vehemently that I thought we'd have to take the scenes over, but when we saw the rushes, all you could hear was the sound of the motor. But Kibbee wasn't acting when he registered fright—he was scared stiff.

I never had so much fun with a new toy since I was a

246

kid. I broke up everything on the Warner lot. An old railroad station they'd been using for years—they never used again. And there was a large iron statue on the lot I never had liked. I pretended the tractor was out of control and I went right for it—though it wasn't in the script. It flattened like a penny on a railroad track and the cameraman kept cranking, so it was left in the picture.

In one of the scenes I was to back my tractor into an old car, back right over the top and crush it flat to the ground. Strangely, although the car was of 1920 vintage and the tractor a mere behemoth of twenty tons, the top of the car held and the tractor passed over it without doing much damage (and they talk about "hard tops" today!). The shot was spoiled and they had to get a weaker and older car.

But the hard work I did in that picture didn't end with the last turn of the camera. The public appearance tour that helped promote the film in the theatres was nearly as strenuous. Comedy, when you take it apart, is, basically, serious business. And it doesn't take much analysis to discover that a clown is not a comedian.

The difference between a clown and a comedian is this: The clown makes the audience laugh at him, while the comedian strives to make the audience laugh with him. It's fairly easy to be a clown. It's a complicated and difficult thing to be a comedian. And there is a vast difference between the two.

To be a comedian the actor must create a sympathetic bond between himself and his audience. He must remind the audience of some person (perhaps even themselves) that they have known. And to give the effect of being real, there must be some serious moments in every play for the comedian.

Some folks seem to have the idea that comedians must be always funny, but the same principle applies off stage too. The comedian that is always funny in real life is a clown,

247

not a comedian. Comedy is and has always been serious business with me, so I never attempted to be funny when the role—on stage or off—didn't call for it.

Old Ma Nature said a mouthful to me, as I've often been told, and I have cashed in on my physical imperfections, but my mouth also serves me as an audience barometer. If I find the going difficult at the outset of any performance, I wait for a chance to open wide, and if they fail to respond then, I know that it's going to be a cold, cruel evening.

This has always been an interesting thing to me, the reaction of various audiences to the same jokes. For instance an audience in the evening, made up of a great many men, will laugh louder but not as long as an afternoon gathering composed of women. The latter seem to take longer to get a joke and then when they do they chuckle over it until the next one. When a man has laughed, however, he is through until the next one.

But audiences, like Bret Harte's "Heathen Chinee," are peculiar. I never saw any two that were alike, although there were general patterns that fit all of them. Matinees, usually, were predominantly feminine. One of the hardest audiences was Monday night, and it was also the worst night for business. People were less relaxed on Monday; they were thinking of tomorrow and the week to come. Thursday nights used to be the cook's night out, and so the audience, at least in New York, was largely a family audience on that night.

Audiences improved toward the end of the week and Saturday night was always the best. People were louder then, more relaxed, the next day was a day of rest and they were in a mood to enjoy themselves.

Away from Broadway, one was likely to encounter almost anything. Shows that tried out in Boston, Philly, or Washington didn't do it expecting their reception in those places to be an exact gauge of what they would encounter on Broadway.

The Crowley All-Stars were a top Toledo semipro club in 1909. All managers have troubles, therefore my serious kisser (second row, r.) as I try to puzzle out my batting order.

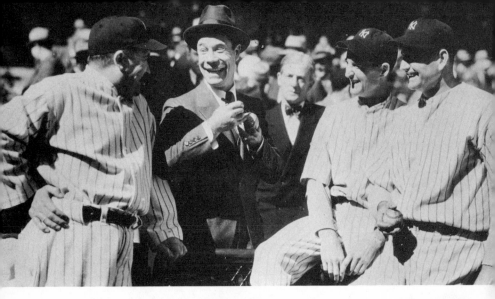

Joe McCarthy (l.) I always thought knew as much about show business as baseball. In 1931 the situation was reversed when the Yankee manager asked me to autograph baseballs for Herb Pennock and Wilcey Moore. *(Culver Service)*

The 1934 World Series was thrilling—but Schoolboy Rowe said it was painful, after he shook my hand before this group collected. Rowe lost his game, and the papers quoted him as saying my powerful paw injured his pitching hand. This was the handshake felt around the baseball world.

Dizzy Dean and I record baseball history—at least the way Schoolboy Rowe said it happened in the '34 Series. Could be, too—after all, didn't I once balance Man Mountain Dean on one hand?

Raising funds for our Olympic team is nothing new. Back in 1932 the lovable Buster Keaton and I managed teams consisting of major league players. Here we choose our squads which later played an exhibition for the benefit of the Olympic Fund. *(Culver Service)*

Here's one of the nicest guys and certainly an all-time baseball great. Tris Speaker and I were part owners of the Kansas City Club, then in the American Association.

In 1935 Don, Joe and I were Polo Ground visitors with National League president Ford Frick, my old sports writing friend.

I interviewed Detroit manager Fred Hutchinson when I was TV announcer (1953) for New York Yankee home games. I first saw Fred as a 17-year-old hurler, and even then thought he had all the necessary equipment.

My job as international president of the P-O-N-Y League brings me in contact with budding big leaguers. At China Lake, California, I explain the meaning of sportsmanship—but seconds later sent them on the field with a good loooong laugh.

It's '43 at New Farm Wharf in Brisbane, Australia aboard the U.S. *Fulton*. It was a heaven-sent audience, and the kids couldn't stop laughing. After all, they just had to look at that kisser.

I met an old friend in t
Philippines, Jacobo Zobel, w
fought in the undergrou
while the Japs ruled his stur
Luzon. Jake and his wife Jeb
were old friends of ours.

Heng Yang, China can never
replace the American Stage
but these appreciative Air
Force kids made me think I
was a pretty funny fellow.
(Culver Service)

Members of the 1st Marine Division stand in line for autographs. Kids will be kids—even on Guadalcanal. Hungry kids, hungry for laughs.

I'm honored when Frank Pace (l.), Secretary of Defense, and General Omar Bradley present me with this Certificate of Appreciation, in '45.

We were in Columbus, Ohio for the first convention of the Air Force Association, along with General Spaatz (l.) and Ohio Governor Frank Lausche. We get a laugh from a great soldier, General Dwight D. Eisenhower.

Of course, I was thrilled by the presence of Mrs. Sara Delano Roosevelt (sitting), mother of the late President, as I addressed the Boys Club of America.

I was proud and quite solemn on this occasion in 1945 when the University of Toledo awarded me with an Honorary Master of Arts Degree.

I had just finished a performance of *Courtin' Time* in 1950 when General Douglas MacArthur and his lovely wife were good enough to visit with Kathryn and me in my New York dressing room. Kathryn Frances is at the General's side.

President Eisenhower was host to stage and sports celebrities when I was caught looking the wrong way. Liberace (r.) is magnificent in his handmade silk suit. Ray Bolger and Howard Keel are on my left and Lena Horne is the beauty next to Liberace. *(Reni photos)*

My Room of Love, surrounded by the great trophies of the past—but always with a twinkling eye on the future.

Life has been wonderful for Kathryn and me. We have our health, humor and each other. And we look forward to years more of the same.

I never knew there were so many in the Brown family until Ralph Edwards surprised me when I was a subject on *This Is Your Life*.

No one could predict how Broadway would take it ur
opened on Broadway.

And road shows that might be highly successful in
town were sorry flops in others. There used to be a say
in show business that the worst weeks were Easter, the w
before Christmas, and Salt Lake.

Our Orpheum circuit vaudeville show, which was almo
intact for twenty weeks during the season 1923–24, was or
of the best shows that ever toured the country. The whol
bill was a comedy and it went like wildfire everywhere
everywhere, that is, except Salt Lake City. Throughout the
tour before we reached Salt Lake, the old timers kept saying
wait 'till we get to Salt Lake, there's a town that'll take the
wind out of our sails. But the youngsters in the troupe just
laughed. We were like a group of college kids. We had that
old spirit. "We'll knock their brains out!" "We'll take care
of Salt Lake, brother!" "We'll lay 'em in the aisles!"

Well, we went on in Salt Lake but it wasn't the audience
that laid. That show lay down and died in the first act and
it never got up. We couldn't see how such a thing was possible. But it was. They are good people in Salt Lake City.
They are right people, liberal, God-fearing, and honest. But
they didn't laugh. And I learned the big axiom of all comedians: *Nothing is funny if the audience doesn't laugh.*

The best comedy is that which the audience itself helps to
build. The experienced comedian is always on the lookout
for the hints and suggestions that come to him through audience reaction. Once in the *Greenwich Village Follies*, I
came on stage selling lollypops as part of a gag, as I think I
mentioned. I wore no funny makeup or costume except a
derby hat and my customary kisser. I had worked out a
funny way to yell "Lollypops" and it got pretty good laughs
—using the big-opening-small-voice technique. But there
was another laugh that came when I wasn't trying for one,
and it puzzled me. I started getting it in the middle of the

scene and it kept getting bigger and bigger and I whispered to one of the girls near me "What are they laughing at?" She shook her head. She didn't get it either.

When I came off stage I said to the stage manager "What-inhell are they laughing at?"

Standing off stage where he could see both the audience and me, he was a better judge of the situation than I. He pointed out to me how the audience was getting an off-color thought that wasn't in my mind at all. So I cut out the whole sequence, even though I was doing nothing intentional that would project a dirty thought.

Other times you sit around a table with the author and the director and you kick it around for awhile and come up with an idea, or you think of one while shaving some morning and you try it out on the audience. Often the audience's reaction will tip you off to certain nuances you never thought of before and you say to yourself, oh, so there's a laugh in that, so you give it a little boost and you polish it a little and you have a good laugh.

Thus comedy, apparently the most extemporaneous form of entertainment, is apt to be the most studied and most carefully worked out. And nowhere is this truer, I was to discover, than it is in motion pictures.

My first insight into the real importance of comedy came during the out-of-town tryouts of *Twinkle Twinkle*, a year or so before I got into pictures. We had played Detroit, Pittsburgh, Baltimore, Washington and were in Brooklyn playing our last week before opening on Broadway. I was doing a simple dance step in the last act one night when I felt the muscle of my leg explode. My doctor put a cast on the leg and I went back to the theatre. I was able to hobble around a bit and even danced a little.

When my doctor heard about that he said "Joe, you're insane," and he threatened to put me in bed.

Without arguing the point too much, I was able to con-

250

vince him that without me there wouldn't be a show. Ona Munson was the feminine star of that show and neither of us had an understudy. And, anyway, the trite philosophy of the trouper, "The show must go on," was law and gospel to me in those days and I felt the responsibility for the entire cast lay on my shoulders. I always felt I was letting everyone down the few times when I couldn't go on.

The doctor looked at me and shook his head, and then he smiled. "Well," he said, "I give up, Joe." Then he told me something that may or may not be strictly accurate scientifically or medically, but it sounded like common sense.

"I don't blame you for wanting to make people laugh," he said. "Do you know what physical good you are doing when you cause your audiences to guffaw and roar with pleasure?"

I said I hadn't thought much about it in that way.

"I value laughter a great deal," he continued. "I firmly believe that laughter means a lot to the health of a man. Ten good laughs a day will add a day to a man's life. I don't mean just giggles or titters; I mean the good hearty guffaw, the belly laugh that exercises all the stomach and abdomen muscles."

I was highly flattered to think that I was in a business that could be awfully good for people. On my way back to the theatre I got to thinking about the show and how many really good laughs there were in it.

I was reminded of the doctor's theory a few years later when some reviewer remarked that one of my movies had at least 40 good laughs in it. Considering the millions who saw that picture, you can imagine how I felt about the job I was doing.

When I first began to be funny in a serious way, I used to take quite a little pride in my ability to handle impromptu comedy. That was possible and in fact it was encouraged on the burlesque stage. Later, too, in musical comedy, I might suddenly decide to change my entire gag routine during a performance. I would ad lib the whole routine and it was fun. I really enjoyed myself.

When I got into pictures, however, I found out right away that screen comedy is something else again. It is practically impossible to ad lib in a picture. Everything about the making of a picture is arranged with the precision of a battle campaign. Cues mean a great deal not only to the other actors, but to the army of technicians off stage. A cue, either in gesture or word, that has come too late because of an ad libbing actor can spoil a day's work. Retakes are expensive and an ad libber who won't conform can do more harm than he is worth. Even if he ad libs a gag and it goes over, it is seldom worth the wear and tear on studio nerves.

The only exceptions to this rule were the infrequent accidental tricks that the cameramen caught and were thought so good the script was rewritten to include them.

When we were making the picture *You Said a Mouthful*, it was at first thought I wouldn't be able to make all the ludicrous underwater scenes in this feature and a double, Stubby Krueger, the noted Olympic swimmer, was hired to impersonate me in the long undersea shots.

Krueger worked for two weeks in the cold waters of the Pacific off Catalina Island. Then, it was decided to take a few closeups of me in a tank at the studio. These were so successful that they were continued for eight days, with me spending six hours daily in the huge tank. At one time I remained under water for one minute and eight seconds— the longest I ever kept my mouth closed in a picture.

In the final assembling of the picture, only one brief shot of Krueger was used. My tank scenes had turned out so well that every one was used. And accidental situations again made the best shots.

During the making of *You Said a Mouthful*, a half dozen trout were placed in the tank with me to stir up the water and add to the realism of the undersea scene. In one sequence where I am supposed to be swimming the channel from Catalina to Los Angeles, what appeared to be a good sized whale swam past me and harassed me no end.

This was really one of the trout. The fish just happened to swim past and it came so close to the lens of the camera that it was magnified into the size of a whale. The scene caused a loud howl everywhere the movie was shown.

There was a scene in *Broadminded* in which I was hiding under a bed. A fly lit on my nose and my facial contortions in a big close-up brought on an avalanche of guffaws. I imagine the screen fans thought the fly was supposed to light there—that it was part of the plot. It wasn't. It was simply an accidental happening I took advantage of and turned into an hilarious comic scene.

But whether deliberate or accidental, it's the final results, laughter, that count.

Did you ever make a telephone call from one of those streamlined drug-store phone booths—the kind which are almost form-fitting? I got into one once that was so suffocatingly small that I could barely close the door. And I had to close the door before the light would go on. Then I found I couldn't get the phone book far enough from my eyes to read it. In order to get more distance I pushed the door open—while still holding the book open in both hands— and the light went out. I tried to carry the book outside the booth to look at it but it was chained to the telephone.

Now, what would the average man have said when he found himself in such a situation? Naturally, and for a moment I started to say it too. Then I thought, Boy! This is good enough to put in a show! I'll save it. And I did. It was one of the best gags in *Earthworm Tractors*.

After I began to get a foothold in pictures, old friends used to say to me: "Joe, you have the best racket in the world. You like to be funny and here you are, getting a swell salary for having a good time."

Huh! If Mrs. Brown were writing this book she'd tell you how I used to burn the midnight oil studying my lines and working on my routines, and then how I'd mope disconsolately because I wasn't satisfied with the rushes or daily showings of the previous day's work on a picture. Or my kids might tell you that the reason they were such good students in school was because of the example they had in their old man. They could tell anyone who asked that their Dad planned a campaign of comedy with as much care as any general plans an attack.

But at least my family had one relief. They knew that if Dad was serious about being funny, he could be just as funny in his attitude toward something serious.

But perhaps the greatest single advantage which motion pictures offer the actor is something one might call freshness.

In the legitimate theatre there are three definite stages in an actor's performance. First is that period when he is reciting lines, whose meaning he really doesn't know; next that period when he reads lines he understands; and finally that period when he becomes so smooth that he is mechanical and superficial.

An actor, general speaking of course, mentally photographs his role. If you stop him during the first period of his interpretation he can visualize each page of his part, and he has to keep looking, with his mind's eye, to see the line he will read next. The result is a halting performance with a split second's pause between each line.

Later, as he becomes familiar with the lines and scenes, he is unable to tell you, on order, the next line in a speech. If he stops to think of it, he usually forgets it. Then he is able to lose himself in the role, to make responses that come as second nature, and thus have spontaneity and speed. It is in this period that he gives his best performances.

254

Finally, as time goes on and the role begins to drape itself around him in the manner of an old overcoat, he begins to give bad performances. His work is superficial. He has said and done the same things so often that he can only get out of the slump by taking the part anew and starting to study it line for line all over again.

Therein lies the greatest advantage the screen has over the stage. One never gets so familiar with a role, learning it by short scenes, that one becomes stale. You study a scene one afternoon or evening and you play it the next morning. Naturally, there are times when the playing might be improved by additional effort, but taken by and large, it is less likely to result in laxity.

Getting back to the premise with which I started this chapter, the biggest disadvantage of working in pictures is the lack of audience reaction. That is the reason why I always enjoy an occasional sortie into the legitimate stage. Only those who are in the business have any idea what a stimulus the stage is. Once I had attained stardom in the movies I could have made (and did) a lot more in point of dollars by personal appearances in the movie houses. But there were several occasions when I turned down personal appearance offers to accept a role in some play I liked. My engagements in *Elmer the Great* in 1931 and *Square Crooks* in 1932, squeezed in between picture shooting schedules, were examples. These engagments were not nearly as profitable financially as a personal appearance tie-up with one of my movies would have been, but the boost to my morale exceeded anything I did in Hollywood.

My own criticism of my work in pictures got me into a lot more hot water than anything the professional critics ever said. After a few years of strenuous work in Hollywood, Mrs. Brown and I decided to take that long postponed honeymoon in 1934. We booked passage for a tour of the

255

Orient and for four months tried to put pictures and shooting schedules and press agents and the whole Hollywood merry-go-round out of our minds.

On our return we were met by a large group of newspaper people. Finally, after all the usual questions and typical American tourist answers, one of them said: "Joe, I'd like to get something different, a different angle. Wasn't there any other reason for your trip that you haven't mentioned?"

After a little more such persuasion and a little thought I said, "Yes, there was. I made a picture five months ago called *A Very Honorable Guy*. It was from a story by Damon Runyon. It was no fault of Runyon's, but that was a bad picture and I know it. I went on this trip actually to be out of the country when they released it."

"That's a Warners' release, isn't it Joe?"

"Warner Brothers made it, but it wasn't released, it escaped!" I said.

"Wait a minute," said one of the reporters, pulling a newspaper from his pocket. "Did you say *A Very Honorable Guy?*" He opened the paper to the drama page and showed me a big advertisement and press release. *A Very Honorable Guy* was opening at Warners' Hollywood that very day.

Well, they all printed that story and my remarks and Jack Warner wouldn't speak to me for six months.

Give What You Have

No comedian ever got big enough reaction to suit him, but any that ventured into the combat zones during the late war was overpaid for his trouble. The South Pacific theatre of operations, especially, was a green hell for the thousands of American G.I.'s, but it was seventh heaven for any comedian who would risk his neck in it.

I appeared at hundreds of places in this area where no professional entertainer had been before. Comedy-starved audiences in these places became hysterical at the smallest quip about Brooklyn and practically died at any joke about the "M.P." They had been storing up laughs for months and released them in explosions that would turn any comedian's head. My baseball pantomime went over like laughing gas on laughing hyenas. Probably no other comedian had ever had such a glorious experience. It was as if practically a third of the globe was inhabited by my own paid claque. I combed the coral reefs to harvest laughs. I dug through jungles and climbed trees and waded through infested water to find an audience, and it didn't matter that frequently it consisted of only one or two. On the island of Canton, I climbed a palm tree to catch my smallest audience. The entire "house" was one soldier from Houston, who had missed my regular performance because he was on lookout duty. At a hospital in the New Hebrides, Johnny Marvin, the Hillbilly King, and I put on a complete show, with encores, for two sick soldiers in a small tent.

Even sciatica, which had troubled me for years, was not enough to stop a comedian who was surrounded by such delirious senses of humor. Lying flat on my back on a stretcher for three weeks, I continued on the trail of this hair-trigger hilariousness. The reception I got on Christmas Island exhilarated me to such an extent that, forgetting my sciatica, I did an eccentric dance and cured myself. I put on acts in jungle grass so tall that my audiences had to hang from branches of trees to see me, and I made night appearances by electric torchlights when stronger lighting effects were forbidden because of the nearness of the enemy. Leaving the Pacific, I did India, China, the Near East, Africa, Italy, and other theatres. Altogether, I traveled over 200,000 miles. I received the Bronze Star and commendations from President Roosevelt and from many generals. And if it is difficult to understand why anyone would give so much time and energy just to get a laugh, let me explain.

I never went to college and I only got one foot in the door of a high school, but when my two boys were attending U.C.L.A. I was on campus almost as much as they were. (Actually I became a Bruin five years before, when Mike enrolled in 1930.) Don and Joe L. were varsity athletes; Don later was elected student-body president and eventually R.O.T.C. commander. From the day my sons enrolled I practically overran the campus, making myself jester and spark plug of student projects, giving fight talks and monologues to the team and rooting section. And although I am an uneducated man, in the academic sense, I was invited to join my sons' fraternity, Zeta Psi. The only catch was that the

258

fraternity accepted no honorary members. I had to be an accredited undergraduate.

Waiving my lack of a high school diploma, U.C.L.A. let me pay tuition fees as a "special student" and I enrolled. That fixed up my qualifications for the fraternity all right, but I wanted to go the whole hog. I enrolled for a course in physics under Professor Joe Kaplan.

At the first class, I opened my big mouth and challenged the professor's statements. I asserted, with some truth, that Albert Einstein frequently telephoned me for advice (I didn't say what kind). Proceedings became so uproarious that the professor bargained privately with me afterward. "Stay away from my class and I'll give you an A," he told me. "But if you ever show your face in here again, I'll flunk you."

I even staged the annual football banquet at my own home, inviting the 58 varsity and frosh players plus 98 other guests. Of course, I stood guard at the front door just to make sure there were no Stanford or other "foreign" scouts in the crowd.

I was the first non-player ever voted a letter-man's sweater by the U.C.L.A. football squad. A U.C.L.A. yearbook (1949) was dedicated to me, "for what he inspired us to do." The baseball field at the University was named for me. I was living in the atmosphere I had wanted so badly when I was a kid.

It was about this time that I made a switch in agents. Mike Levee became my agent after Ivan Kahn and I parted, and Mike advised me to strike out on my own with the independent producers. He got me a contract with David Loew for six pictures at $100,000 a picture. But it was bad advice and a disastrous move. None of the independent pictures were up to the standards set at Warners. In addition to which some extraordinary things began to happen to me personally that changed the whole course of my life.

I was making a movie at Universal, which called for me to

twirl the giant wrestler, Man Mountain Dean, over my head. The prop department had installed an arrangement of invisible wires to help me do the trick, but Man Mountain insisted I could do it without the wires.

"You're a strong fellow, Joe," he said. "You can do it. I'll help you."

"Are you kidding?" I asked. "What do you weigh?"

"Only 327 pounds."

"We'll do it with wires," I said.

But he kept insisting, and there were about 400 extras standing around looking on, so when the time came for me to lift him I didn't stop and wait for the cut and the hook up with the wires. I just lifted and he gave a little push and I had him up there. And once I got him up in the air I found I could twirl him around without much trouble.

It was so good the director, Eddie Sedgwick, yelled, "Fine, Joe, now let's shoot it once more from this angle."

Well, with all those extras looking on, the ham in me came out and at the director's urging, I did it five times. On the fifth try, however, I felt something tear inside me. The pain was like two red-hot drills grinding into my groin.

The sawbones patched up my double hernia and I was about ready to go back to work. Then one morning I was driving along Sunset Boulevard where it passes through the U.C.L.A. campus, proudly surveying Joe E. Brown field. There's a bad curve right there and a steep 30-foot embankment on the outside. I braked for the curve, but there weren't any brakes. The station wagon somersaulted down the hillside. It landed in a mass of splinters, twisted metal, and me. I was barely conscious and almost totally paralyzed. Blood was flowing from a wound somewhere on my face.

My first sensation was not of pain, but the fear that the car might catch on fire. I managed to open the door with my elbow and fall clear of the car. I lay in a heap, repeating over and over to myself, "I don't want to die, I don't want to die."

It was early in the morning and few cars were on the street, but Jane Withers' mother lived nearby and she heard the crash. She called the police and came to my rescue. The police arrived and took me not to the hospital, but the West Los Angeles Police Station where they waited for an ambulance.

Although I was in pretty bad shape, I remember the various stages my mind passed through. At the police station my thoughts changed from the negative "I don't want to die," to the more positive, "I'm not going to die," and I kept saying it over and over, "I'm not going to die, I'm not going to die."

By the time they got me to the hospital and put me on the operating table, I was repeating, "I want to live, I want to live."

My own personal physician checked me. I had a severe septum (which had caused all the bleeding) and my back was broken in two places. And, though they didn't discover it until later, one lung had collapsed.

Had the doctor examined me more completely, I doubt if he would have dared to administer ether. For as I learned later, one of the worst things you can do to a patient with a collapsed lung is to give him ether. It is apt to bring on pneumonia or lead to fatal complications.

The doctor began stitching up my face. While the operation went on, Kathryn watched through a glass door that separated the operating room from the corridor. She was a trained nurse before we were married and she understood all that was going on in that room. She beheld what some people would call a miracle.

Suddenly the interne whispered, "Doctor, no pulse."

The doctor looked at him. "What?" he said.

He repeated, "No pulse."

Kathryn saw the doctor feel my pulse, shake his head, then take off his gloves and start to walk away.

The interne said, "Oxygen, doctor?"

"What?" asked the doctor, pausing. "Oh, yes, O.K." He came back and gave me a shot of oxygen.

Afterwards they said I was dead for 40 seconds. The doctor was ready to reach for a spade, but I held the best cards in the deck.

What brought me back from the brink of death? Some will say it was the shot of oxygen; some will attribute it to the positive thought, the will to live, which I held in my mind as I went under the anesthetic. I'm sure that both of these things helped—I believe that positive thoughts can influence life and death—but I attribute my return to life to the fact that my number hadn't come up. I am a fatalist and I believe that most of what happens to us is preordained.

When one plays a game, one plays to win, and surely that is true of life, the supreme game. One hates to lose anything, and the same feeling to a greater degree is attached to the thought of losing oneself. However, much of the fear of death departs if one acquires a helpful philosophy. Though I don't want to die, I have no fear of death. If I knew I were going to die tomorrow, it would make no difference in the way I live today. I've looked right at death and have found that it didn't cause any great change in my attitude. A man should do the best he can, regardless of when death may knock at the door.

Once before I had been pronounced dead and this was not the first time my back was broken.

The first time I "died," I was making my second movie, *Hit of the Show*. On the set was a successful doctor who had recently retired from practice and was playing a small part in the picture. I played a stage actor, who always carried a small ivory elephant with him for luck.

One day I had some particularly strenuous scenes to play. It was a hot afternoon and perspiration was pouring from my brow. I went through a very long and difficult close-up, becoming more and more tired as the day wore on. The scenes in which I had to appear were almost unbelievably tense. So was I.

Finally we came to the death scene. I was to lie down on a couch in a theatrical dressing room and repeat the words of the character I was playing—"This is the place to die, doing the thing I love." Toward the end of the scene, I was to let my right hand drop down and the elephant fall from it.

The scene ended. I was told later that Ralph Ince, the director, came over and said, "Swell, Joe. This shot is fine. I won't have to take another."

I was lying back with my eyes closed, in the "death" position. I didn't move.

"He's exhausted," Ince said. "Turn off the lights and let him rest."

Some fifteen minutes later, Ralph came over to me and said, "O.K., Joe. You can get up now. We're going to change the set." I didn't stir. He nudged me. Still I didn't move.

In panic, he turned to the retired doctor on the set. "What's the matter with him?" he asked.

The doctor felt my pulse, then turned to Ralph Ince with a set and grave face. "He's dead," he said. "He has no pulse."

There was a man from one of the wire services present who rushed out and sent the news to his syndicate. The late afternoon and evening papers carried the story, "Joe E. Brown Dies on Movie Set."

Fifteen minutes later, I came to. As soon as I got up and learned what had happened, I sent telegrams to all my nearest and dearest, so that they wouldn't be upset by the newspaper reports of my supposed death.

These events happened so long ago that I have little recollection of my thoughts as I went into the sleep that was almost like death. I only know that from my youth I have had no fear of death. I will go when my number is called, not before.

The first time I broke my back was during my early trampoline and burlesque days. We were playing at the Academy Theatre in Pittsburgh. I either miscalculated the position of the trampoline or someone had jostled it out of position, for I came down flat on my back on one of the steel braces that supported it. The curtain was rung down but I was back again the next day.

My back hurt, but I paid little attention to it. I went on doing my work twice a day, doing the same somersaults. Later, when I played baseball, it annoyed me a lot. I noticed that if I played several innings and got warmed up, then sat on the beach for awhile, I suffered a painful stiffness all over. That stiffness and pain lasted through a number of years. I decided I must have lumbago and I remembered wondering just how long it took one to outgrow lumbago.

Twelve years after I took that fall, I went to a hospital for a check-up and an X-ray showed that I had broken my spine in two separate places.

The old scars of those two places still showed clearly on the X-rays they took after the automobile accident.

But the strange part about this second break is one for the book. They measured me in the hospital after I got out of bed and discovered that I had grown a half inch.

It sounds silly, but it seems I have a strange spine. The vertebrae were "frozen" close together and it seems they shouldn't be. There should be a little gap between them. Well, this second break seems to have sprung them apart, which gave me the extra height. Old Doc Cooper and a quart of his Sagwa couldn't have done more to improve my figure.

But something else in me grew a little to. Lying in a cast for several months I had a chance to take stock of my career.

Hollywood, in its usual routine, leaves little opportunity to stop and think.

I had been in a few bad pictures. Martha Raye and I had played in *Thousand Dollars a Touchdown* and it was terrible. My box office appeal had fallen off and I wondered if I was slipping. I thought that when I got well I'd better go back to the stage and learn how the public felt about it.

An actor loves to see people when he is playing, to obtain their reaction, to hear their applause. Applause is his greatest stimulus. It is the barometer of his ability. I was offered the part of Aubrey Piper in the George Kelly farce *The Show-Off*. This, I thought, is the great test. If I can still get a laugh, it's not me that's slipping. I could blame any recent movie failure on the directors, the producers, the stories, or all of them together. At least I'd prove whether or not Joe E. Brown on his own had the same old appeal.

The Show-Off played to sell-out houses wherever it appeared and I got back more morale than I lost.

Meanwhile, however, something bigger and more horrible than anyone ever dreamed could happen was happening to the world. Men were forgetting laughter in a holocaust that threatened to envelop us all. My two boys graduated from the University and went into the air corps. Mrs. Brown became involved in Red Cross work and other wartime activities. And the Brown household took on the same tense atmosphere that gripped millions of homes in 1940–41.

Everybody seemed to be getting into the act but me. I did an occasional personal appearance at army camps, but that didn't satisfy me. We didn't need entertainment so much then; it was training and discipline all of us needed at that time. I felt useless. I felt, in fact, fifty.

"I've got to do something," I kept mumbling to myself. "But what in heck can you do, you big jerk?" I'd scold myself. The only thing I ever could do was make people laugh. And I could take little credit for that talent. Nature met me more than halfway when it threw a handful of features together and called it a face.

"I gotta help win this war," I kept on muttering to myself, and every time I said it the answer came back to me from my own mind. "What could *you* do? Laughter never helped win any wars, you know."

Then one day at the studio I got a letter from Artie Reichle. Artie was one of "my boys" from U.C.L.A., Class of 1938. He was in the Army and his letter was postmarked Anchorage, Alaska. It said, "Please, for Pete's sake, come up here and talk to the men the way you used to talk to us kids at U.C.L.A." Of course the request floated on a lot of soft soap but this line seemed to jump out in bold type. And another word, kind of new then, stood out too: morale. But I had an idea what it meant. It meant helping people to do their own jobs better.

Artie went on talking about Anchorage. Dull place, he said. Fellows were a little low. Would I come?

Would I? But where was Anchorage? I dug through the studio library and found a map of Alaska and, finally, Anchorage.

Well, I had my job. I knew it. In the next ten minutes I'd put in three long distance calls. "Get me Washington. Get me my wife. Get me Anchorage, Alaska." (The only call that came through was the one to my wife, and she said no. "Joe," she said, "you're crazy. Alaska in February, at your age! Come home and let me put compresses on your head!")

The next few days I was a nuisance to everybody. I got myself all tangled up in red tape with the Government. Things take time, everybody said; just go at this in an orderly way, pal. But I didn't have time to be orderly. I couldn't do any slow motion on this; the brisk overture was coming from the pit, and the curtain was already up on the swiftest drama in history. Artie said the kids needed me, so what were we waiting for?

266

I couldn't telephone to Anchorage, but we burned up a few cables. Artie and his kids wired they'd gladly pay my expenses out of some "tobacco fund" they had. That nearly threw me. Kids up there in the ice and snow, offering to pay my expenses just to see me! Thanks fellows, but I'll buy my own tickets, of course.

Unsponsored, unauthorized, unassisted, I got to Alaska. This was before the U.S.O. troupes; no Army regulations covered visits of entertainers to military posts. My request for permission to go bogged down in red tape and I left it there. I simply flew north without permission and spent three winter months in Alaska and the Aleutians entertaining Army units illegally. The kids in uniform loved it.

"For crying out loud! He came up here . . . *and he didn't even have to,*" they said, over and over.

The whole trip from start to finish was one long grin. I never in my life saw men who needed fun as badly as those boys did. After I came home I got an official report which said that my visit had caused an 85 percent increase in outgoing mail. The lads had something "to write home about" and they certainly wrote. Years later I continued to get letters from mothers of those boys who wanted to thank me for that bit of entertaining. "God bless you for what you did for my boy," they said over and over.

General Simon Bolivar Buckner, Jr. (killed in the Pacific in 1945) was the commanding officer at Anchorage when I was there. There was a tough, rugged, old-school military man if there ever was one! When he talked to me about his men it made my blood tingle with fighting ambition. He gave those kids a report card any parent would have been proud of. General Buckner assigned Lieutenant Natzel to by my official aide, supporter, and abettor. The Air Force, not to be outdone, put a lad by the name of Marston, with the rank of major, at my disposal. I'd have had to be twins to avail myself of all the kindness and care those two energetic guys wanted to give me. Sometimes I felt like an old lady being helped across a street by two boy scouts going in opposite directions. My biggest problem was trying to get a realistic taste of the hardships I knew they were enduring. But somehow they never let me do that. They had some crazy notion that they ought to be "grateful" to me—*they grateful to me!* So they always tried to give me the best they had.

At the end of my first show in Anchorage I knew I had found my job. Drained and limp, I said to myself, "Brother, this is your job. From now on." Government and red tape hardly entered my mind.

I had intended to play only Anchorage. But I had barely reached there when youngsters began saying to me:

"Say, Joe E., we're not so badly off here at Anchorage. The kids that really need some fun are up at Kodiak in the Aleutians. Now *there's* a hole inside of a hole. Too bad you can't run up there and give those fellas a break!"

"Why *can't* I go?" I said.

And later, when I did go to Kodiak, the chaps there said, "It's been swell having you. But the boys who would *really* appreciate you are at Long Island. They've never had anything. They sure need something like you, Joe."

When I got to that outpost the lads there said, and I could hear it coming, "Joe E., long as you're this far, wouldn't it be swell if you could go out to Dutch Harbor?"

That's the way it was all along: the kids themselves kept pushing me on! Kids that probably never before in their lives had been guilty of much unselfishness were thinking about fellows they didn't even know who were a little worse off than they were themselves.

On the way from Kodiak to Dutch Harbor our plane was lost for several hours. Looked as if we'd never make it. Weather had been sour day after day, and we kept putting off the trip, but the boys were expecting us and we wanted terribly to go. You can see how important the officers felt

268

entertainment was for the men, when they let us set out at a time when flight men stationed at various spots were betting three to one we'd never make it. Three weeks later, in Sitka, I was told that during the hours we were lost odds went up to 30 to one.

Wherever I could find an audience, whether military or civilian (thousands of American construction men were in the area building defense posts) or Eskimo, I literally knocked myself groggy to make it laugh. The Eskimo populace of Gambell, on remote St. Lawrence Island, still celebrates the anniversary of my visit as a holiday and telegraphs thanks to me annually.

It was a wonderful, exciting, and stimulating trip. I stayed just twice as long as I intended to when I set out. And I came back with a sober determination. As soon as I could I would start out again to other battle fronts where our kids needed giggles and guffaws.

I had found my war work.

Kathryn helped me see it. She tells a little French fable about a poor juggler who knelt before the Virgin Mother's shrine and prayed that he might have something he could give, for he had no money. He thought perhaps some money would fall from heaven into his outstretched hand, so he could give that. But no money fell. Then into his heart came the voice of the Virgin.

"Rise, my son, and give what you have," she said. So he rose from his trembling knees and drew the three little balls from his pocket and juggled those as beautifully as he could. Then he heard laughter—the loveliest laughter ever heard on earth. The Babe Himself was laughing with joy.

There was also a job I felt could be done at home. I talked to everyone everywhere that anyone would listen about sending recreation material and entertainment to our boys on the fighting fronts. Meanwhile I sold bonds and gave broadcasts; I made a movie and appeared in a play. But

269

under everything I was doing, I was hammering on official doors to get extended permission to make another trip to entertain troops. No entertainer had yet gone to our Pacific front, and the officials weren't sure it was "practical" to send me. But I kept at it.

Early in September I went to Detroit to appear again in *The Show-Off* at the Shubert Theatre. Don, who was by then a captain, and ten of his fellow pilot officers were on a delivery trip and brought their planes around in a detour in order to help us put over a bond drive in Detroit. We had a fine time.

Just before they left, when Don and I were having our last talk—our last, although of course we didn't know it then! —he said, "Dad, if you can keep a secret . . ."

"I've kept a lot of them, son."

"I believe I'm going to be sent to Australia in a very little while."

"I'm glad, Bud," I said.

"We're out to get Japs," Don said, and then he reached out and patted me on the shoulder. "Gosh, Dad . . . you know what I wish? I wish we were going to take you with us."

I was so pleased that I had to brush the whole thing off the way people do when feeling touches them suddenly. "Zat so? Fine thing. Can't go out fightin' unless you've got your old man with you." Then I saw that Don knew how proud I was, so there wasn't much use pretending about it and trying to make it into a gag. I said seriously, "Tell you what, Bud. Maybe I'll meet you out there. Maybe I'll run into you out there, you doing your job and me doing mine."

Later when I was out there alone—well, as much alone as anybody can be with hundreds of thousands of American kids in the Pacific—I sometimes thought of that thing we had said to each other. Sometimes when I'd be clowning on some messhall stage I'd see a lad down in the audience who looked like my son, and I'd remember. I did meet him out

270

there hundreds of times—not his body, of course, but the spirit of my son and the cheerfulness and straightness.

But that's ahead of this part of the story. I went on with the show in Detroit, and on this evening of the eighth of October I was hoping perhaps he'd telephone me and say exactly when he was leaving. Sometimes when I'm playing I like to go out in the box office just for fun—just to see the amazed look of people who come up to the window. Their mouths fall open and then they recover and try to look dignified, as if they didn't recognize me.

"Hiya, folks!" I say. "Just picking up a little pin money on the side." The crowd always gets a kick out of it, and I do too. So this night there I was and the telephone rang.

"This is the Army Ferry Command in Long Beach, California," a voice said, and I said "Sure. Let's have the call. I'm expecting it."

"We want to reach Joe E. Brown to tell him that his son has just been killed in a routine flight . . . Will you get the message to him?"

"Yes," I said. "I'll get it to him. Thank you very much."

I don't know much about the next 40 hours. They were only a blur of disbelief, as sudden loss always is. There had been some mistake; there must be. Why, Don was so full of life. He was the boy other youngsters depended on. He had such plans. And over all this I heard people coming in and out of my dressing room, the telephone ringing, people trying to get Kathryn in Los Angeles, strangers crying, my producer, Henry Duffy, explaining to the audience out front, Doug whispering in my ear, "Joe E., don't you want to take off that zoot suit?" My face in the mirror, hardly recognizable without its grin. The crazy costume I was wearing seemed like my whole life itself—just a fool's garb to make other people laugh. Then finally the airport, cold and windy, and strangers' faces weeping when they recognized me, and the airways officials shaking their heads—no seats on any plane.

271

Then there was something solid that my eyes rested on. Something that had no connection with all this nightmare. It was the shoulder patch of which we were so proud in my house, the emblem of Don's own company, the gold circle and the white Grecian ship.

"Those boys—those fliers. Who are they?" I said to someone. And there, sure enough, were ten of Don's fellow officers returning on a plane to Long Beach. They hadn't heard until I told them, and we all stood there weeping together, those boys and I, not caring that a curious crowd stood around us, gaping.

"We're taking charge from here on," they said. "You're not flying with anybody else, sir. We all want to be together, don't we?"

It was in that moment that I felt that first stirring in me of the truth that many bereaved men and women came to know in those days. *When you have lost your own boy all other lads become your sons.*

I felt it that night, but I was too stunned to accept it then; acceptance came much later, and then it came through action.

The next few days were a dark abyss. I seemed to be falling through endless chaos; I couldn't get hold of myself. And then one night when I was alone, I felt something I never had known before. It was the presence of God. It was a peace that passes understanding. I felt God's arms around me, in a way I cannot possibly describe.

From then on, I knew that everything was going to go on; that I would do my work, my crazy juggling act before the shrine. I knew that as long as there is breath in this body I shall go on clowning and strutting and screaming my loudest, if that's what makes people laugh.

No Hot Water

My work is laughter. Ever since my early days with Prevost I have wanted to make people laugh when they looked at me —beggars and big businessmen, the unknown and the notorious, babies and grown-ups, the sick and the well. And above all, I wanted to make those laugh who needed laughter most.

I had said to my son that we'd meet out there in the Pacific. Well, I would keep my rendezvous, not with my son, but with hundreds of thousands of Dons, other people's Dons, who needed laughter more than anyone on earth, for they were engaged in the world's biggest job.

The Government red tape finally got itself tied into a pretty little bow on a package that contained the words ". . . official permission to proceed . . ." and I was on my way. From then on I covered the Pacific like a Fuller Brush man ringing doorbells. I had Johnny Marvin and his hillbilly gee-tar to make music and Lieutenant Ed Virgin assigned to me by the Army to make arrangements for the shows.

Hawaii was already having some entertainment; after all, it was practically at our back door, only 2100 miles from San

273

Francisco. So we did only twenty shows or so around there and then struck out for the rest of the Pacific, where no entertainers had yet gone.

We covered the whole Pacific front, clear up to the spots where bullets were flying. We didn't miss an island, for they were all important. Specks that used to be just pepper spilled on the map had become Main Street to hundreds of thousands of American kids. Islands with the width of our continent between them were next-door neighbors in this weird new neighborhood. You met and passed people you knew and ran into them again 3000 miles away, and the whole thing seemed utterly impossible, except that it was really happening. And I soon came to realize that the space I was taking up in a plane or in somebody's tent was worth a whale of a lot. I knew I'd have to be funnier than I had ever been in my life if I was going to be worth my weight in war effort.

It's difficult to weigh a laugh and find out just what it's worth. To a boy lying under a shade tree beside his favorite fishin' spot on a lazy morning, one laugh more or less doesn't count up to anything. They come easy there.

But you put that same boy in the broiling mud of a Pacific island, with mosquitoes and flies and hardship in eternal monotony, and you multiply that by hundreds of thousands, and you've got a war job for a comedian. A laugh there was as important as quinine; a laugh was a kind of quinine when morale had bogged down.

Medical men in the Army and Navy explained the therapeutic value of laughter to me and I was reminded of my early days on Broadway. I hadn't gone far along the Pacific route before I had all my old psychological and physiological theories of comedy confirmed beyond any question of doubt. Out on the fringe of the fight, a show wasn't just something to while away the time. It was a therapeutic treatment, and utterly necessary. Naturally the youngsters never thought

274

of it that way. But you may be sure that General MacArthur and Admiral Halsey and the officers on their staffs did. They were all very serious about the subject of nonsense.

Our kids were living under constant tension, day after day, night after night. It was a grilling and galling combination; extreme danger and extreme monotony. The boys' nervous systems became like clenched fists, tight and jumpy.

One Army doctor said to me, "Only thing that can relax a body as taut as these bodies is a tub of hot water—or a good belly laugh. And we can't get the hot water."

There was no danger of getting a big head in a situation like that. Your ego had little to feed on when it was a case of hot water or you—and they couldn't get the hot water.

Show time was any time at the front. Often we would begin our first show early in the morning. Once when I was taking a 9:00 A.M. plane in the New Hebrides Islands I jeeped sixteen miles out into the jungle and did a show for Carlson's Raiders and got back before the plane left.

The smallest audience I had, the one I mentioned, was one youngster on lookout duty who had had to miss all the shows. I shinnied up the tree to a platform where he was sitting. He said he was from Houston, Texas, and I asked him "How come you got this assignment in a tree?"

"Well, I'll tell you," he said with a grin and a nice soft drawl. "Fact is, I didn't have me no shoes. So I couldn't work any other way."

That was on the island of Canton, which was pretty short of supplies just then: no bread or butter, and not an extra pair of shoes to be had. But in spite of all the difficulties and the temporary shortages, the boys everywhere were doing a fine job.

One of the difficulties was rain. It was hard to do anything in the kind of rain they had on those tropical islands. It was almost impossible to do a show. But the boys didn't see any reason why sheets of rain couldn't be used as a backdrop for our act, and I got so I could accept it myself. It just meant screaming a little louder to get above the roar of the rain.

Once in New Guinea, when I got to a certain place where we had scheduled a show, I found it had been raining for hours. The mud was almost knee deep, and I couldn't imagine how I could stand on some rickety, wobbly platform, much less try to do my act. I asked the Special Services officer to announce that the show would be postponed until the next day.

Then I heard a terrible outcry. "What's that?" I asked the colonel who was putting me up in his tent.

"That's your audience," he said. "Listen!"

I listened. "We want him now. We want Joe E., we want Joe E.," they were chanting. Their voices came in waves that went up and down my spine.

"Where are those kids?"

"They're waiting in the rain," the colonel said. "They've been there for two hours—twenty-five hundred of 'em, Mr. Brown."

I don't need to add any "P.S., they got their show." And not one kid left throughout the whole hour that I sloshed around on that "stage," trying to keep on my feet and deliver the goods they had ordered.

Another time I remember kids waiting in the rain was in Iran, on a later trip to that war area, only there it was as cold as it had been hot in the South Pacific. And in Iran there was ice on the stage instead of mud.

Many times in the Pacific I stumbled along in utter darkness to reach a makeshift platform of boxes where my guide would say "This is the stage, sir." I'd look around and say "But where is the audience?"

"They're all around you, sir." And sure enough they were, crouching there in the darkness waiting for the show. We were so close to the Japs we couldn't risk much light; just

276

enough for the boys to make out that I was a reasonably accurate facsimile of Joe E. Brown.

Sometimes the mental atmosphere surrounding the shows was so charged with emotion you could cut it with a knife. I remember, for instance, a show I did one night in Italy.

The boys had been out on a bombing mission, and they knew that when they came back we were going to have some fun. You wouldn't think fun would be much good just after a bombing mission.

But I'll never forget that field in the chill dusk, while I waited for my audience to come back from a brush with death itself. "What comedy can you offer men at such a moment?" I kept thinking. "No comedy—prayer," I said earnestly to myself. But I knew most of the kids would have taken care of the prayers; you realized that about our boys after you had been in danger with them a little while. No, the prayers were their business; the comedy was mine.

I stood with the C.O. at the head of the field, and in a little while the planes came in zoom-zoom out of the cold emptiness of the sky. They were B-17s, and they all looked alike, but the C.O. identified them as they returned to the base by the way they peeled off.

"One missing," he said shortly.

At last all that were coming in were in, and the boys were out of the planes and running down to the mess hall where we were going to have the show. There was coffee and doughnuts and noise and tight sentences. They were too excited to do anything much; it was the time they needed laughter the most.

Once I was on the stage of that mess hall, I knew from their faces, young and dirty and strained, it wouldn't be hard to do a show for them. I could see how much they needed to laugh. I wasn't Joe E. Brown standing up there. I watched from somewhere outside, and I saw myself giving a show with an extra portion of talent loaned to me for that moment, as if God Himself knew how great was the need of these kids and was supplying it.

And the stuff those kids laughed at! I'm afraid most of the things the kids in the front lines laughed at would be considered pretty dull stuff by you. You can turn on your radio and yawn your way through a half hour of humor any time you want to, but out there it was different. Brother, it was terribly different.

You would have to listen to those jokes against a backdrop of G.I. hardship and boredom: days of monotony, each one a carbon copy of the one before; same old food in tin plates, canned corn, canned peaches, and Spam, all on the same plate. Everywhere about you there was the woolly, thoroughly male smell of G.I. clothes, a smell you'll never forget to your dying day. And there was the same old fat to chew, the same old wrangling; the kid with the gripe, the kid who was an optimistic nuisance; the letters from home that didn't come; the worry about the girl friend forgetting you. And there was the mud when it rained, or the dust when it didn't. All this over and over, day after day.

You've got to take all that into account when you try to understand why 4000 kids would sit in the rain for an hour or two just waiting for the show to begin. It wasn't that I'm such a whale of a comedian. I wasn't ever fooled about that, even when they applauded so you could have heard them a mile away, when they yelled my name until the very stars in the sky must have heard it, when a hospital in Melbourne, Australia, had kids hanging from every window and crowded from every balcony shouting "So long, Joe," and "Thanks for everything, fella." I didn't fool myself that that was *me*. I knew what it was all right.

It was American kidhood, the noisiest, cheerfullest, make-the-best-of-it race on earth. Humor to Americans is daily bread. They've got to have it if they're going to stay normal. If they haven't got it, they make it up—not very good hu-

I mumbled. "I thought so too. Well, just shows you how wrong a guy can be." I've never been troubled by sciatica since.

I used to tell my sons that opportunity begins inside a man. When you become qualified enough inside yourself for any job, that job knocks on your door.

Taking my own advice, I never missed an opportunity to qualify for the one thing I wanted so terribly: the chance to go on some kind of mission, to get in a few licks on my own. It wasn't easy, the way they were all watching out for me and doing everything they could to protect me, but I managed to get in a lot of flying practice and even learned to handle some of the regulation small arms. Before it was over I had all I wanted of it. Contrary to military regulations and the laws of war, I managed to participate in a tank attack, an infantry engagement, and eleven bombing raids. I personally was credited with killing at least two Jap soldiers in a tank battle and later took one prisoner—all this as a civilian.

Frequently, when I arrived at a military base, I was welcomed with considerable pomp by high officers. The pomp soon disintegrated, I saw to that. When introduced to a general, my usual remark was, "At ease, general." Of course that tickled the enlisted men more than it did the generals, but high brass, being American too, had a sense of humor equal to any G.I.'s. I'm sure they all knew that underneath all my joshing was sincere admiration for the big job they were doing. And they understood why I wanted so terribly to get in a few licks on my own.

On Luzon I talked Major General Robert S. Beightler into letting me ride in a medium tank while it led the 37th Division's attack on Bamboeng. The soldier next to me in the tank was shot through the head. It was Beightler who later publicly credited me with killing two Japs during the fight.

It was General MacArthur who gave the orders permitting

mor always, but the best they can do. But I guess kids all over the world would be the same—given the same opportunities.

But, occasionally, under such circumstances, humor may run down hill. Like water, it seeks its lowest level. If somebody isn't around to pass out new material, jokes deteriorate. Like everything else that's used too much, jokes get dirty. And when the jokes get dirty, everything else gets dirty.

That's why I took my job so seriously. Because, with everything else I believe, I have faith that people honestly prefer things clean. And everywhere I went in all those miles I proved over and over that kids want good humor, and clean humor.

Once (and I like to tell this story), at Dobodura, a little tip of land in New Guinea, I was doing a show for fourteen or fifteen hundred kids gathered down at one end of the airfield where the crews could be handy to their planes if trouble started dropping from the sky.

It had been a long show, for those kids were simply starved for some fun. Every time I got ready to stop, they'd scream and applaud and make me go on. I'd just about reached the end, but they kept shouting.

"Listen, you guys," I said, "that's all I know."

"Give us more, Joe," they roared.

We argued like this awhile, and then there was a little slit of silence in the noise, as sometimes happens, and way back on the edge of the crowd a youngster shouted: "Hey, Joe, tell us some dirty stories."

You could have heard a pin drop, and not a big pin either. The kids looked at me, every one of 'em. I could feel 'em wondering what I was going to do. I stood there a minute, not quite knowing myself how to turn it off. And then I just forgot I was a comedian. I said to them, just the way I'd have said it to my own sons:

"Listen, you kids. I've been on the stage since I was ten

years old. I've told all kinds of jokes to all kinds of people. I've been in little flea-bitten vaudeville theatres and in big first-class houses. I've been in movies, I've made 65 pictures in my life—and there's one thing I've been proud about. In all that time I've never had to stoop to a dirty story to get a laugh."

They were quiet and they looked a little guilty, the way kids do when somebody speaks out loud about something like this.

"I know some dirty stories," I went on. "I've heard plenty of 'em in my time. I could tell them to you fellows if I wanted to. But I made a rule a long time ago that I'd never tell a story that I wouldn't want my mother to hear me telling."

Then the applause came. Not just a trickle of it but the biggest, noisiest gale of hand clapping I've ever heard anywhere. It went on and on. Seemed to me it went on for five minutes. And back on the edge of the crowd, the youngster who had asked for the dirty story was applauding with the rest of them. He was clapping his hands off.

And it didn't end there. Cardinal (then Archbishop) Spellman said that within two weeks after that happened in New Guinea he heard about it in North Africa, halfway around the world. There's something inspiring and heartening about that to me; shows that good news travels as fast as bad news and people are just as eager to pass along something good as the other plentiful stuff.

Then the letters began coming to me from parents. You'd never guess how many people back home sat down and wrote to tell me what their boy had said about that afternoon. Most of them thought nobody else would ever get around to telling me, and they wanted me to know.

I've got a big carton full of those letters, and I wouldn't take anything for them. They made the whole trip worth doing from my point of view. There were letters from all kinds of people. Ten chaplains wrote to me; there were sim-

280

ple letters carefully spelled out on ruled tablet paper by people who didn't often take pen in hand; there were typewritten letters from prominent men whose sons had been in that crowd; some people sent me the boys' own letters. And more than one said: "I'm going to pray for you every night for the rest of my life for what you've done for my boy."

They said things like that to a little guy with a big mouth who once thought a laugh was pay enough for knocking himself out.

The rains and the travel schedule I maintained took their toll. I lost a lot of weight and the sciatica I had been bothered with in recent years began acting up again. It became so bad finally that I had to be carried on a stretcher. But I always attempted to stride onto the stage without a hint of distress, after getting off the stretcher in some secluded spot where my audience couldn't see me. If I limped too badly to conceal it, I pretended this was a comedy routine. When any of them saw me in an ambulance, I gagged this up too, putting on an elaborate act of a lazy civilian traveling in supine comfort.

Meanwhile I prayed constantly. Friends and fans who heard of my handicap prayed too, and wrote to tell me so. I still have many of those letters and they still make good reading, for the prayers were answered.

One night on Christmas Island, in the midst of my show, I remembered a wild dance from vaudeville days. I spontaneously broke into it, and carried it through without a thought of sciatica. When I came offstage my stretcher bearers were aghast. "You danced!" they cried.

"Sure, I always used to," I said, mopping my face. "Didn't I ever tell you I could dance?"

"Well, yeah, but we thought you were practically a cripple now."

Suddenly I froze in my tracks. "By golly! That's right!"

281

me to go along on air raids. I spent 50 minutes alone with MacArthur in Brisbane. The chat began on a humorous note, but before long we were talking about our sons, and we weren't ashamed of tears, either of us. The general understood why I wanted to go on a bombing raid. He picked up a phone and issued the necessary instructions before I left his office.

"Take care of yourself, general," I said as I departed.

"The bullet hasn't been made nor the disease found that will kill me before I lead my men back into Manila," the general answered.

Our next meeting was in Manila early in May, 1945.

"Well, well, Joe," he said. "It is grand to see you." And for over an hour we just sat and talked. He told me of his entrance into Manila and Corregidor. I didn't know whether I should remind him of a promise he had made to take me into Manila with him when he returned victorious, but he remembered anyway. He had not forgotten, he said, but things moved much faster than he expected. After taking Corregidor he found an opening in the middle of the Jap defenses and decided to move in at once. I was amazed that he, with the thousand and one things he had to think about, would remember a half-joking promise he'd made to me months before.

In a ceremony at City Hall the next day he pinned the Asiatic Pacific service ribbon on my shirt "for your meritorious service and in appreciation of what your efforts have meant to my troops." He added that it was the first time he had made this presentation. Perhaps you can understand that it was a little difficult for me to see or say anything for several moments.

I helped shoot guns and drop bombs during air raids in China, Burma, New Guinea, and Italy, without any known results. Except once, when we flew low enough for me to throw hand grenades at Jap snipers roosting in the tops of

283

palm trees. At Palom Pom, near Leyte, I saw one tree and all its inhabitants disappear the way a kid's baloon bursts and disappears when you touch it with a match.

My feat in taking a prisoner gave me material for many animated monologues. It happened while I was entertaining soldiers around a campfire on Jolo in the Sulu Sea. Gradually I became aware of a ragged little figure tottering just outside the firelight, grinning hopefully. It was a starving Jap sniper who had come to give himself up. I jumped off the stage and yelled "Stand back, everybody," and I ran over and put my arm around the Jap's shoulders. "This guy's too ferocious for anyone but me," I said as I led him off to the guardhouse.

Later I built it up. "We fought hand-to-hand for an hour before I subdued him," I related, with strenuous pantomime. "My life was in danger each instant, yet somehow I never felt frightened."

Wonderful, generous Jacobo "Jake" Zobel and his señora, Doña Jellie, whom Kathryn and I met first in Manila on our trip to Asia in 1934, were among the many friends I found when I returned to the Philippines. They were all doing their bit to repair the destruction left by the Japs. Jake was lending a hand with the guerrillas and "Hellie" was helping to restore the capital.

I hopped all over the Philippines, by Jeep, Cub, and C-47 on my second trip to the Far Pacific in 1945, and in little places like San Marcelino, Subic Bay, Lingayen, Luna, Bam Bang, Batangas, Zamboanga, and on the islands of Jolo, Saipan, Iwo Jima, Guam, Kwajalein, Okinawa it was like old home week. A lot of the kids and officers I met on this trip were the same ones I had entertained two years before in New Caledonia, New Guinea (where official maps now show a hill named in my honor), Guadalcanal, Fiji, and points farther south.

When I had a short-snorter bill long enough to wrap

284

mor always, but the best they can do. But I guess kids all over the world would be the same—given the same opportunities.

But, occasionally, under such circumstances, humor may run down hill. Like water, it seeks its lowest level. If somebody isn't around to pass out new material, jokes deteriorate. Like everything else that's used too much, jokes get dirty. And when the jokes get dirty, everything else gets dirty.

That's why I took my job so seriously. Because, with everything else I believe, I have faith that people honestly prefer things clean. And everywhere I went in all those miles I proved over and over that kids want good humor, and clean humor.

Once (and I like to tell this story), at Dobodura, a little tip of land in New Guinea, I was doing a show for fourteen or fifteen hundred kids gathered down at one end of the airfield where the crews could be handy to their planes if trouble started dropping from the sky.

It had been a long show, for those kids were simply starved for some fun. Every time I got ready to stop, they'd scream and applaud and make me go on. I'd just about reached the end, but they kept shouting.

"Listen, you guys," I said, "that's all I know."

"Give us more, Joe," they roared.

We argued like this awhile, and then there was a little slit of silence in the noise, as sometimes happens, and way back on the edge of the crowd a youngster shouted: "Hey, Joe, tell us some dirty stories."

You could have heard a pin drop, and not a big pin either. The kids looked at me, every one of 'em. I could feel 'em wondering what I was going to do. I stood there a minute, not quite knowing myself how to turn it off. And then I just forgot I was a comedian. I said to them, just the way I'd have said it to my own sons:

"Listen, you kids. I've been on the stage since I was ten

279

years old. I've told all kinds of jokes to all kinds of people. I've been in little flea-bitten vaudeville theatres and in big first-class houses. I've been in movies, I've made 65 pictures in my life—and there's one thing I've been proud about. In all that time I've never had to stoop to a dirty story to get a laugh."

They were quiet and they looked a little guilty, the way kids do when somebody speaks out loud about something like this.

"I know some dirty stories," I went on. "I've heard plenty of 'em in my time. I could tell them to you fellows if I wanted to. But I made a rule a long time ago that I'd never tell a story that I wouldn't want my mother to hear me telling."

Then the applause came. Not just a trickle of it but the biggest, noisiest gale of hand clapping I've ever heard anywhere. It went on and on. Seemed to me it went on for five minutes. And back on the edge of the crowd, the youngster who had asked for the dirty story was applauding with the rest of them. He was clapping his hands off.

And it didn't end there. Cardinal (then Archbishop) Spellman said that within two weeks after that happened in New Guinea he heard about it in North Africa, halfway around the world. There's something inspiring and heartening about that to me; shows that good news travels as fast as bad news and people are just as eager to pass along something good as the other plentiful stuff.

Then the letters began coming to me from parents. You'd never guess how many people back home sat down and wrote to tell me what their boy had said about that afternoon. Most of them thought nobody else would ever get around to telling me, and they wanted me to know.

I've got a big carton full of those letters, and I wouldn't take anything for them. They made the whole trip worth doing from my point of view. There were letters from all kinds of people. Ten chaplains wrote to me; there were sim-

ple letters carefully spelled out on ruled tablet paper by
people who didn't often take pen in hand; there were typewritten letters from prominent men whose sons had been
in that crowd; some people sent me the boys' own letters.
And more than one said: "I'm going to pray for you every
night for the rest of my life for what you've done for my
boy."

They said things like that to a little guy with a big mouth
who once thought a laugh was pay enough for knocking himself out.

The rains and the travel schedule I maintained took their
toll. I lost a lot of weight and the sciatica I had been bothered with in recent years began acting up again. It became
so bad finally that I had to be carried on a stretcher. But I
always attempted to stride onto the stage without a hint
of distress, after getting off the stretcher in some secluded
spot where my audience couldn't see me. If I limped too
badly to conceal it, I pretended this was a comedy routine.
When any of them saw me in an ambulance, I gagged this
up too, putting on an elaborate act of a lazy civilian traveling
in supine comfort.

Meanwhile I prayed constantly. Friends and fans who
heard of my handicap prayed too, and wrote to tell me so.
I still have many of those letters and they still make good
reading, for the prayers were answered.

One night on Christmas Island, in the midst of my show,
I remembered a wild dance from vaudeville days. I spontaneously broke into it, and carried it through without a
thought of sciatica. When I came offstage my stretcher bearers were aghast. "You danced!" they cried.

"Sure, I always used to," I said, mopping my face. "Didn't
I ever tell you I could dance?"

"Well, yeah, but we thought you were practically a cripple now."

Suddenly I froze in my tracks. "By golly! That's right!"

I mumbled. "I thought so too. Well, just shows you how wrong a guy can be." I've never been troubled by sciatica since.

I used to tell my sons that opportunity begins inside a man. When you become qualified enough inside yourself for any job, that job knocks on your door.

Taking my own advice, I never missed an opportunity to qualify for the one thing I wanted so terribly: the chance to go on some kind of mission, to get in a few licks on my own. It wasn't easy, the way they were all watching out for me and doing everything they could to protect me, but I managed to get in a lot of flying practice and even learned to handle some of the regulation small arms. Before it was over I had all I wanted of it. Contrary to military regulations and the laws of war, I managed to participate in a tank attack, an infantry engagement, and eleven bombing raids. I personally was credited with killing at least two Jap soldiers in a tank battle and later took one prisoner—all this as a civilian.

Frequently, when I arrived at a military base, I was welcomed with considerable pomp by high officers. The pomp soon disintegrated, I saw to that. When introduced to a general, my usual remark was, "At ease, general." Of course that tickled the enlisted men more than it did the generals, but high brass, being American too, had a sense of humor equal to any G.I.'s. I'm sure they all knew that underneath all my joshing was sincere admiration for the big job they were doing. And they understood why I wanted so terribly to get in a few licks on my own.

On Luzon I talked Major General Robert S. Beightler into letting me ride in a medium tank while it led the 37th Division's attack on Bamboeng. The soldier next to me in the tank was shot through the head. It was Beightler who later publicly credited me with killing two Japs during the fight.

It was General MacArthur who gave the orders permitting

me to go along on air raids. I spent 50 minutes alone with MacArthur in Brisbane. The chat began on a humorous note, but before long we were talking about our sons, and we weren't ashamed of tears, either of us. The general understood why I wanted to go on a bombing raid. He picked up a phone and issued the necessary instructions before I left his office.

"Take care of yourself, general," I said as I departed.

"The bullet hasn't been made nor the disease found that will kill me before I lead my men back into Manila," the general answered.

Our next meeting was in Manila early in May, 1945.

"Well, well, Joe," he said. "It is grand to see you." And for over an hour we just sat and talked. He told me of his entrance into Manila and Corregidor. I didn't know whether I should remind him of a promise he had made to take me into Manila with him when he returned victorious, but he remembered anyway. He had not forgotten, he said, but things moved much faster than he expected. After taking Corregidor he found an opening in the middle of the Jap defenses and decided to move in at once. I was amazed that he, with the thousand and one things he had to think about, would remember a half-joking promise he'd made to me months before.

In a ceremony at City Hall the next day he pinned the Asiatic Pacific service ribbon on my shirt "for your meritorious service and in appreciation of what your efforts have meant to my troops." He added that it was the first time he had made this presentation. Perhaps you can understand that it was a little difficult for me to see or say anything for several moments.

I helped shoot guns and drop bombs during air raids in China, Burma, New Guinea, and Italy, without any known results. Except once, when we flew low enough for me to throw hand grenades at Jap snipers roosting in the tops of

283

palm trees. At Palom Pom, near Leyte, I saw one tree and all its inhabitants disappear the way a kid's baloon bursts and disappears when you touch it with a match.

My feat in taking a prisoner gave me material for many animated monologues. It happened while I was entertaining soldiers around a campfire on Jolo in the Sulu Sea. Gradually I became aware of a ragged little figure tottering just outside the firelight, grinning hopefully. It was a starving Jap sniper who had come to give himself up. I jumped off the stage and yelled "Stand back, everybody," and I ran over and put my arm around the Jap's shoulders. "This guy's too ferocious for anyone but me," I said as I led him off to the guardhouse.

Later I built it up. "We fought hand-to-hand for an hour before I subdued him," I related, with strenuous pantomime. "My life was in danger each instant, yet somehow I never felt frightened."

Wonderful, generous Jacobo "Jake" Zobel and his señora, Doña Jellie, whom Kathryn and I met first in Manila on our trip to Asia in 1934, were among the many friends I found when I returned to the Philippines. They were all doing their bit to repair the destruction left by the Japs. Jake was lending a hand with the guerrillas and "Hellie" was helping to restore the capital.

I hopped all over the Philippines, by Jeep, Cub, and C-47 on my second trip to the Far Pacific in 1945, and in little places like San Marcelino, Subic Bay, Lingayen, Luna, Bam Bang, Batangas, Zamboanga, and on the islands of Jolo, Saipan, Iwo Jima, Guam, Kwajalein, Okinawa it was like old home week. A lot of the kids and officers I met on this trip were the same ones I had entertained two years before in New Caledonia, New Guinea (where official maps now show a hill named in my honor), Guadalcanal, Fiji, and points farther south.

When I had a short-snorter bill long enough to wrap

around the Pentagon building, I was persuaded it was time to come home. Military hospitals in this country were beginning to fill up and there was plenty of work for me to do here. Today, with most of us back in civilian life, I never visit a town that I don't run into someone I met "out there," in Wagga-Wagga, Dutch Harbor, or some little place in Italy or Iran or India. I shared hundreds of exciting adventures with these fellows. Is it any wonder that I enjoy hopping about the country the way I do?

I did 742 shows overseas during the war, and each one was just as important to me as the first night of any show I did on Broadway.

Perhaps that's why I get so much out of life—I take it seriously and I play it hard. I accepted the responsibility of bringing laughter to those boys of ours and I wanted always to furnish the funniest and cleanest shows possible. But there were times when my own morale was so low I felt I simply could not go on. Unfortunately, I am one of those whose face reflects every inner emotion. After half a century of acting, I still cannot make my face say one thing when my heart says something else. I've got to believe what I say and say what I believe, act what I feel and feel what I act. It's just like the old circus clown, One-Eye Murph, told me. "If you want people to believe what you're doing, always believe it yourself."

Only Murph never told me what to do when my morale was low. The cure for that was something I had to learn for myself.

There was the morning, for instance, when I was slated to do a show for Carlson's Second Raider Battalion. The day before had been particularly trying and the night that followed was a sleepless one. As I rolled off my cot at dawn I was dreading that early morning show. How could anyone in my physical and mental condition be funny? I crawled into a Jeep with a youngster from Oklahoma to drive the eight miles to camp. Although it was a beautiful day, I seemed unable to shake my depression.

Driving along the jungle road I spied a little church on a hill not far away. I asked the boy to stop and I got out and went into the tiny House of God. It was a crude little place, with benches for about 40 people. I went to the altar and got down on my knees.

There are modern intellectuals who say that religion is only a crutch, that man must originate his own strength and not try to shift the burden off onto God. Perhaps so, but I am humble enough to admit that I could use a crutch now and then.

Call it what you like, but after I talked to God for ten minutes, I came out of that little church feeling as though a weight had been lifted from my shoulders. When I came down the hill and got into the Jeep I was actually gay, and never have I done a more inspired show than that one for Colonel Carlson and his Raider Battalion.

To this day I do not know the denomination of that church, for I am not a religious man in the sense that most people speak of religion. I believe in God because everything around us proclaims Him. I respect His Universal Laws which are wondrous indeed. I live the Golden Rule to my fullest capabilities. As the years have passed, I have worked out a philosophy for myself that convinces me God is universal and that I may incorporate into my daily life and thoughts as much of Him as I wish.

I believe we should carry our love of God out of the church and into our daily lives. If we do we will be looking for good in the other person—and finding it. We will be looking up at God's heavens and the beauties He fashioned for us to enjoy. We won't be so conscious of the shape of a man's nose or the color of his skin. We will be a living sermon.

After the war and while I was playing in *Harvey*, I had a letter from a boy that serves to illustrate how our actions

286

can be an influence for good or bad, without our knowledge. This is the letter:

Dear Mr. Brown:

This is a fan letter, written without motive, with hardly a reason, and sent in a form which I hope will resemble a sort of "written applause."

I have seen you twice, met you once, and watched you take a shower. (According to theory, that sentence should be an interest-catcher. Is it?)

The first time I saw you was in Luzon, about four miles behind the town of Bayombong, which was then under seige. I was a machine-gunner with the Thirty-seventh Infantry Division. You were a guest. That evening, I watched you play a role which contained as much drama as any you have ever played on the stage or in pictures. Since many things have happened to you since then, it is possible that you have forgotten it. I'd like to refresh you, if I may.

Thirty-six bedraggled, wounded, near-dead Japanese had been captured and were being interrogated in our Language Section. You came into the tent for another look at the people who were making such an awful stench upon the world. As soon as you entered, I was conscious of seeing the bright light of recognition twinkling in their numb eyes. They knew you almost as well as we did. After the first shock of seeing you in the flesh was over, one of them, a graduate of an American college, asked why you had to fight. I remember it was with great difficulty that you made him understand what you were doing. Finally, he grasped it, and one did not need to know Japanese to understand the story he told his friends. With wonderment and awe ogling out of their sunken faces, they learned that Joe E. Brown had come all the way to the front to make soldiers laugh!

That threw a new light on it for me, too. It made me realize that you and the other entertainers who came to us had no commercial motives, but actually *came for no other reason than to make us feel better. But that isn't the point of the story. The climax of it came when you were about to leave. You shook hands with the M.P.s, and with the interrogators and with us, then turned to leave the tent. But as you did, from the center of this beaten, motley group of trained savages there was extended the skinny arm of a Jap who had become a kid again. He had forgotten all the nonsense he had been taught, he must even have forgotten that he was a prisoner. All he knew at the moment was that Elmer the Great and Alibi Ike and the Biggest Mouth in the World were in the tent, and he wanted to shake hands with them. That thin hand was in the dead center of the tent—everyone saw it and wondered what you would do. It was an enemy's hand, a hand that may have killed a lot of us. But then too, it was a human hand, and though it reeked with the stench of being unwashed for weeks, it sang of friendship, forgiveness, and a lot of other fine things that soldiers had got sour on. It was a pretty rough moment. The silence swelled so that it seemed to billow the tent. Some of us leered at the soldier, others looked at you wonderingly. And you paused.*

That pause may have been your trained sense of timing, but I don't think so. I think you paused so that this Jap and all the others would know the simple symbolism of what you were about to do. You leaned over into the group and shook the prisoner's hand. You shook it, I am sure, as warmly as you had just shaken mine, and I wanted to shake with you again, that some of the act would be on me. You smiled too but that was incidental. The climax for all of us had been when flesh turned into understanding and solidified our attitude toward the men we had been sent to kill. For the first time then, I felt sorry for our enemy. Perhaps I shouldn't have. Perhaps the United States War Department would have been furious that one of its soldiers was propitious toward the foe. But I think it was a healthy sympathy. Anyway, when the surrender came, I wasn't so anxious to have Japan systematically dynamited as I had been. Instead, I sort of hoped we'd try to teach them a little bit about standing on soap boxes and calling umpires bums and perhaps even sending irate telegrams to their new Nippongo Senators.

This year has justified that hope I think. But I also think that you had a pretty good idea of it when you shook the dirty hand of the guy who forgot his hate and made us forget ours. Such handshakes accomplished more than my machine gun.

Well, that was the first time I saw you. The second time was last night when I watched you and your handsome white friend parade from bar to bar. Harvey was up here this morning, so I showed him this letter and asked him if he thought you'd like it. He encouraged me to send it right away, so I shall. But what I want to say is this: When you and Harvey came out after the play last night, and sat and talked with us, it reminded me of the guy who was taking a shower from an oil drum in the Pacific and hollering a holler that we had known since the days when we cashed in milk bottles to get the dime for the show.

And you know what I think? I think that the night you shook hands with the Japanese prisoner, Harvey must have encouraged you to do so. He's so persuasive, isn't he?

Yours truly,

(Signed)   Paul Benzaquin
1108 North Dearborn, Chicago, Illinois.

That letter served to strength my resolve that my life will be as near a living sermon as I can make it. And if that sounds strange coming from a comedian, let me add: I have said that laughter is good medicine. It is a recognized therapy, a real specific for disease. Experts state that the first test of sanity is whether the patient has humor and can laugh at himself.

So laughter is healing.

And laughter is holy.

I could not be interested in any man's religion if his knowledge of God did not bring more joy, did not brighten his life, and did not make him want to carry this light into every dark corner of the world. I have no understanding of a long-faced Christian. If God is anything, He must be joy.

Around the World in 80 Days

Few thrills in a man's life surpass a triumphant return to his home town. To be welcomed back by old friends and be admired for success, however small, is a thrill that comes once in a lifetime to some men. It was a thrill I had not once but many times. And though the size of the welcome and the importance of the success may have grown with the years, my enjoyment was always as if it were the first and only time.

Any boy can understand the thrill I got when I appeared in Toledo for the first time as a professional entertainer. I was eleven years old and just back from my first summer with the circus. (Billy Ashe always booked the act locally whenever he could. It kept us in practice and in spending money.) In this, our first local engagement, I wore the beautiful plum-colored velvet pants I'd worn in the circus and I was sure all the neighbor kids were green with envy.

We played in Toledo's Bellview Park and we didn't have very big audiences at the afternoon performances. One afternoon it rained and only three youngsters showed up in the seats.

Our agreement with the management was that we would go on even if the audience comprised only a single customer. George and cross-eyed Grover thought it a waste of effort to put on the act just for three kids, so they went outside and chased the entire audience away. But the manager caught them doing it, so we had to go on anyway—and played to empty seats.

If I can be credited with the attainment of any pinnacle of success, then I want it known that my friends were responsible for a large share of it.

Mitchell Woodbury is one of these. I have known Mitch for a long time. With Jimmie and Jerry Shea, Connie Desmond, and a great many others, we used to be part of the same gang at Stop 42, old Toledo Beach, when we were regular summer boarders in the cottage occupied by "Mother" McGinn.

Mitch was working for the *Toledo Bee* when Prevost and I were with vaudeville and his review of our engagement in Toledo was one of the first times my name got more than a one-line mention in the press. On a return engagement, a year or two later, he helped organize a Joe E. Brown Night, when everyone I knew in Toledo turned out to see our act. It was a gala evening, for half the audience were personal friends and neighbors.

Mitch and I carried on a lively feud for years over which could down the most chocolate ice cream "bittersweet" sundaes. In the days when I was manager of the Coliseum Bowling Alleys, over Faber's Drug Store at Ashland and Bancroft, we used to "join battle" at least once a week. No records were kept of these contests except the fond memory of how those sundaes used to taste—even after the fifth or sixth. Years later when I installed my own private soda fountain in our Beverly Hills home, it was not only the realization of another youthful dream but an excuse to invite Mitch and Jean, his missus, out to visit us.

We planned a "little" reception for the Woodbury's and invited 280 guests. It was intended as a kind of gesture, to entertain Mitch and Jean, and to show off our affluence. They were entertained all right, for instead of 280 guests, 450 showed up. There was no opportunity for us to renew our sundae feud; there was scarcely enough to go around.

The braggart always gets his comeuppance. One evening Charlie (the late Charles S.) Howard and his wife, Marcella came out to our house for dinner. Charlie was the west coast distributor for Buick automobiles, but he is best remembered as the owner of Seabiscuit. We had owned Buicks for years but at this particular time we had switched to a Packard under the impression that the Buicks that year were not up to standard.

On the place we had at that time were twenty-eight big avocado trees. They bore such a bounteous crop every year that they were the pride and joy of the whole Brown family. We gave them to friends and sent fancy boxes of them all over the country. Our gardener Davis (still with us) took a great deal of pride in them.

Charlie and I were talking about the avocados on the way up to the house and as usual I was bragging about them. "You never saw such avocados," I said. "There must be half a dozen varieties and each one is better than the next," and so on and on.

Davis had picked several bushel baskets of them and they were lined up along a workbench in one side of a two-car garage. "Just let me show you a few," I said.

Davis was working near the garage and I asked him to open the door. But he hadn't heard our conversation and he didn't know I was boasting about the avocados. He opened the door to the garage where the new Packard car sat. Charlie knew I wanted to show off my avocados, but here was a new Packard, polished and bright. He laughed and laughed at my embarrassment and for years he kept the joke alive.

But the party we gave for Jean and Mitch Woodbury could hardly compare with the one the whole town of Toledo gave me in 1945. December 7th, that year, was set aside as Joe E. Brown Day, with an official proclamation by his honor, Lloyd E. Roulet, Mayor of Toledo:

"Whereas, one of our illustrious citizens, Joe E. Brown, has distinguished himself as a star in movie, radio, and stage; and

"Whereas, in this role, he has traveled over 200,000 miles and made 742 personal appearances to entertain the members of our armed forces in this country and in all parts of the world; and. . . ."

That was about the biggest day of my whole life. It began when "Dorm" Richardson, program chairman, met me at Toledo's Union Station and drove me to the Commodore Perry Hotel for breakfast. After that an official car, with motorcycle police escort, whisked me about Toledo, from one function to another for twelve busy hours. First there was the Memorial Convocation at the University of Toledo where I received an honorary Master of Arts Degree from President Phillip C. Nash, and an informal reception in his office later. At noon I was honor guest at a luncheon given by George A. Vradenburg at the Toledo Club. In the afternoon I visited the Auto Lite plant, where I used to work, and made a personal appearance before a thousand enlisted sailors and Waves at the U.S. Naval Armory in Bay View Park.

I barely had time to freshen up a bit before the big event of the day, a testimonial dinner at the Commodore Perry. My old friend Judge Aaron B. Cohn was toastmaster for that event. It was a real oldtimers' get-together and no one had more fun than myself, Mitch Woodbury, Jack Haggerty, Ted Donoher, etc. It would take several pages to list them all and another book to describe my own feelings. Perhaps that which pleased me most was the presence of Billy Ashe, aged and quite feeble, but still able to recall the day he signed me up for $1.50 a week. It was our last public appearance together.

After the dinner there was a big public reception for me in the Civic Auditorium, more nice speeches, more honors, and more people than I thought they could squeeze into the place. All told, it was a pretty big day. It exceeded any thrill I've had, before or since, though there was to be still another homecoming celebration for me in Holgate a few years later. And this one too was the culmination of another dream I'd had—a dream I'd had ever since the days when I stood with Grandfather Evans and watched the Clover Leaf Express high-ball through town.

Maybe I ought to let Harvey tell about that one. A guy gets a little self-conscious telling such things about himself and a gimmick like Harvey would come in handy.

Just in case you are not familiar with the content of Mary Chase's *Harvey*, the Pulitzer-prize winning comedy about a friendly alcoholic and his bunny buddy, here's the gist:

Elwood P. Dowd, who lives in the ancestral mansion of his "loving sister and charming niece," is a man who discovered long before he reached the age of 47 that to get along in the world "you've got to be smart or pleasant." He gave up being smart, finding it much more fun just being amiable to strangers and asking them home for dinner. His favorite pastime is going to bars, Charlie's place in particular, and imbibing a few until all the wonderful people there look at him and smile, as if to say, "You're a swell guy, Mr. Dowd."

His companion at these times is Harvey, a rabbit six feet 1½ inches tall, invisible to everyone except Elwood and maybe some of Elwood's friends, if they've been imbibing too. Harvey and Elwood go everywhere together; and whenever they enter a room, Elwood always seats Harvey next to him so they can have a nice, quiet chat, which gives others the impression that Elwood is merely talking to himself.

295

His widowed sister, Veta Louise Simmons, and her slightly ungainly daughter, Myrtle Mae, never acquired Elwood's easy philosophy or equilibrium. They knock around in that frustrated element of society made up of ladies' clubs, musicales, and coming-out teas, trying to pave the way for Myrtle Mae's social future. Elwood and Harvey put them at a great disadvantage.

When Veta decides that she "can't bear sitting next to that rabbit at dinner again," she commits her brother to an institution, where the psychiatrists in charge first mistake her for the unbalanced member of the family but change their minds when Elwood returns looking for his rabbit friend. Elwood is to have an injection of insulin to restore him to normalcy, and he's not looking forward to it one little bit. It is the taxi driver, who has been driving patients to the institution for fifteen years, who makes Veta reconsider. To paraphrase his words: "On the way back, after one of them shots, they just sit there looking glum; they gripe if I drive too fast and they gripe if I drive too slow. They tell me to watch every curve and to be careful to keep on my side of the road. They've lost their confidence, and when they get out they don't tip me. In short, they've become normal human beings and you know what they can be." So Elwood and Harvey are allowed to live happily ever after.

Mixing fact and farce, the play, beneath its surface of comedy, has its reflective moments that coax the specator to re-examine his concept of normalcy, that make him wonder if, in the case of Dowd vs. the World, the former hasn't won out in the sanest, most logical way open to him, not in being an alcoholic, but in keeping whatever proof he can that human beings are good guys who like to get along.

So much has been written about the play since its premiere in New York on the night after Hallowe'en in 1944 that it is hardly necessary to go into its ramifications now. Frank Fay and Josephine Hull were the original stars in the Broadway production produced by Brock Pemberton.

That's why people laughed when Pemberton sat down at the typewriter and tapped out the announcement that I would play the lead in the road company.

"Sure, Joe is a good comedian," said the scoffers. "But his style is too broad for *Harvey*. He'll clown. He'll make Joe Brown funny faces and people will laugh, but he won't have that 'fay' quality—that Frank Fay quality—that you need for Elwood P. Dowd."

Many drama lovers were indignant at the mere rumor that I would play the gentle, bemused Elwood. "Brown will clown and do double-takes all over the stage," they predicted. "He's strictly for the sticks. Why, that guy would hold himself at arm's length and kick himself to underline a joke."

Despite such catcalls, director Antoinette Perry and producer Pemberton went ahead with their plans and I signed to play the role.

I rehearsed for several weeks and then one day Pemberton and Miss Perry summoned me to a conference.

They seemed hesitant and embarrassed. I sensed what was causing their discomfort and decided to grasp the nettle for them.

"You keep hearing sour talk on Broadway, don't you? They say, 'You want a hammed-up *Harvey*? You gonna have that clown with the big mouth do it? And you let it frighten you.'"

After some hand-fluttering, they admitted that this was approximately the case.

"Then tear up the contract," I offered.

"No. No, we just want to be sure you don't intend to play it too broadly."

"I refuse to imitate Frank Fay," I said. "If I do this part, it will be a Joe E. Brown interpretation. I'll take your direction, but you mustn't put handcuffs on me."

They looked anguished. "If we could only be sure . . ."

"Tear up the contract after opening night in Columbus, if I flop," I said. "Or tear it up now, if you won't trust me till then."

They were still unhappy about it but they promised to trust me.

After the first performance, drama columnist Bud Kissel of the *Columbus Citizen*, came backstage. "Mr. Brown," he said, "you probably didn't see what I wrote about you before you came to town."

"Oh, yes, I did," I retorted, interrupting him. "You wrote that I wouldn't be 'subtle' enough for this play."

"That I did. I was wrong. I'm going to take it all back tomorrow." Sure enough, Kissel wrote in the next day's *Citizen*:

> *I saw Fay in the role, and it was my belief that Brown could not handle it as deftly and convincingly. I was wrong. Others who saw the show in New York agreed . . . Brown gave a magnificent performance, straight and sincere. He has what show people call the "heart" for the role.*

This was the first of a torrent of favorable reviews which was to flow for five years. We played to sell-out audiences in thirty-odd cities, and in city after city the engagement was lengthened by several weeks. What started as a nine-week San Francisco stand was extended to thirteen weeks.

There were similar jackpots throughout the tour. Because of the bigger theatres in which I played, I even made more money out of it than Frank Fay. Finally Fay quit the Broadway production and I returned to New York to replace him. The jaded Broadway audience was the toughest test of all. I guess I passed because I stayed twenty weeks with the SRO sign up. Then I went on tour again, played for months in London and Australia, and wound up with a record for the fifth longest run in American theatrical history.

During Fay's run on Broadway, there were vacation periods when other stars replaced him. I suggested movie actor Jimmie Stewart for one of these replacements. The suggestion led to bigger things than I bargained for. Stewart eventually landed the starring role in the movie version of *Harvey*.

It was a part I wanted to play, naturally. I felt it would have been one of my greatest hits. But Stewart was a hot attraction for younger movie fans, so maybe he was a logical choice. He was fine in the movie.

The play got some unusual publicity breaks. We took it to Australia at the height of that country's campaign to rid the land of rabbit pests.

They told me that a Mr. Thomas Austin is credited with creating the extraordinary pest problem that has plagued Australia for the past several years. The twenty-four English rabbits he released near Melbourne in 1859 have multiplied until they and the depredations of their descendants have made headlines in the newspapers "down under." Millions of rabbits running over gardens and fields, devouring everything in sight, would make the word "rabbit" unpopular in any community. But no one who had anything to do with my tour knew beforehand that such a strange publicity gimmick would be encountered. Considering the nature of the play and the intensity of local feeling, it is surprising that the play was as successful as it was. Just goes to prove that the Aussies have a wonderful sense of humor.

And I'm inclined to disagree with those who say the British sense of humor is a little weak. I saw no evidence of any lack of it. One evening, in the midst of the curtain talk I usually gave at the end, someone in the audience kept interrupting. At first I couldn't understand what he was saying, then, despite the accent, I got it.

299

"I say, old boy," he was repeating. "Give us Mousie, Mousie."

It had been years since I had given my Little Mousie story, and I wondered who in this audience could have heard me in those long-gone years. Finally, while I continued my curtain speech, I spotted the owner of that voice. It was my old friend William Henry Pratt, better known to movie fans as Boris Karloff.

So it was during my American tour in Harvey that I experienced my next big homecoming thrill. We were playing in St. Louis when a friend of mine, John Davin, Chairman of the Board of the New York, Chicago, and St. Louis Railroad Company, broached the subject.

"Joe," he said, "I hear your next stop is Cleveland, that right?"

I said it was.

"Then you're going as my guest," he said.

"Huh?" I said, raising a quizzical eyebrow.

"Yes, I want you and your whole show to go as guests of the Nickel Plate. What do you need in the way of cars?"

"Cars?" I said, raising both eyebrows.

"Sure, we'll make up a private train for you."

"A private train?"

"Yes, and you can take as long as you want and make any stops you want. And, of course, Joe, you remember that the Nickel Plate runs through Holgate."

"Gosh!" I said. Did I remember! Only in my day the part of the line that ran through Holgate was called the Clover Leaf. And I remembered, as though it were only yesterday, the little boy who stood in the shadow of the big water tank and watched the Express as it thundered past and, in awe, hearing his grandfather say, "It'll be in Toledo tonight!"

They made up a special train for the *Harvey* troupe. A private car for me, a car for the company, a dining and buffet car, and two baggage cars, with food and drinks for the entire company. There were four big stage hands with that company that together weighed nearly 1000 pounds. After they had loaded the baggage after the last show that night in St. Louis, they went aboard our special and put away the darndest meals and the most beer I ever saw four men eat.

That was quite a ride. In my youth I had played baseball at practically every little crossroads and town we passed, and in each place we stopped and I'd wave to the crowd that had gathered. By the time we pulled into Holgate, the trip had attained something of the proportions of that of a Caesar returning from the wars. And this time the Express didn't high-ball through Holgate. It pulled right across the two main streets of the town and stopped, and there it stayed for several hours while half of Henry County turned out to honor its native son.

Mayor Mike Horning, H. G. Fitzwater (publisher of the Henry County Review) and all the leading citizens of my birthplace were on hand to welcome me.

The Holgate Fire Department had just purchased a new fire truck and this is what they met me with. I climbed aboard and we started out, then I noticed the "fireman" beside me was wearing a dress. I looked under the fireman's hat and discovered it was my mother. They had brought her down from Toledo for the occasion and she was getting as big a thrill out of it as I. They named a street in my honor and dedicated a new stadium to me. And A. B. (Happy) Chandler, U.S. Commissioner of Major League Baseball, made the dedicatory speech. May I repeat, it was a wonderful, thrilling day.

So I'm convinced that if you live long enough, every piece of bread you cast on the waters will return with butter and jam on it. The returns I still get today for my wartime tours, the thrill I get when someone remembers some little something I did or said years ago, that is what makes life a real satisfaction. It has built up in me a faith in my fellow man that is akin to a religion. It is this faith that has kept me bouncing up from all sorts of misfortune.

Once our daughters, Kathryn and Mary Elizabeth, were critically hurt in an auto accident, on a Saturday night when Los Angeles had one of its near-record totals of crashes. The emergency hospital was overwhelmed. Mary Elizabeth was unconscious and barely breathing. I rampaged through the jammed halls trying furiously to get a doctor or even a nurse, but everyone was too busy.

Finally I spotted one doctor just dragging off duty after a day and night of work. "Wish I could help you," he said. "Too tired to keep my eyes open. You'll have to find another . . . wait! Aren't you Joe E. Brown? That's different. Where is your daughter?"

The doctor (I learned later he was Dr. Lawrence Leidig) stayed for seven hours, plying himself with wake-up powders, and finally pulled her out of danger.

Afterward I tried to stammer my thanks. "You must be a Joe E. Brown fan," I said. "You weren't going to help me until you recognized me."

The doctor looked at me a moment and then he said, "On Christmas Eve, fifteen years ago, I sent out a call for movie stars to come to the Children's Orthopedic Hospital and cheer up the patients. The only ones who came were Bill Robinson and you."

Good old "Bojangles!" In 1931 I was attending a ball game in New York and Bill came over and sat with me. A bunch of kids gathered around for autographs and I whispered to one of them that he ought to get Bill's autograph. "He's a bigger man than I am," I said. The youngster approached Bill, pad and pencil in hand, and then I discovered something I had never known. Bill Robinson couldn't sign his name!

302

But that little fault in his education never bothered his acting ability. He was one of the greatest.

Now you can understand, perhaps, why I can claim charter membership in the Club of No Regrets. I've lived it and I've loved it and the happiest thing I do today is remembering it. And no matter what extreme my morale hits, I know a little trick that always brings it back to an even keel. There's not much danger of getting the big-head or an outsize opinion of myself when I use it. The same trick also works in reverse when I find myself in the dumps. No matter where I am, New York, Chicago, San Francisco, Boston, Atlanta, St. Louis, or Kalamazoo, I can always find something to remind me of the days when I had nothing to be big-headed about—or of the days when I was too busy to have the blues.

I woke up one morning recently in Chicago with such a depressed feeling I thought I simply could not go on and do my act. I got in a taxi and went down to a little humpty-dumpty theatre on lower State Street called the Follies. The doorman recognized me and I asked if I could go in and look around.

"Sure, Mr. Brown, go right in," he said.

The place hadn't changed much since 1910 when I played there with Pre and Uncle Sam's Belles. But I had, and so had my sense of values, so I thought to myself, what a nice men's room I played in! It was a far cry from the sumptuous palace where I was scheduled to make a personal appearance that afternoon. When I got back in the taxi my morale was back on level ground again.

During my heyday in motion pictures, when I had tasted success and gone on to stardom, there was a period when I felt I was pretty good. I was accused of going high-hat, and I guess I was. But I stopped off in Cleveland one trip and dropped in at the shabby little Star Theatre (where I had played also in the old days) to see my brother Paul.

303

Paul, though he never regained his eyesight, had grown to manhood, married, and built a reputation for himself as a musician. He gained no fame beyond the middlewest, but he supported himself and his wife, who, too, was blind. He would never let me or anyone else in the family help him, and of the whole Brown brood he was always the most cheerful. So I came away from my visit with Paul thinking how thankful I should be for every bit of success I'd had. Thereafter any inflated ego I might have had always got put back in its place by such reminders.

My kids have had another effect on me. They have been the source of more real satisfaction and pride than I ever got from my work. Take Joe L., for instance.

I don't know whether young Joe's love for baseball came from environment or inheritance. Probably it was a little of both. Certainly he was a very little guy when he first began to play, to talk, to live baseball. Later his love developed into something near an obsession. No one ever had to ask him what he wanted to be when he grew up. It was pretty obvious that he intended to make baseball a career. He did make it a career all right but not in the way any of us thought he would.

He was not yet sixteen when Honus Wagner invited him to work out with the Pittsburgh Pirates at their Paso Robles training camp. It was only a friendly gesture to the boy although by now he was already almost big enough to qualify. But his enthusiasm and his desire to measure up proved his undoing. In throwing a ball to first base during infield practice he attempted to impress the club officials with his strong throwing arm. Somehow one of his pegs caused his arm severe pain and his dream of a big league playing career was ended when examination disclosed he had broken all the bones in his right elbow.

No amount of surgery was ever able to restore the full use of that arm and though he never complained or bemoaned his fate, we all felt his great disappointment. But no one knew the

304

extent of his determination or the strength of his ambition. It was a source of power he was to draw on for a long time before it paid off.

He captained the baseball team at Mercersberg and he went on to play varsity football at U.C.L.A. And then when his brother Don graduated Joe figured he had had all the schooling he wanted too. He quit at the end of his sophomore year and took a job as assistant general manager of the Lubbock, Texas team. He went from there to general manager of the Waterloo, Iowa outfit before the war and the Air Corps put a temporary halt to his baseball life.

My own struggles to get a little education made me want to give my kids every advantage that I had missed. Kathryn and I would have preferred that he go on and finish school, but there was never any argument about it.

"This is what I want to do, Dad," he said, and though I knew he had a good head and abilities that would take him far in some commercial field, I didn't try very hard to influence him. It wouldn't have changed him anyway. He never for a moment ever considered anything but baseball.

When the war was over we had a talk about his future and I asked him what he was going to do.

"I'm going back into baseball," he said.

"But don't you realize there are only nineteen good jobs in baseball?" I was counting the sixteen major league general managers, two league presidents and the commissioner. It looked like a hard climb.

"Maybe I can make one of those spots," he said. "Dad, that's what I want to do."

I reminded him that he had a family (his first child was born while I was in the South Pacific), that it might be a long time before he would earn anything like the kind of money he could be making in industry or commerce.

"Have you talked it over with Din?" I asked.

"Yes," he said, "I have."

305

"How does she feel about it?"

"She said she didn't think I was cut out for anything but baseball."

My mouth fell open. Hadn't I heard those exact words once before? History was repeating itself as I recalled the dark days back in Toledo when I had tried so hard to be a business man. So what could I say, what could I do but give him my blessing?

If you are a baseball fan you know the rest of the story for Joe's rise was rapid and a little spectacular. He got one of those nineteen top jobs last year when he became general manager of the Pittsburgh Pirates. So perhaps you can imagine the satisfaction and pride I feel in his accomplishments. He is everything that I wanted to be but could never quite attain myself.

In December, 1955, en route to my *Harvey* engagement at Milburn, New Jersey, I stopped off in Toledo for a few days' visit with Mother. It, too, was the kind of homecoming that I always enjoy, for mothers never change. Mine, especially, has always seemed like an imperishable rock of strong will, her arms a haven of comfort. And I suppose I will always be her "little man." Her intuition and understanding are most remarkable. I was complaining that age was beginning to dull my memory as it also dulled my physical activity.

She gave a little snort of derision to remind me that my years were not much compared to her nearly ninety.

"Still," I said, "I think it's time I slowed down, settled down."

She laughed. "Wasn't it fifty years ago that I asked you to do just that?" There was nothing wrong with her memory. It was nearly fifty years to the day that I returned from my last tour with Billy Ashe, after the earthquake in San Francisco.

306

"Well, I've lived it and I've loved it," I said. "There's not much I'd change if I had it to do over. But I really am going to take it easy from here on out."

"Anyway, Evan, I'm sure glad to hear you say it." There was no sarcasm in mother's voice, but there was a twinkle in her eye. "By the way," she continued, "there's a pile of mail for you on the hall table, and there was a call from a Mr. Todd in Hollywood."

"Oh, is that so? Good old Mike," I said. "What'd he want?"

"Said something about wanting you to meet him in Durango, Colorado, for a bit part in a picture they were doing —something he called *Around the World in 80 Days*."

"Is that so? He did? Where's the number?"

I could hear mother chuckling to herself as I went out to the telephone in the hall. "*Around the World in 80 Days*," she said. "H'm-m, that's Evan all right!"

Mother may be a little old fashioned but she had the right idea. She understood me, probably better than I understand myself. As I see it, around the world in eight days would be more in character for Joe Evan Brown. I've been in a hurry ever since I can remember because I've always felt there was so much to do and so little time to do it in.

Now I've reached the age when I should retire, settle down to a "life with grandfather" pattern, and relax, but I find that old habits are much too strong. I'm still in a hurry. The pressure is the same. The only thing about it that is different is the force that applies the pressure. Where once I was driven to seek success and fame, I want now to repay some of the debt I owe my country and my fellow man.

I can't reminisce without remembering hundreds of friends, and I can't recall a friend to whom I don't owe some debt. I enjoy my children and my grandchildren and I'm proud of the things they have accomplished on their own, but I have no feeling that any of this has paid off my personal

307

obligations. Success, money, fame—they have all been mine and I'm grateful for having had them, but I feel I earned them. Friendship is a different matter. The more you earn, the more in debt you become. I like to think of myself as the man with the biggest debt in the U.S.A.

Index

309

310